EBURY PRESS
HEAD HELD HIGH

Vishwas Nangre Patil is the joint commissioner of police (law and order), Mumbai City, and former commissioner of police, Nashik City. He is an Indian Police Service officer from the 1997 batch. In 2015, he was awarded the President's Police Medal for Gallantry, for his role in the counterterrorism operations during the 2008 Mumbai attacks.

ADVANCE PRAISE FOR THE BOOK

'The Maharashtra Police motto is "सद्रक्षणाय खलनिग्रहणाय"—"सद्रक्षणाय" means to "protect the good", "खलनिग्रहणाय" means to "destroy the evil". Vishwas Nangre Patil is one such officer of the force he represents, who has always, in my eyes, lived up to the meaning of this motto. Upright, straightforward and fearless in the line of duty. May this book be an inspiration to not just the force, but to every individual'—Amitabh Bachchan

'Translated from the Marathi, *Head Held High* beautifully captures the magic of *Mann Mein Hai Vishwas*. A must-read for the youth of today'—Sachin Tendulkar

HEAD
HELD
HIGH

Vishwas Nangre Patil

Foreword by **JULIO RIBEIRO**

Translated by Vinita Deshmukh and Prasannakumar Keskar

EBURY
PRESS

An imprint of Penguin Random House

EBURY PRESS

USA | Canada | UK | Ireland | Australia
New Zealand | India | South Africa | China | Singapore

Ebury Press is part of the Penguin Random House group of companies
whose addresses can be found at global.penguinrandomhouse.com

Published by Penguin Random House India Pvt. Ltd
4th Floor, Capital Tower 1, MG Road,
Gurugram 122 002, Haryana, India

Penguin
Random House
India

First published in Ebury Press by Penguin Random House India 2022

Originally published in Marathi as *Mann Mein Hai Vishwas*,
Rajhans Prakashan, 2016

ISBN 9780143454960

Typeset in Adobe Caslon Pro by MAP Systems, Bengaluru, India
Printed at Repro India Limited

www.penguin.co.in

MIX
Paper from
responsible sources
FSC® C047271

*Dedicated to the martyrs
who sacrificed their lives for the country
while bravely battling the terrorists
on the fateful night of 26/11*

Contents

Foreword

Head Held High is the story of a simple village boy who made good. Born in rural Maharashtra, where the pinnacle of ambition is to become a police sub-inspector, Vishwasrao Nangre Patil, the protagonist of the tale, was selected for the prestigious Indian Police Service, where probationers begin life as assistant superintendents of police and at the end of their careers retire at the very top, if all goes well!

Vishwas had the brains. He needed opportunity, besides hard work and application of mind. Considering that his parents had hardly crossed the barrier of primary school, there was no one at home to mentor him. The closest to have had the fortune of a decent education was his father's brother, who studied basic engineering and was employed in an engineering company in a mid-level job.

Vishwasrao did get shelter and support at his uncle's home in a neighbouring town when he entered middle school, but after that he had to find his own way to continue his studies in high school. This final school lap he completed in Kolhapur, the big city closest to his village, Kokrud.

The life of a young boy growing up in a village is described in minute detail in this book. To say the least, it is fascinating.

The simple pleasures one experiences, and the not-so-pleasant experience of being rammed and thrown into the air by a rampaging bull are detailed in this book. Fortunately, Vishwasrao's physique, agility and presence of mind—which served him well during the ordeal of 26/11 at the Taj hotel in 2008—saved him from being actually gored by that bull!

At a very early age, our hero acquired the intellectual habit of reading. When he was engrossed in reading, neither hunger nor thirst could affect his concentration! The habit must have stood him in good stead in his plans for a future career. A shot at the UPSC's All-India and Civil Services examinations requires not only above-average intelligence but vast knowledge, based on wide reading, and the ability to analyze and take positions. After my commerce degree I studied law. As soon as I cleared the LLB, I joined the *National Standard*, now renamed the *Indian Express*, as a sub-editor to expose myself to all that was happening in India and the world beyond. Vishwasrao's preparations five decades later were more elaborate and much better planned!

I had the advantage of an English education in a big city (Mumbai), and exposure to teachers and mentors who were always around to solve doubts. Finally, I spent four months at my maternal grandmother's home in her village in Goa, revising my stuff under the light of a petromax since there was no electricity in Goa's villages in 1952, when I appeared for the competitive examination.

Vishwasrao had to shift from hostel to hostel with numerous distractions to overcome, including, at times, rowdy visitors from the village. He had to make the most of his opportunities. He was lucky to meet some very successful and serious-minded personalities, like the IAS officer Bushan Gagrani; Dr S.N. Patil, whom he refers to as 'Doctor Uncle' in this book; and also two friends, Vikas Kharge and Prakash

Pote, who, like him, were students at the government's pre-IAS training centre in Mumbai.

Kharge and Pote dissuaded him from wasting his time fruitlessly with rowdy rural boys who came to meet him at the hostel. 'Doctor Uncle' inculcated in him good and healthy habits of hygiene and daily exercise, which stood him in good stead throughout his career. Vikas Kharge went on to top the IAS exam a couple of years before Vishwasrao himself got selected.

In his account of his efforts and struggles to achieve success, Vishwasrao speaks to young men and women of rural background, egging them on to emulate him and march determinedly to the goal of becoming 'sahebs' and 'madams'. It is, as I said earlier, a fascinating account of the life of a young man growing up in a village, whose steely determination and extraordinary courage aided him to become an IPS officer, despite the odds stacked against him.

That same village lad—now a joint commissioner of police in Mumbai—on 26 November 2008, at Mumbai's iconic Taj Mahal Palace hotel, led his team of the Mumbai Police against the Pakistani terrorists who had sneaked in and caused untold havoc and mayhem never before experienced. All his cognitive senses, developed from infancy in his native village, were in play at that critical time, when out-of-the-box thinking, quick decision-making, cautious but determined action and, above all, extraordinary leadership qualities were required. Vishwasrao had all those qualities. They won him the President's Police Medal for Gallantry.

Some of my ex-colleagues, now retired, tell me that they have read another account in Hindi, written by a Maharashtra-cadre IPS officer hailing from the Bhind–Morena dacoit-infested area of Madhya Pradesh. I have not read that account, but I was happy to learn that IPS officers from rural backgrounds are writing their stories. It will encourage boys and girls from the hinterland to enter the Class I services and thus introduce a measure of egalitarianism in our society.

Before I end, I wish to record my deep appreciation of the skills displayed by Vinita Deshmukh and Prasannakumar Keskar in translating Vishwasrao's book from Marathi into English. It was a pleasure to read the translated version. At no time did I feel bored! The narrative was almost 'racy', like an action movie!

And to my friend Vishwas, I say this: Now that you have shown your brothers and sisters of rural Maharashtra the way to advance in life, spend the rest of your life in the service of the people and guide future IPS officers on the path of truth, justice and integrity, for that is why the IPS was constituted by Sardar Vallabhbhai Patel, that great son of India.

February 2022   Julio Ribeiro
                                Former police commissioner of Mumbai

Preface

My Kaleidoscope

My ancestral village, Kokrud, is tucked atop a mountain range of the mighty Sahyadris, bordered by the River Warna. Every morning, it wakes up to the sound of the azan (prayer calls), emanating from a nearby mosque or to the melodious recital of Dnyaneshwari. The sounds of people professing different religions, and of all communities living happily in harmony. Whenever I hark back to the past, I can hear my grandmother affectionately imploring me to eat bhakri with milk. I recall diving into the holes dug in the sandy riverbed during the summer. I can hear our cheerful cries when we caught tiny fish; I can hear the satisfied burps after polishing off the free glass of milk served as a part of the nutritious food scheme for schoolchildren. I recollect the thump on my back given by Chaugule Sir. I remember the burfi that was given even if one lost the wrestling match. I remember the recitation of the Marathi alphabet. I relive the rhythm of the raindrops falling on water puddles in the sugarcane fields. I remember the taste of the fresh sugarcane juice and relive jumping on the heaps of bagasse. The strong odour of the illicit liquor consumed on the day of the festival of Ghandevi, our village deity, lingers. I remember the puran poli cooked by my mother. I recall the bullocks decorated to mark the Pola festival, dedicated to bullocks. I can again hear the beats of the *halgi* (an instrument akin to a drum) during Lezim performances. I remember the pitter-patter of rolling caps and the booming sound of Laxmi bombs during Diwali. The memory of these sounds sometimes mingles with the sound of rounds fired at shooting practice during police training. Sometimes they merge with the din of grenade blasts on the night of 26/11. In the deep corners of my mind, this cacophony resonates constantly.

Rural children are like wildflowers. Given fertile black soil, fertilizer, water and sunlight, they will bloom so beautifully that no rose, lotus or daffodil will be able to hold a candle to them. Some such wildflowers that blossomed on the banks of River Warna conquered the throne of Delhi. I was one such wildflower, which blossomed in 1997.

After my selection to the Indian Police Service, I visited schools and colleges in various villages located in the nooks and corners of Maharashtra, in a bid to inspire Marathi boys to take up the gauntlet of appearing for and succeeding in the Union Public Service Commission examination. During these visits I would have a dialogue with the students, resolving their doubts and answering their questions. Some students uploaded the recordings of my lectures on YouTube, which were watched by millions. Several people sent me emails and letters, insisting that I pen down my journey; my school, college, preparation for the competitive examinations and my final selection for the IPS cadre. They insisted that this would inspire the shorts-clad young warriors like them who travel to places like Mumbai and Pune to chase their dreams. I was convinced.

Just like I had so many years ago, many join the milling crowds of Mumbai and Pune to fulfil their dream of being selected in the competitive examinations. Four or five such students share a room in the MLA Hostel or live together in a 10x10 ft cubbyhole, rented on a cot basis. Hoping that their child would one day become a tehsildar or a police sub-inspector, their rural parents live frugally, at times even mortgaging their farmland, to sponsor their son. These boys enrol themselves in coaching classes, serious about their studies. Some stray from their path, distracted by the dazzle of the city, only to find themselves in a tight spot. There is no one to rescue them or guide them to the right path. What emerges is a big zero, a failure. Their youth is wasted in the mistakes they made, the years of maturity are spent in constant struggle and old age, in repentance. Some study like men possessed and even find the right direction. However, much to their misfortune, sometimes the examinations are not conducted, or there is a lack of vacancies. In the three-stage process of the UPSC examination, some get eliminated in the first stage itself, some in the second and some in the third. Despite slaving away for four to five years, they come away empty-handed. Some even surpass the eligibility age before they can appear for the examination and are hence elbowed out of it. Such youngsters spend their lives carrying a deep hatred for the system and a rather cynical attitude towards the world around them.

My journey too had undergone such stages. Had I taken a wrong turn, I could have been mired in a whirlpool of frustration and negativity. Nevertheless, I realized my dream with hard work, suffered the blows of reality, stumbled but regained my strength and took off. Having made my wings strong, my dreams took flight and conquered the heights of the vast syllabus. However, I never lost my footing on the ground. That is why I remained stable, even modestly successful, in my journey.

I faltered many times while chasing my dream; in the journey from the tiny Kokrud village to the *taluka* headquarters of Shirala; from Shirala to the district headquarters of Kolhapur; and from Kolhapur to the financial capital of the country, Mumbai. I had my friends and family to support and reassure me until I was in Kolhapur. However, upon reaching Mumbai, I was on my own, like a kite without a string, flying aimlessly.

Mumbai has two faces: one Mumbai is grand, glittering and ostentatious while the other is ugly, poverty-stricken and dirty. I lingered on the border of these two facets of Mumbai. Such was my aim that if I succeeded, I would enter the high-class society of Mumbai but if I failed, I would be forced to find a 6×3 ft space in the room of a fellow villager to sleep in, in Wanichawl on Delight Road.

I lived in a hostel in the plush Churchgate area of Mumbai but could not afford more than a Rs 15 plate of rice. Often, I would stroll along the Marine Drive or the Gateway of India with my friends, who were as poor as I was. We would witness the dazzle and glitter of the Taj, Ambassador and Oberoi hotels, guests from abroad alighting from luxury cars. We would try to peep inside the tall compounds of the CCI Club and the Bombay Gymkhana to find out what the world was like inside. The vehicles of the Indian Administrative Service and Indian Police Service officers, with red lights flashing atop them, would halt at the apartments of IAS and IPS officers nearby, at the Yashodhan, Suniti and Suruchi buildings. Smartly dressed sahebs would alight from them. When I was yet to be admitted into the hostel, I had tried looking for accommodation in the servants' quarters of this

Yashodhan building. Even this modest dream of studying in the library throughout the day and spending the night at the servants' quarters could not be fulfilled. Finally, I settled on the Majestic MLA Hostel and started studying. The Metro Cinema was at a meagre five-minute walking distance. On the days of film premieres I would stand there for hours, suffering abuses from bouncers and being shoved, all the while hoping to catch a glimpse of a Bollywood star.

I had big dreams; I was able to accomplish them with perseverance and hard work. The bigger the struggle, the greater the success! I had a never-say-die attitude and limitless willpower. I studied tirelessly until my back ached, without feeling defeated. I worked hard, was selected for the IPS and my life changed. Today, I live in a spacious 2200 square foot government flat in the same Yashodhan building where I had once looked for accommodation in the servants' quarters. The clubs I used to try to peep in offered me and my family their honorary membership when I was appointed as the deputy commissioner of police for the South Mumbai Zone. My children play squash and tennis at the sports clubs I used to gaze at with envy. When I became additional commissioner of police for the Western Mumbai range, the Bollywood stars, for a glimpse of whom I would suffer abuses, would book an appointment, two days prior, to meet me. I had never thought that I would be able to have a cup of tea at the Taj Hotel. On the night of 26/11, my arrival was awaited at the Taj. Moreover, I was honoured with the President's Medal for Gallantry for combating terrorists.

Times change, characters change and roles change as well. All one needs to achieve is the zest to live up to one's dreams, strengthen one's wings and have the willingness to work hard. I have written this book for youngsters who, like me, are born to labourers belonging to the lowest strata of society and are studying hard, in a lone corner of their homes, to make their dreams a reality.

I picked up a pen and started writing everything I could recollect of my twenty-four-year journey, from 1973 to 1997. I have written this account of my journey, my quest for knowledge, keeping students, parents, teachers and society in mind. There is a deep relation between studies and the minute observations of daily life, examination preparations and common sense. While I was penning this down, I would interact with my wife Rupali every day. Though she holds a BE in computer science, she sacrificed her career and focused on raising our children, simply because I am a police officer. She shouldered the responsibility of bringing up both of our children and took up their studies in earnest, changing my outdated notions about parenting. Thanks to a consistent dialogue with her, the expanse of my knowledge on modern parenting has widened. My children, Janhavi and Ranveer, are my teachers as well, teaching me something new every day. Though I am old-fashioned, my children never allow me to be wrongly exposed. Of course, occasionally my wrong pronunciation of English words becomes the butt of their jokes. In this book, I have also tried putting forth my conclusions about parenting, which are the outcomes of discussions in my family life.

Further, I have tried to review the good and bad tendencies in society while handling the void of frustration among urban as well as rural youths due to unemployment and poverty. Moreover, I have touched upon the rise in addiction and substance abuse due to a hedonistic culture, which I have witnessed while handling rave parties, especially among children studying in the tenth and twelfth grades, who often lean towards emotional and psychological frustration. I have tried to present my own experience during my teenage years in an inspirational form for their benefit.

Overall, the book is about my journey from darkness to light, from negativity to positivity, from frustration to hope. This book is an appeal to children, parents, teachers and every member of society who contributes to moulding the personality of students and helps them attain emotional maturity.

At some places, I have changed the names of people. I have used my imagination to make the dialogue more effective and cited some famous poems throughout the book. I have commented on topics not related to my professional life; my opinions on such topics are solely personal. From the bottom of my heart, I am thankful to all those who helped make this book a reality.

My writing is neither sophisticated nor poetic. I do not have a literary style. It is simply an expression of what I see on the screen of my mind. My emotional world is no different from that of any child living in a village. However, when I narrate the tale of the never-say-die approach that I adopted while treading the treacherous path of my life, I find several incidents which inspired me along the way. Linking them together is like taking a walk down memory lane. I recall several bittersweet memories, moments of hope and despair, tales of defeat and victory, to spice up all that I have experienced.

I found new contexts to my old struggles after joining the Indian Police Service which helped me realize the meaning of life, and gave my life a purpose. They answered old questions and gave rise to several new ones. This amalgamation of my experiences is dedicated to my innumerable siblings living in the villages and facing the same situations I have lived through.

Vishwas Nangre Patil

Chapter 1

The Rustic Reality

I consider myself fortunate to have been born and raised in the rustic environment of Kokrud village, living a pastoral lifestyle. Located atop a mountain range, it separates the Konkan coastal belt from the Maharashtra plateau. River Warna ensconces it from three sides and the Gawloba Hill, which resembles the shape of a Shivling, stands guard on the fourth side.

If one were to describe the sociocultural milieu of my village, it would be pertinent to mention the lush greenery by way of trees and sugarcane cultivation. And amid these sylvan surroundings, the aura of snooty wrestlers in a game of one-upmanship, patting their arms to challenge adversaries; the beats of dhol-Lezim inspiring us to do a jig; the lucid Kolhapuri dialect; and the spicy mutton curry added to the village charm.

Paradoxically, though, the powerful families which dominated the village were not as harmonious as nature was, for they always had their daggers drawn against each other.

Thus, even joyous occasions like the village fair and festivities reflected rivalry instead of celebration. At the centre of this conflict were the Nangre and Ghode brethren, who were responsible for the downslide of the village. They crossed swords (literally and metaphorically) for trivial reasons, indulging in one-upmanship. They would confront each other at the slightest provocation, eye to eye, spit on one another, even attack each other with sticks and axes. Of course, unlike the present-day era, the power of money was of little use to settle scores.

Mr Deshmukh, fondly known as Deshmukh Saheb, was the local political leader who, with his political astuteness, maintained a cordial atmosphere in the village. He had become a member of the Legislative Assembly at a very young age. He was an influential man, mature and ambitious in his leadership. Not only was he well educated, he also had an affable and affectionate personality. His influence went beyond the village; it shadowed over the entire tehsil. Although he hailed from an erstwhile feudal family, he had to maintain friendly relations with the mighty Nangre and Ghode clans. If he showed preferential treatment to one, the other would distance themselves from him. Keeping them both in good humour was a tightrope walk.

My family oversaw the leadership for the Nangre family clan. My grandfather was at the forefront of it. He passed away before I was born but the villagers regaled his legends. During the *patrisarkar*—the parallel government that sprouted during the 1942 Quit India Movement against the British Raj—my grandfather had mercilessly thrashed a police sub-inspector into the dust for his unjustified behaviour, leading him to go underground for several months. However, the police sub-inspector who had been beaten up did not dare to file a police complaint against my grandfather, fearing his reputation would be maligned. Had he done so, my grandfather would probably have been arrested, and this evidence of 'arrest' would have helped him claim the freedom fighter's pension for a lifetime. However, being a man of principles, he despised easy rewards. His motto was, 'I do not deserve even the light of the lamp, which is lit with the oil that comes free as a result of a corrupt system.'

Our family was cut above the rest. In the present era, even brothers born of the same womb do not live as a united family. However, in our family, not only the family members but also the domestic servants under our employ lived together, amiably. There was no discrimination. My grandfather had employed a youngster by the name of Dhondiram from a nearby village, to work on our farm fields. His brother-in-law too had accompanied him. Imagine the magnanimity of my family—they got them both married, and they in turn had five children each. Eventually, these children too got married and a kindred of 20–25 people would have meals together with us. My grandmother, a warm-hearted, motherly figure, would relentlessly care for each one of us in an affectionate yet responsible manner.

The concept of family planning had no relevance for people in those days. Every household would have enough siblings to form a basketball team, if not a cricket team. My grandparents were no exception. My grandmother gave birth to seven children—five daughters and two sons! My father was fondly called Tatya. Being the eldest male child in the household, born after four daughters, he was pampered by everyone. His younger brother was not as indulged, would be engrossed in studies and spent most of his academic years in hostels, away from home.

My uncle contracted the infectious disease of varicella soon after birth. To ensure that Tatya too did not contract the infection, a decision was taken to keep my newborn uncle in a heap of cow dung and waste in the cattle shed. Despite several days there, he somehow survived. In his youth, he studied hard, and did his engineering from Karad. He settled down in Pune where he was able to get an attractive job.

Tatya had a stout physique and a fair complexion. To add a cherry on top, he was a formidable wrestler, all credit to my grandfather. A strict disciplinarian, my grandfather had a strong affinity for the red soil in the wrestling ring. He would keep a stern watch on Tatya's diet and exercise regimen. He monitored Tatya at such an obsessive and micro level that he would even examine his stool, to ensure that the diet was right. A carefully planned diet, consisting of desi ghee, thandai and nutritious food. My five aunts would compete to prepare him a balanced meal. Tatya was made to complete sets of 1000 push-ups and sit-ups every day and consume a glass filled to the top with desi ghee. Therefore, when the charismatic, fair-complexioned Tatya, with an enviable physique, would challenge the opponent by beating his hand on his chest, even well-acclaimed wrestlers would shudder at their fate. Wrestling became his magnificent obsession, and he gave up his studies to make his career as a wrestler.

Though Tatya had crossed into his thirties, he remained a bachelor as he had rejected every marriage proposal that was brought before him. Being the elder son, the family waited patiently for him to get married but in vain. Therefore, the search began for my uncle, who soon got engaged in a ceremony in Pune. Tatya met my mother, a cousin of my younger uncle's wife, at their wedding ceremony, and cupid's arrow struck. The two families met at Baramati and finalized the marriage. My parents' elaborate wedding celebration lasted for three days. Legend has it that it was the first-ever wedding in the village which had a public procession, with the bride and the bridegroom seated in a chariot.

The lifestyle, values, rituals and tastes of my mother's maternal home were different from those in our village. This difference in cultures often led to verbal clashes between my mother and grandmother. My mother also belonged to a family which was poorer than the one she had married into. Since she did not bring many valuables to her in-laws' home, she would often be subjected to taunts and sarcasm.

All my paternal aunts were married off at an early age, as was customary. They would return to their maternal home during the last stages of their pregnancies for delivery and post-natal care. There was a superstition that if the woman delivered the child in the room located in the centre of our earthen-roof house, she was destined to deliver a boy child. However, my mother defied this superstition, much to the consternation of the family, and went to her mother's house to deliver her first baby. While the family prayed for a boy, to everyone's disappointment, she gave birth to a girl. The depth of Tatya's disappointment can be gauged from the fact that he did not even go to see his newborn daughter. He even named her Seema, which in the Marathi language means 'the end', further implying that he had had 'enough of the girl child'. This hurt my mother deeply.

However, she remained adamant about not opting for the 'lucky room' and insisted on going to her maternal home when she was pregnant with me. This perturbed not only the family members but also the people of our village. They racked their brains over how to ensure that a male child be born. My grandmother began looking for a suitable matrimonial match, intending to get Tatya remarried. She almost zeroed in on a girl from Kotoli village. If my mother delivered another girl child, she had made up her mind to get him remarried with the hope that it would enhance the chances of begetting a son. When my younger aunt found out about this strategy, she immediately wrote a letter to my mother. Panicking, my mother rushed to her in-laws' home, carrying me in her womb, in the eighth month of her pregnancy. She offered prayers at the temple of the village deity, seeking the faith she needed to live with her husband and in-laws.

I was born.

For my mother, I was the personification of the faith she had prayed for in the Ninai Temple. Therefore, she named me Vishwas.

Vishwas, in Marathi, means faith; faith in Ninabai. This is the story behind my name.

For my parents, my younger sibling, who was also a boy, was the personification of further progress and therefore he was named Vikas.

My mother was twelve years younger than my father. Due to this age difference, she never asserted herself over him. For example, when I was born, my mother insisted that the polio vaccine be administered to me. But Tatya would have none of it. He maintained, 'He is the offspring of a genuine wrestler. I have never allowed a syringe to be pierced in my body. Why inflict the mark on the arm of such a tender child?' My mother relented.

However, a year later, I suffered from a fever because of polio. The fever would not subside. The village doctor advised my parents to take me to Sangli. It was raining heavily, and I was taken to Shirala in a covered bullock cart and from there to Sangli in the State Transport bus. Thanks to the timely treatment administered by Dr Karmarkar, I was saved from being crippled for life. Apparently, he told my mother, 'Your son is fortunate. He was saved because he reached here in the nick of time. Otherwise, he would have been forced to carry the burden of disability for the rest of his life. Mark my words, one day he will become a big officer.'

Time and again, my mother narrates this incident proudly, her eyes welling up with tears. When I was selected for the Indian Police Service (IPS), she bought a box of pedhas and went to meet Dr Karmarkar. The doctor had aged. My mother touched his feet and, expressing her gratitude, said, 'Today my son has become a big officer, because of your graciousness. It has all been made possible because you saved him.' Such was his humility that all he said was, 'I just did my duty. The rest is all because of the blessings of Mauli.'

People from neighbouring villages would visit Kokrud for shopping. Besides, our village had a school with classes up to the tenth standard. Children from neighbouring villages would flock to our village to attend school. Since my aunts were married within a five-kilometre distance from Kokrud, their children attended the same school. All the cousins would gather at our house for lunch. They would live in our house when examinations approached, so that they would get the maximum time to study. They would also spend the summer and Diwali vacations at our house. Thus, my two siblings and I grew up alongside my cousins. Since they would address my father as 'Mama' (maternal uncle), we too initially called him 'Mama'. Later, influenced by other members of the family, we started calling him 'Tatya'. The residents of surrounding villages would call him 'Aaba'. We addressed our mother as 'Aai' and grandmother as 'Mhatariaiee' (older mother). I have no recollection of my mother or Tatya ever asking us to

address them as 'Baba', 'Pappa' or just plain 'Aai' (mother) or
'Aaji' (grandmother).

My uncle worked in respectable positions with big
companies. He had also bought his own flat in Pune. He never
had any expectations from his farmer brother, of a share in the
land or a part of the earnings from the agriculture.

Occasionally, my uncle would visit Kokrud to attend
festivities or in grieving. He would always be dressed in formal
suits. All three of my cousins were very sweet and always tried
to connect with us, but the prejudices and apprehensions
created in our mind by the villagers never allowed any strong
and emotional bonding among us. Uncle would tell us stories
about the struggle he underwent during his childhood.
He would say, 'Every problem is solved once you do away
with your inferiority complex. You should never consider
yourself inferior to anyone. You should never cover up your
shortcomings. You should never be afraid.'

About fear, he would say, 'Fear is nothing but anxiety
for the future! Fear means a refusal to accept uncertainty.
One who accepts uncertainty as a part of life finds out that
life is like an adventure sport. One should not hate anyone or
feel jealous of anyone. Refusal to accept goodness in others
results in jealousy; respect for the virtues of others proves
to be an inspiration. Acceptance of any person without any
precondition or expectation is love. When we have expectations
from others, we start hating that person. We get frustrated
about things we cannot change. When we become mature
enough to understand whether we can change such things or
not, we become tolerant.' I used to find his words of wisdom
very inspiring and felt that I could hear him speak forever.

He was my idol. I would always dream of studying and
becoming someone big like him, migrating to a big city like

he did and making a name for myself. However, I always seemed to have had too little of my uncle. He would visit us like a stranger, share some gems of wisdom and leave in a jiffy. We were left watching his Fiat car speed away, leaving clouds of dust behind it.

Chapter 2

Stepping into School

On the auspicious day of Gudi Padva, I stepped inside the school to take admission. My father was the sarpanch of our village, which got me a bit of VIP treatment, with Kadam Guruji himself welcoming me. He jotted down my date of birth in the school records and thereafter, the school reopened in June.

Since it was the rainy season, reaching school was quite a feat. Donning the improvised raincoat, with a hood made with a gunny bag, and clutching the textbook and slate in hand, we had to wade, barefoot, through the slushy road. By the time we reached school, wet mud stuck to our feet. The first thing we did was wash our feet with the rainwater that noisily fell from the rooftop of our school building.

I still recall how I was seized with the curiosity to learn when I entered the classroom for the first time. I was the first boy to learn to write the Marathi alphabet, which made me the teacher's pet. Besides this accomplishment, I was viewed as a cut above the rest, being the son of a noted wrestler and sarpanch and belonging to the farming community. This further enhanced my reputation at school. When I was in the second standard, our class teacher, Chaugule Sir, would reprimand others, sometimes using corporal punishment. I was the privileged one to be served, in front of the entire class, an over-brimming glass of milk. Naturally, some classmates looked at me with awe, others with jealousy.

My school was simply known as the Zilla Parishad Boy's School No. 1. Located near the farm fields, on the outskirts of the village, the building was impressive, with a lot of open space. The school's backyard was used for slaughtering goats and the courtyard in front of the school would be littered with garbage, especially human hair, thanks to the haircutting salon in front. We would spend the recess sadistically watching the writhing body of a freshly slaughtered goat or finding pieces of used blades thrown out by the barber, along with the hair. The other prank was to stand on the platform built around the trunk of a tree and compete with my peers to see who could pee the furthest.

I am filled with nostalgia whenever I think about my school days—it feels like a pleasant dream, perceived in the wee hours of the morning. It is almost like a hallucination, hearing the familiar voices, calling out to my friends, Tanya, Mujbya and Parshya, and remembering my teachers with fondness. I also remember the joy I would feel when the school bell rang to mark the end of the day. We would run out of school like newborn calves—playful and energetic.

After school, we would go to a particular elevated open space behind the school and partake in a skating competition on the slopes of that little plateau-like space. We used a piece of stick as a skating board, extending our arms to maintain our balance. I have lost count of the number of times we tumbled and suffered bruises on our knees while 'skating'.

Tatya had bought two buffaloes, of good pedigree, which produced a lot of milk. The surplus milk would be sold to the milk collection centre. However, there would still be a surfeit of milk, curd and ghee, which we would savour. When I returned home from school, my grandmother would serve us pieces of leftover bhakri (roti made of jowar or bajra) soaked in milk, which I used to consider a 'feast'.

In school, it was a rule to write an inspirational quote on the blackboard every day. It was also mandatory for everyone to recite mathematical tables up to thirty in front of the whole class. Thanks to this daily regimen, I can still recall my tables well. Our teachers would be meticulously dressed in spotless white shirts and pyjamas; some would wear a dhoti.

Corporal punishment was very common; pinching the belly button and caning on the back, depending on the intensity of mischief or bad behaviour. The quote, 'One who gets beaten, learns the fastest' was written on the walls of the school. I would feel anxious, as I was rarely ever punished, over the prospect that I would learn less! In sharp contrast, several students in my class hated attending school. Their parents would bring them to school forcibly, wielding canes. Once these wayward students were handed over to the teachers, they would be whipped even more. However, punishment hardly ever fazed these students; they would think of ways to run away the moment the teacher stepped out of the classroom. Even the iron bars fitted on the windows were not a deterrent. Their bodies were lithe and slender, and the joy of manoeuvring through these windows and breaking free was akin to a prisoner escaping from jail.

Our uniform comprised of a loose-fitting shirt and shorts, patched in several places. Our play area was the open space behind the school as well as the lake where we swam with the buffaloes.

On Dussehra, we would pluck the freshly grown wheat grass that had sprouted from the seeds sown on the first day of Navratri, collect it in a bowl at the sanctum sanctorum of the Ninabai Temple and walk pompously to school, carrying it in the folds of our arms or in our Gandhi caps.

On the auspicious Gudi Padva Day, we would pray to our slates with the utmost devotion, having coloured its borders and written 'Shree Ganesha' in its centre and drawn a *gudi* (a cloth hung on a stick, covered from atop with a copper or steel vessel and bedecked with neem leaves and sugar candies). I learnt to write countless words and solved innumerable sums on my jet-black slate with white chalk. The zeal to keep my slate impeccably clean prompted me to use my saliva. My teachers considered this offensive and whenever they noticed me doing it, I would receive a thorough scolding and a few blows on my back.

The tiffin would be simple; my mother would tie bhakri with spicy chutney made of chilli and oil, and a piece of onion tied in a cloth cut from Dada's old dhoti. This frugal meal was oh-so-delicious! Today, my children eat pizzas, but I challenge them to find the authentic taste of my childhood meal in the best pizza outlets of the world.

Once a fortnight, we were made to sit before the village barber, Shyamu Aaba, to get a haircut. This proved to be the most miserable time of our lives. He would use a noisy machine to crop the hair and virtually tonsure our heads, leaving a few long hairs, like a tail, at the top. It would make me look so comical; I hated myself whenever I looked at my reflection in a piece of broken mirror, and would cry my lungs out. Finally, Tatya took mercy on us, and we were allowed to keep our hair short. However, despite the neatly trimmed hair, my grandmother would apply so much oil on my head that it would trickle down my face.

In kindergarten and the first standard, we had to study only the primer book, which contained the basic alphabets of Marathi. Subsequently, the teacher asked us to bring textbooks of history, depicted in the form of a story, mathematics and Balbharati, the Marathi-language book. Notebooks were recycled from the ones used by our elder cousins, the blank pages were torn and stitched together, compressing a section of the lines under the stitches.

In the adjoining village of Chincholi, Bali Jadhav had a bookstall. Tatya would ask us to buy books from him on credit. However, Jadhav would humiliate us by tersely saying, 'Get cash first, only then can you get the books.' I felt insulted and my blood boiled. However, as he possessed a treasure of books, it was better to suppress my anger.

On Sunday morning, the classes would be conducted outside. Studying under the open sky was especially enjoyable during the winters, with the sunrays on our heads. On the flip side, the winter chill would make our tender skin dry and cause rashes.

My classmate Ghanshyam Pise was my toughest competitor in studies. His handwriting was better than mine and he had a good diction. However, he would become an example of how addiction can destroy the life of a bright youngster. His father, who was differently abled, was a tailor and his income was meagre. To augment his family's earnings, Ghanshyam made use of his good handwriting to paint movie posters at the newly opened Video Centre in our village. He began to spend more time there than in the school. Soon, he fell into bad company and took to substance abuse and addiction. Recently, I found out about his demise, due to a serious liver ailment. He was, most probably, the first victim of overindulgence in the modern vices and entertainment that invaded our village.

On Saturday, school would conclude early, leaving us free to enjoy ourselves however we liked. We would consider ourselves fortunate if we could catch a film at Bapu's Talkies, which toured from place to place. To enter the tent of the talkies and watch the night show required some adroitness and proved to be quite an adventure. We, the children, would sleep together in the shed, outside the house. After all the elders in the house were asleep, we would get up and run to the talkies. The film used to be shown through a series of reels. The first of the reel would be over within ten to fifteen minutes after the show started. The next reel required ten minutes to fix on to the projector. The audience would use this break to answer nature's call in the open field. As they returned to the tent, we would cheekily join them and sneak into the talkies tent, watching the film without buying any tickets. In those days, Dara Singh and Dharmendra were the most popular actors, in action-packed stunt films. We would whistle away in appreciation of a good scene and enjoyed ourselves to the fullest. However, some of the films shown at Bapu's Talkies were old ones, in black and white, which we found boring. We would doze off while they were playing. In the morning, we would awaken to hurls of abuses from the men who were folding up the tent and would run back home to receive an earful from the elders in the family. My mother would give us a thrashing too.

Since we were a joint family, we would often not meet Aai and Tatya for two consecutive days. Today, my wife becomes restless if our children are out of her sight even for a few minutes. Such is the difference of lifestyle between then and now. If anyone gave us a mango or a banana, we would eat it like monkeys, skin and flesh whole. We would crave chapatis made of wheat, as they were served only once a week. If we saw a water tanker along the road, we would rush to drink from it. We would attend weddings and meals served in the memory of the deceased called *shraddh*, irrespective of whether we were invited, only because we wanted to savour rice, vegetable curry and bundi.

We ate when we were hungry and slept when drowsy. We lived a natural life. Today, we need to use hot water to wash the plates that our children use for eating. If we visit a restaurant, we need mineral water to drink. We need to cajole our children to eat fruits. We need to reprimand them to use sanitizer every ten minutes. I do not remember a single occasion when I was hospitalized. We would routinely catch a cold and recover without any medicine. Nobody would even know that we had a cold, except when we wiped our runny noses with the sleeves of our shirts. Today, our child sneezes and we rush them to the paediatrician and administer too many medicines. What a contrast! I wonder if it is we who have changed or if the environment is responsible. What has been polluted—the atmosphere or our minds? Only God holds the answers to these questions.

Ghosts and evil spirits like Satwai, Khavis and Lavastin had their own designated places in our village and its outskirts. It was ingrained in our minds that every tree, well, river, hill and open space outside the village was haunted. Such was the impact of these superstitions that we could never enjoy the beauty and serenity of these places after 7 p.m. People believed that at the stroke of midnight, the evil spirit Khavis wakes up the wrestler sleeping alone in the *talim* and forces him to a wrestling match until the latter drops onto the mat, exhausted. No one slept alone in the talim, out of fear.

The thought of a devil entering the talim, which was blessed by Lord Hanuman, puzzled me endlessly. I took up the challenge of spending a night, all by myself, in the talim to confront Khavis. I was drenched in cold sweat at around 11 p.m., but I had accepted the challenge, there was no way out. Moreover, the wrestlers had locked the talim from the outside. If I chickened out, I would have become the laughing stock of the village. The fear of humiliation overpowered my fear of the ghost. I just lay there, with my eyes shut, chanting the name of Bajrangbali. I did not have a watch so I didn't realize when I dozed off. When I woke up in the morning, the wrestling coach, Vastad, looked at me appreciatively. 'This kid is lion-hearted,' he commented. Owing to this, I overcame fear at an early age, even when I took on terrorists, the real devils, at the Hotel Taj, on that fateful night of 26/11 Mumbai terror attack.

As I learnt the alphabet, I found myself able to read and write words. Soon, I began understanding sentences. When one learns to ride a bicycle, one begins enjoying pedalling it; when a child learns to walk, he is thrilled to totter around; it takes the synchronisation of beats and tunes to play a symphony. Similarly, when we learn to form words from individual letters and ascribe meaning to those words, we start enjoying them. Until I learnt how to read, my grandmother would tell me stories, after a lot of cajoling and pleading.

Once, I found a history book, written in a story form. I settled into the corner of a room on the first floor of our house and read it, cover to cover, in one sitting, so engrossed that I felt neither hunger nor thirst. Thus, I developed the habit of reading; I read anything that I could lay my hands on—*Chandoba, Champak, Panchatantra*, stories of Akbar and Birbal, stories of Sahdeo-Bhadali, to name a few. We subscribed to several Sunday newspapers. I found the children's section in the special supplements of the newspapers an intellectual feast and would throw myself into them. The other children wondered why I no longer accompanied them to swim in the river or play Sur Parambi on the mango and tamarind trees. They passed sarcastic remarks like, 'He is so obsessed with reading, as if he is going to become a teacher.'

When I started displaying academic excellence, Tatya began encouraging me. If my report card stated that I had stood first in the class, Tatya would give me Rs 10 to buy pedhas. I would eat as many watermelons and mangoes as I liked, and get a one-rupee coin to buy ice cream. Tatya loved watching movies, so he never stopped me from watching films on video or at the Bapu's Talkies tent. As a child, I was exposed to a different world through the silver screen. Those were the days when the climax of every movie would depict the triumph of truth; the hero would always defeat the villain. One could imagine Sulochana or Nirupama Roy as one's own mother or grandmother. Mythological and historical films would give us glimpses of our rich culture and longstanding traditions. The powerful on-screen presence of the Angry Young Man, Amitabh, would make us feel heroic. The cinema hall would resonate with the deafening sound of whistles and claps when he single-handedly beat up a dozen goons.

Initially, I found romantic song sequences very boring, but gradually I developed an ear for them. I also began to understand Hindi and the meaning behind dialogues unravelled before me. I started following films depicting serious issues. Whenever Tatya attended Zilla Parishad meetings, he would take me along. During those tours, he would show me the films of his favourite Bollywood star, Hema Malini, the dream girl, at the theatre in Sangli. I watched all her films, from *Seeta Aur Geeta* to *Andha Kanoon*—both of which I saw twice. Many a time, I would eat from Tatya's plate. I savoured the taste of chapati with jaggery and ghee. Occasionally, I would sleep next to him in his bed, resting my head on his muscular arm, and he would nurture my ambition, fondly saying, 'Study hard, become a big saheb!' These words ring in my ears even today.

We would hear tales of Tatya's heroics in the wrestling ring and his gruelling exercise regimen from my grandmother and aunts. I would probe him with questions about his career in wrestling which he answered unenthusiastically. I yearned to hear about his prowess in the ring, patting his arms and thighs formidably, hailing the master who had trained him. Instead, he would give me the example of my uncle, who had concentrated on his studies and become a respected officer. He taught me that education uplifts one's life and that the answers to all problems can be found in the cities. He would also tell me about the problems faced by the rural economy such as inadequate yield in agriculture, despite slaving away on the fields. He would rue how pests destroy sugarcane fields, resulting in uncontrollable losses for the farmer; how a farmer labours hard to make the best quality jaggery but the commission agent pockets all the profit, leaving him in the lurch. In sharp contrast, at school we would be taught that, 'Farming is the best profession, trade is even better, and a job is the worst.' However, Tatya regretted not having pursued his studies and nursed his unfulfilled dreams through me. This motivated me to work hard and score well to ensure that there was not a single remark in red ink in my report card.

Time passed by. Three video centres cropped up in our village, bringing the curtains down on Bapu's touring talkies business, and redefining entertainment for the entire village. The Indian cricket team, captained by Kapil Dev, won the 1983 World Cup. People thronged to these video centres to watch the screening of that match, captured in video cassettes. The excitement of watching a new film manifested in the crowd that excitedly gathered at the video centre at 9 a.m. to find out the film that was scheduled to be screened that day.

People from the surrounding villages would flock to the video centres during the week-long village fare. Marathi action films starring Sushama Shiromani would be the major crowd-puller. I have seen cloth tents being torn apart by jostling crowds during the screening of films like *Mardani, Mosambi-Naringi* and *Jakhami Waghin*. The titillating dance performances of popular tamasha troupes were another major attraction. Even the circus would put up shows to mark the occasion.

The week-long fair was jampacked with entertaining attractions, with wrestling matches being the final icing on the cake. The wrestling rings, the powerful physique of wrestlers and their fighting spirit emanating out of chest-thumping and war cries, villagers cheering for the incumbent winner or the underdog by tossing their *phetas* high in the air, reflected the liveliness of the village.

At least 100 goats would be slaughtered on the last day of the fair. Guests from the surrounding villages would cook and serve meat curry and other delicacies. Although farmers could ill-afford country liquor, the aroma of the illicit spirit would tempt them. There would be intense arguments over the quality of meat and liquor served, but the farmers took it in their stride, as it was their only available entertainment.

Festivals and celebrations were lined up in the month of Shravan. However, I would be busy with schoolwork, so I could hardly ever enjoy the festivities. The Fair of 'Nath' (The Nath Sampradaya is an ancient lineage of spiritual masters, highly revered in Maharashtra) would be organized in the Shirala village around Christmas time. Hence, for several years, I believed that Christmas was, in some way, related to Saint Gorakshanath.

My happiness knew no bounds during Diwali, as the school would have a three-week-long vacation, following the terminal examinations. Diwali meant firecrackers, feasting on sweet delicacies like faral and building miniature mud replicas of Shivaji's forts. After I joined the Indian Police Service, I realized that Diwali is the only festival that is celebrated with merriment, and without tensions between the different strata of society. The significance of festivals and celebrations undergoes change too, like the transition from childhood to adulthood and the lifestyle differences between a city and a village.

I vividly remember the way we used to celebrate Diwali. As soon as our examinations ended we would start planning; purchasing firecrackers was our biggest priority. It was a game of one-upmanship to be the first one to burst crackers, at the crack of dawn which signifies the beginning of Diwali. I would sleep in my grandmother's bed and repeatedly request her to wake me up before anybody else. However, she would wake me up only after every adult in the house had had a bath and was ready to celebrate. Upon waking, I would find the air charged with firecrackers, each bursting distinctly. My mother would give me a full body massage on a low, wooden *paath* (seat) with sandalwood oil, which I found most boring. I would be eager to be done with it, fretting the delay in bursting firecrackers. A bath with hot water, nearly scalding my skin, would follow. On the previous day, a decision had been made as to which perfumed soap to buy for the grand Diwali celebration, usually Moti. For the rest of the year, we would bathe with Nirma or some other detergent powder.

Our joint family comprised forty members; therefore, by the time it was my turn to take a bath, the soap was reduced to a small piece. My mother would then mark my forehead with a tika, perform *aarti* and dress me up in new clothes, ironed by burning coal in a pot. Every year, I would argue with everyone as I wanted to buy a police or army uniform, available in the departmental store, instead of settling for the traditional shirt and trousers. Of course, I had no idea then that I was destined to wear the police uniform for the rest of my life. Having donned our clothes, we would spray perfume on our neck and wrists, and apply perfumed oil on the head. Finally, we would be all set to celebrate Diwali. My mother would serve faral, and we would feast on typical Maharashtrian delicacies like kanawale, ladoos made of rawa and bundi, chiwda, kadakanis, anarse, shankarpalya and chaklis. We were allowed to taste these delicacies as they were being prepared, but that was a limited supply. We could eat to our hearts' content only on the day of Diwali. I still remember how we used to bite into the hard ladoos with our milk teeth, compete to see who could eat the maximum number of groundnuts in the chiwda and savour as many karanjis as we could. After eating, we would begin by lighting Laxmi Bombs, which were tied in a chain-like series. We would fuse the cracker before lighting it to delay the explosion. We would wait for ten to fifteen seconds for it to explode with a boom. At times the firecracker would not burst, but this never discouraged us. We would strip off the paper cover to remove the explosive material and repack it in another piece of paper. Placing it on a rock with a pebble atop it, we would throw a rock from a height, and this improvised firecracker would burst, making a deafening sound. At times, we would cover a firecracker with a plastic container. The container would be flung high in the air as the cracker burst. This simple thing amused us greatly.

Every day, we would take stock of how many firecrackers were burst and how many were left. In the evening, we would burst illuminating fire sparklers, ground *chakkars*, rockets and more. At least one case of burn injuries would occur every Diwali, but that never dampened our spirits. We dangerously indulged in flinging the fire sparklers in the air, kicking the ground chakkar while it was still burning, holding a fiery flowerpot cracker in our hands—all of which would give us immense thrill. Initially, we had a black plastic toy gun, that cost one and a half rupees, for bursting the rolling caps. Later, as we grew older, we got a steel toy gun, long-lasting and sturdy. If ever we were given a roll instead of caps, we would enjoy a round of rapid firing. The caps which did not burst would not be wasted; they would be torn from the roll and burst by holding it in our fingers and rubbing them against the wall. Our hands, with bits of explosives stuck on them, would look as if they had been painted with varnish.

The day of Laxmi Puja marked the opening of new shops in the village, with traders praying to their account books. We would visit our friends and seek the blessings of the elders at home, as well as our teachers.

There is a large settlement of Muslims near Nangre Wada in our village. My childhood buddies, Mujbya, Rafikya and Hanfya, would join me in bursting firecrackers. Their mothers, whom each called Ammi, would also prepare a limited quantity of Diwali faral like karanjis and ladoos. When I return to my village today, I feel saddened that the children of Hanifya and Mujbya do not burst firecrackers during Diwali. Something feels amiss. If there is *Ali* in Deepavali and *Ram* in Ramzan, why should there be a difference in karanji and shurkurma? This is the question that haunts me.

Bhaubeej, also known as Bhaiyya Dooj, is the festival which cements the relationship between brothers and sisters.

However, as children, we didn't have cordial relations with our sisters. Therefore, we would be misers when it came to giving gifts (*ovalni*) to them. In fact, my mother would not allow Tai to play as much as she wanted. She would get fewer firecrackers than us; my brother and I would get our pick of the sweets and she, though elder to us, would get the leftovers. We considered this blatant discrimination our birthright. We would tease and taunt her, angering her greatly. She would also taunt us and, at times, scratch us with her nails. But now, we do not meet her often because her husband is a police officer as well. Neither of us gets leave at the same time. When I talk to her over the phone, the bittersweet memories of our childhood come rushing back and our eyes well with tears. My children do not have the magnificent obsession with Diwali that I do. If I buy them firecrackers, they preach about protecting the environment, saying, 'Daddy, no more air and sound pollution, please.' When I consider my daughter in the position that my sister was in as a child, my guilt propels me to ensure that she always gets the same treatment as her brother.

As Diwali concluded, we would gear up for the end of vacations. Tatya would save some of the firecrackers for Tulsi Poojan. We would count every passing day of the twenty-one-day-long vacation. During the winter, the bonfire lit in the morning would burn till the afternoon. Rashes would break out on our skin and our lips would crack. We would huddle under Godhadi blankets, made of an assortment of appliques woven together. In the fields, crop cutting would be in full swing. One spent the day watching the hustle and bustle that surrounded the harvesting of paddy and wheat. My children will probably never experience it. Still, they may read about it in books or watch it on the internet. When I recall these memories of Diwali, I can almost taste the chakli testing the strength of our teeth, karanjis and ladoos. No sweetmeat made by any famous sweet shop can compete with the taste of those homemade goodies.

I recollect an incident. On a school holiday, I had gone to our field where they were crop-cutting during the wee hours of the day. Two rugged bullocks were trampling the crops to separate the grain. Half-asleep, I was helping with the work and did not see the bullocks approaching me. One of them, an aggressive, youthful bullock, rammed into me with its horns. Fortunately, my body, agile and slender, missed the horns and instead hit between them. The impact of the encounter flung me high in the air, landing on a heap of grass. Thankfully, I escaped with only a few minor bruises on my abdomen. We witnessed many disasters and mishaps like this one. They only made us tougher.

My favourite pastime was to go to the jaggery mill, drink sugarcane juice and savour the hot, sticky, fresh jaggery we called 'soda gul'. Semi-liquid jaggery is made by boiling sugarcane juice for three hours. We would then add baking soda to it to make soda gul. When I was in the fourth standard, I visited the jaggery mill during my vacations. I was walking towards the makeshift shed nearby, holding the pot of fresh jaggery in hand, when I tripped on a solid block of jaggery. The boiling-hot jaggery spilled on my leg. I suffered burns and three boils promptly surfaced on my left ankle. I burst into tears. Terrified, my sister used a rug made of sheep's wool to rub off the boils. This blunder caused the burnt skin to peel, exposing fleshy muscles and bones. Panicked, the workers picked me up and took me near the *kahil*, the pot in which the sugarcane juice was boiling, and applied lime on the burns. I was writhing in pain. While this was going on, other workers were busy taking the jaggery out of the pot.

The workers holding the pot lost their balance and dropped it. The entire pot of boiling hot jaggery rolled towards us. Datta Dada used all his might to push the pot away. Thus, I was saved but Datta Dada suffered severe burns on both of his hands. Such disastrous incidents were common but the heroic workers never shied away from risking their lives to save another. My childhood was rife with such dangerous experiences, which is why I never lost grip on the situation trying to find my way into the raging fire at the Taj on the night of 26/11. Rewinding to these childhood experiences in my mind stirred me to fight against the terrorists, whom I could witness from the CCTV room.

By the time I reached the fifth standard, I had developed a keen interest in my studies. I liked attending school and thought it my right to bully my classmates. I was mighty proud of the fact that I was brilliant and that my father was the sarpanch. I used to cane my classmates, pretending to be a teacher myself. To use modern terminology, this behaviour was akin to ragging. Once, a new teacher was supposed to teach us. Everybody was excited. I was sitting on the teacher's chair when the new teacher, Kadam Madam, walked into the classroom. I did not notice her. Everybody rose to greet her, but I remained seated. The new teacher walked up to me and, without warning, gave me a tight slap. 'Aren't you the son of a wrestler? Do you want to become a goon? You insult teachers by behaving in this manner. Is it good behaviour? Continue behaving like this and one day you will become a goon and bring shame upon yourself, your parents and us. Why do you harass poor students with the help of the goons belonging to your brethren? You are a coward. You will live a low life, hosting on others like a parasite. What is the image that you have built for yourself? You may be gifted but at your core, you are just a spoilt brat. Talent is a jewel for the modest. Without modesty, your brilliance is useless. Get out of my classroom.'

The teacher's anger knew no bounds. Not that I understood every word of what she was saying but my cheeks went red with the pain and insults. Stung with humiliation, I walked out of the school and went home sobbing. I told Tatya, 'I am not going to school again. I shall become a big wrestler like you and make my own future.' My father had never misused his strength or power. Whatever clout he wielded, he used it to help others. I was hurt because the teacher had spoken about him and my foolishness. I was adamant about not returning to school. I would find petty reasons to get angry and go into hiding. Tatya, afraid that I might give up studying, went to school and spoke to the headmaster, Sutar Sir. Thereafter, my class was changed.

My new class teacher was Lakole Sir. He had studied only up to the tenth grade. He was affectionate and sensitive. It was his warmth, more than his discipline, that attracted us to his class. Dressed in a pyjama and shirt, clean-shaven, always smiling and soft-spoken, he would love all his students as if they were his own children. He would make even tough subjects like mathematics simple by explaining the formulas in the form of a story. His elder son Dilip studied in our school and his younger son Vijay was my classmate and both possessed extraordinary talent. They were so intelligent that they would read something once and comprehend it fully, and both displayed mastery over mathematics. Vijay, a skilful orator, captivated the audience with his speeches. During these speeches, Sir's moist eyes would shine with pride. Thanks to Sir's encouragement, I too started excelling in my studies. He appreciated my tough and ambitious nature. He would tell me, 'Vishwas, you have leadership qualities. You can become a good leader, but for that to happen, you will need to study hard.'

Sir had the ability to gauge a student's strengths and work towards their overall development. Once, he asked every student in the class what they wanted to become when they grew up. I do not know why but I asked him, 'Sir, who is the *biggest* saheb of all?' He replied, 'The Commissioner!' I asked him, 'Sir, can I become a commissioner?' The entire classroom burst into laughter but Sir reprimanded them, saying, 'You should dream of achieving great heights. The heights you achieve are measured in terms of where you start from. You should reach for the moon. You must have the guts to make your dreams a reality. You should put all your efforts into it. If you do this, you will be able to become not only the President of our country but even a world leader.' His words hit me like a tsunami.

He would always say, 'Only those who dare to dream big can fulfil those dreams. Just having wings will not help you. Your wings must be strong enough to take flight in the open skies. Do you know the tale of the eagle? As an eagle grows old, its beak starts weakening, its wings become frail. An eagle can live up to seventy years but it must take some tough decisions. When it becomes weak, it has two options—either accept defeat and end his life or revive its zest for life by undergoing 150 days of excruciating penance, which begins with seclusion in a nest built on a mountainside. There it must batter its beak against the rock until it breaks down. Steadily, it then grows a new strong beak. Then it must start beating its weakened wings and feathers against the mountain rocks. It undergoes intense agony but attains new, powerful wings. The five-month long hibernation rejuvenates it and adds another thirty years to its life. Like the eagle, you must decide whether you want to make your life or break it.'

He would further say, 'Everybody gets the same life. You are going to live as long as Mahatma Gandhi, Lokmanya

Tilak, Babasaheb Ambedkar, Pandit Nehru, Indira Gandhi, Albert Einstein or Newton lived. Then why shouldn't you dream of becoming as big as they did? You should aim to reach the highest peak of your chosen career. Once you get to it, there won't be much of a crowd. Everything falls in line when you introspect on the meaning of life. In this way, you can make the most out of your life.' We would not understand the depth of his words but they would move us from the core of our hearts, energizing us. Whenever he spoke, he would give us the confidence to believe that, 'I too can become someone big, someone great!' I was possessed by the power of such motivation.

Sutar Sir, the headmaster, taught us English. Till date, I have not forgotten the rules of grammar. Like Lakole Sir, Sutar Sir had studied up to the tenth standard. He would draw a humble salary of Rs 550 per month and, in return, provide us with the best education. His repeated mantra was that, 'It is best to do agriculture, better to do business and good to do service.' He would explain that the one who farms with dedication and produces wholesome crops, the one who does business while maintaining high moral grounds, turning away from greed and immorality and the one who does service loyally, putting his employers' interest first, is the real patriot. Those were the days when the country was witnessing the riots of 1984. Sutar Sir would be overwhelmed when he read the newspaper reports.

I recall a story he told us.

Once a hungry baby vulture said to its father, 'Papa, I want to eat the flesh of a human being today.' The father vulture asks it to wait and takes off, looking for the flesh with its sharp eyes. Finding no human flesh, it picks up a piece of the carcass of a pig. However, the baby vulture recognizes it and says, 'Papa, this is a pig's flesh. Can't you fulfil my wish?' The vulture asks it to wait and goes in search of human flesh again. It looks everywhere to fulfil its baby's demand, but in vain. However, this time it finds the carcass of a cow. It offers the cow's flesh to the baby but the latter refuses to eat that too. Vexed, the vulture cooks up a sinister plan. It picks up the two pieces of flesh and flies off. During the night, it drops the pig's flesh in the premises of a mosque and the cow's flesh inside a temple. When the humans wake up and find the pieces of flesh in their respective areas of worship, fanned frenzy takes over reason and they attack each other, bashing each other's heads and setting buildings on fire. Communal violence snuffs out many lives, making the vulture's job easy. It picks up several pieces of human flesh and takes them to his baby. The baby vulture is delighted and asks, 'Papa, how did you achieve this?' The father vulture describes the beast-like, selfish tendency of human beings, saying, 'Human beings, who take pride in calling themselves the best creation of God, are worse than beasts. They are bound by the chains of caste, religion, language, colour, gender and so on. At times, they offer flowers to stones and other times, they crush flowers with stones. They build temples and mosques to worship God but degrade their own sense of self to such an extent that they incite communal riots over petty reasons and suffer in hell for generations.'

Sir would caution us against our own vulture-like tendencies. Human vultures spin deceitful tales to influence and provoke us. This provocation makes us forget the values of humanity, brotherhood and integrity and kills our sense of equality, mercy and love. If each one of us went about the work assigned to us in an honest manner, the country would resolve all its problems and set off on the path of development. Students should study hard, workers should labour in factories, farmers should toil in the field, teachers should impart quality education and politicians should do social work. However, these workers, students, politicians lose their heads if a Ganesh idol is damaged by a calf trying to eat some grass or if a troublemaker throws a pig carcass near a mosque. These acts are enough for them to butcher each other with sticks and axes, become so irrational that they commit gang rapes on streets.

The city of Ahmednagar witnessed communal riots for three consecutive years, from 2002 to 2005, during the Muharrum processions. I was posted at Ahmednagar as district superintendent of police in 2005 and faced the challenge of breaking this vicious cycle of communal riots. I researched the rioting cases filed over the previous three years and profiled the accused. I was shocked to note that 90 per cent of them were ordinary, hardworking people: autorickshaw drivers, handcart pullers, paan-stall owners and school and college students.

The first thing I did was to take all the sections of society into confidence and organize programmes aimed at promoting communal harmony. We invited spiritual leaders from various communities to speak at these programmes, including maulanas, priests and *bhikhus*. These good-hearted people exercised their authority and explained to the youth that the real meaning of religion was to love one another, be compassionate towards everyone and serve society.

I walked on foot, along the procession route, on at least fifteen occasions, carrying out a reconnaissance of the exact spots the riots would spark off. I prepared a twenty-two-point anti-riot scheme and took some bold decisions. One of them was to ban sound systems installed on trucks. I also executed *naka bandi* exercises at a few locations, and conducted rehearsals of riot-control exercises in areas inhabited by a mixed population, intending to showcase police presence. As a result of this strategy, several goons fled to Mumbai and

I called my police officials from there, assuring them that they had indeed left Ahmednagar. I went a step further and reduced the height of torch-flame sticks carried in processions, as the oil poured on these torches posed the danger of instigating fires.

The revenue administration was apprehensive about my plans. They expressed to my senior officers that these measures may flare up riots. However, the intention behind the steps taken by me was clear. I had successfully gained the confidence of the Muslim community, thus re-establishing communal harmony in the city. When the procession, of nearly 75,000 Muslims, stepped outside Delhi Gate without any untoward occurrences, the Muslim brothers shouted slogans hailing the Ahmednagar police.

I was posted at Latur as district superintendent of police when bomb blasts took place near mosques in Purna and Jalna towns of Marathwada. Tensions mounted in the entire Marathwada belt but Latur stayed neutral. A reputed newspaper even published a special editorial article praising the people and the police force of Latur, stating, 'There was no flare up in Latur though its borders were going up in flames.' Such an appreciation of one's achievements is more heartening than any medal. These values were inculcated in me by my teachers when I was a child. I remember Sutar Sir teaching us a Sanskrit shloka and explaining its meaning. It was:

Oṁ Sahanāvavatusahanaubhunaktu,
Sahavīryamkaravāvahai
Tejasvināvadhītamastu Māvidviṣāvahai

(May God protect us together. May God accept us together. Let us achieve strength together. Let our learning always be fresh.)

The most important part of the shloka is '*Māvidviṣāvahai*', which means, 'May we all make a commitment to never hate, detest or abhor each other. Come what may, my religion, creed, region or language will never affect my cordial and humane relationship with others. I shall always respect diversity.'

The story of the six blind men and the elephant is well known. According to the story, six blind men try to figure out what an elephant looks like by touching various parts of its body. The one who feels its trunk says that the elephant is like a snake; the one who feels the leg says it is like a pillar; the one who feels the stomach says it is like a drum; the one who feels its tail says it is like a broom and the one who feels its ear says it is like a winnowing basket. They would be able to comprehend the physical appearance of the elephant only with the help of someone with unimpaired vision. We do not feel safe if our real brother, an alcoholic, is at the steering wheel of our vehicle. If the doctor belonging to our own caste or religion fails to provide good treatment, we avoid consulting him. We value how good the music is over whether the lyrics are sung by Lata Mangeshkar or Mohammed Rafi. We overcome differences of caste and religion on all such occasions. That is why we should respect diversity. How would it be if all the five fingers of our hand were of the same size and shape? What would have happened if the colour and fragrance of all flowers were the same? How would our life be if all foods tasted the same? Our lives would be unbearably monotonous. My secondary school teachers would inculcate such thoughts in our young, impressionable minds, every day.

Sutar Sir narrated one more story, explaining the true nature of religion. The story is so deeply embedded in my being that if anyone tried to tell me otherwise, I would not be fazed. The story is about a virtuous soul, a saint. Once he was bathing in a river when he noticed a scorpion drowning. Filled with pity, he picked up the scorpion with his bare hands to save its life. The nature of the scorpion was to sting; it stung the saint's finger. He suffered unbearable pain and the scorpion slipped out of his hands, drowning again. He picked it up again with his bare hands and was stung again, this time with more intensity. Again, he let go of it. The saint and the scorpion repeated this cycle four or five times. The saint suffered from blood poisoning and his body turned black and blue. A man who was standing on the bank of the river and witnessing this interaction, said, 'Sir, don't you realize that it is a venomous scorpion? It has stung you and if you suffer another couple of stings, you may die. Why are you behaving so recklessly?'

The merciful saint calmly replied, 'I know it is a venomous scorpion. To sting and inflict pain upon others is its Dharma. But being a human being, it is my Dharma to rescue it, save its life. If the scorpion does not change its Dharma, why should I change mine?' Indeed, this is true. Today we see many venomous, destructive scorpions stinging society incessantly. These vainglorious souls, whose only pride is their religion, pollute the entire atmosphere. They intentionally misinterpret the teachings of religion and create disharmony. As a result, communal riots flare up and people find themselves divided by the walls of religions. We need to explain the true meaning of religion to such misguided souls and their polluted brains.

Today, it amazes me that teachers from a rustic, sleepy village, who possessed neither an advanced education nor any urban exposure, had the sense to inculcate such values in us. They reiterated that education must bring wisdom. To achieve this, they would make us recite Swami Samarth Ramdas's 'Manache Shlok' (verses that impart ethical and

moral values). Each of the verses is key to personality
development. We would have reciting competitions; the
school walls, painted with inspiring quotes, would resonate
with the poems that we recited in unison. Portraits of eminent
personalities would be hung at every nook and corner of the
school. Marathi poems enamoured us and poems about valiant
war heroes chilled us to the bone. Poems about nature would
give flight to our imagination. The poem 'Nilya Khadichya
Kathala Majha Ivlasa Gav' (My Little Village on the Banks
of the Blue Lagoon) makes my mind drift to that lush green
village on the banks of River Warna.

Chapter 3

High on High School

My paternal uncle, who worked in the state Water Resource Department, was transferred to Shirala. My father, seeing an opportunity, sent me there to pursue my high-school education. I would live with my uncle and aunt. I enrolled in the sixth standard of New English School in Shirala, known for its disciplined environment and quality education.

My uncle's house was modest, and my aunt was a woman of impressive grit and discipline. Like any true disciplinarian, she would wake up before 5 a.m. every day, deftly managing the household. This meant that we too had to follow her strict regimen. Waking up early was the first item on the list; something that I did not mind at all. I awoke to the lilting sound of devotional music and the news broadcast on All India Radio. The music would fill my ears and heart with joy, and the news kept me abreast of all the current events. My aunt's disciplinary routine affected me in a positive way. I was focused on my studies and became one of the brightest students of my class.

However, helping my aunt with household chores was a must for everyone. Since Shirala suffered from water shortage, we had to take turns once a week to fetch water from the public tap. During the summer, people had to fetch water from wells which were located at quite a distance from my uncle's house. My cousin Rajkumar was pursuing engineering at Sangli and was given privileged treatment in terms of the errands he had to run or the new clothes that were bought for him. We younger siblings would wear his cast-off trousers which didn't fit us and were worn out and shabby. However, I was delighted by the full-length trousers, a pleasant change from the shorts that I used to wear. My aunt would alter the trousers to fit our waist and length, and do applique work on them by stitching patches of cloth to mend the torn portions. Sometimes these patches were stitched on the rear side of the trousers, clearly visible to others.

On my way to school I would spot Abdullya, the lunatic. He was menacingly stationed at the corner of the lane that led to my uncle's house. Many a time, he would stand there stark naked. This sight terrified me, and I would run as fast as I could to the safety of my school.

Back home in Kokrud, the school was run by the Zilla Parishad, and the students would arrange a gunny bag on the floor to sit on. However, at New English School at Shirala, much to my pleasant surprise, students would sit on benches. My cousin Vijay was in my class and though he was naughty and quarrelsome, he excelled in sports. This inadvertently protected me from being bullied despite being new to the school.

The massive school building was located on a campus that sprawled across ten acres of land and had a huge playground. The adjoining building housed the newly established girls' school. The classrooms were spacious, with big blackboards. The teachers were smartly dressed in shirts and trousers. Clean shaven, they looked tidier than the sloppily dressed teachers at Kokrud. Our headmaster, Digwadekar Sir, was a short man, always dressed in spotless white shirts and trousers. He had a quiet disposition and when he did talk, it was always to the point. He held the reins of the school firmly and had zero tolerance for nonsense. There were other teachers who made up for an interesting faculty. Rama Joshi Sir was potbellied, Vedpathak Sir had cat eyes and Deshingkar Madam, with her slim build, had an aura like that of the actress Ashvini Bhave. Hasabnis Sir would always wear half-sleeved shirts, Kulkarni Sir styled the few strands of hair on his head like Nikolai Bulganin and Lawate Sir was feared for his cane-wielding skills. The memories of these unique personalities are still fresh in my mind.

It was here that I first found out what a real library looks like. To begin with, I borrowed two story books from the library. Thereafter, I became a regular patron of the library. The science laboratories were situated in a corner of the building. The chemistry laboratory was infamous for always emitting a pungent, foul smell. I was disinterested in biology because biology students had to conduct a post-mortem examination on frogs, because of which I made a resolution that come what may, I would never become a doctor.

Unfortunately, students from rural areas never receive any career counselling. Their highest goal is to become a doctor or an engineer. To become a teacher or a policeman is an average goal and the aspiration to become a peon in the bank or a worker at a sugar mill is considered the lowest. Students pursued specific careers based on their IQ. When it came to girls, building a career was rarely ever considered. When they passed the tenth or twelfth boards, their family would make efforts to marry them off. Many girls would be married as early as when they attained puberty. At best, and that too rarely, a girl would become a teacher. Otherwise, girls were expected to become homemakers. If girls became highly educated, finding a suitable groom became difficult.

The social and educational setups, be it at villages or at *taluka* places, were practically the same. However, one thing was clear. The teachers in Shirala would not doze off in the classroom or embarrassingly keep re-tying their dhotis, the way the teachers at Kokrud did. They would not work in the fields after school hours. Teaching was their sole occupation.

Gradually, I got accustomed to the new school. At the beginning of the rainy season, as school reopened, a tree plantation programme was held on campus where every student was expected to plant a tree. We would nurture our planted sapling with candid enthusiasm. As a rule, we would water the plant, enclosed within a barbed compound, and till the soil at its roots before attending morning prayers every day. Even today, when I visit Shirala, I see the neem tree, fully matured now, which I had planted as a schoolboy. Thanks to my school, I continue to nurture this love for greenery. During my tenure in Marathwada where I was responsible for supervising the functioning of 178 police stations, each of my subordinate officers made it mandatory for every policeman to plant a tree at the police-station campus during the monsoon. We planted a whopping 18,000 trees. I motivated all the superintendents of police to not only ensure that everyone adopts a tree, but also to ensure it was cared for by making remarks in every policeman's annual report.

Some of my classmates like Ganya Jadhav, Shirpya Kambale, Shivjya Bhosale and Tanya Mohite would come to school from nearby villages. They would either ride bicycles or travel via the State Transport buses. Besides this, there were students who belonged to middle class families like Makrand Deshpande, Samir Mane, Digambar Kulkarni and Abhijit Deshmukh. A student named Kaustubh Wadekar was also a new admission. His name itself hinted at his elite class. He spoke chaste Marathi, and his father was an engineer in the telephone department. All the other students would wear rubber slippers or plastic footwear during the monsoon, whereas Kaustubh would wear black shoes and socks. His uniform would always be clean and crisply ironed. He would flaunt his snobbish attitude at school, arguing with the teacher or bursting into tears if he failed to answer a question. Even while playing, he would be a spoilsport. Once I got into an argument with him during a physical training class and we came to blows. I punched him and started chasing him with an iron ball in my hand. Gaikwad Sir got there in the nick of time, and he was saved. He started throwing a tantrum. Fearing that his parents would come to school, and I would not be spared from punishment, or worse, suspension, I decided to pull a vanishing act. I went to my aunt and narrated the entire episode to her with tears rolling down my cheeks. She gave me money for the bus fare, and I escaped to my village. I did not attend school the following Monday.

When I returned, my father in tow, the school was abuzz with gossip. The headmaster summoned me. Digwadekar Sir advised me to use my gift of the gab and not physical prowess hereafter to make my point.

Digwadekar Sir was a man of discipline. Pin-drop silence would prevail in the school when he stepped into the campus. He conducted a weekly class of Sanskrit *Subhashitas*. A Subhashita (Sanskrit: सुभाषित) is a literary genre

of Sanskrit epigrammatic poems and their message is an
adage filled with useful advice. He made us memorize and
recite the twelfth and eighteenth chapters of the Bhagavad
Gita. His attempts to use the Sanskrit Subhashita to turn
ignorant students into scholars was laudable. My classmates,
who had come from villages, were not fluent in Marathi
and their understanding of Hindi and English was, at best,
barely enough to pass the examination. We believed that
Sanskrit was the prerogative of only the elite scholars whose
knowledge extended so far beyond their brains that they
needed to maintain a pigtail to store it. Moreover, Sanskrit
was an optional subject and therefore not a priority. However,
I developed an affinity for this subject which I believed
imparted vital and comprehensive teachings. We imbibed its
teachings through examples given by Digwadekar Sir in his
lucid, clear voice which would make its way into the deepest
trenches of my mind.

I have still not forgotten two Subhashitas taught by
Digawadekar Sir.

विद्वत्वचनृपत्वचनैवतुल्यकदाचन |
स्वदेशेपूज्यतेराजा, विद्वान्सर्वत्रपूज्यते ||

'There can be no comparison between a king and a learned
scholar. The king is respected only in his kingdom, but
the learned scholar is respected everywhere.' Due to this
Subhashita, I never gave up my studies. When I became
an IPS officer, the only educational qualification I had was
my BA degree in history from Shivaji University, Kolhapur.
Even after being selected for the IPS I pursued my studies,
doing my MA from Bombay University and post-graduation
in police management from Osmania University, Hyderabad

during my training as a police officer. I obtained an LLB degree from Swami Ramanand Tirth University while I was posted at Latur as district superintendent of police. When I was posted with the Anti-Corruption Bureau, I finished a certificate course in peace and conflict management from Chulalongkorn University. I trained in post-blast investigation from the US-based Black Water Academy while I was posted in Mumbai and presently, I am in my first year of LLM at Dr Babasaheb Ambedkar Marathwada University. I had resolved to enhance my knowledge as much as I could in the seventh standard, when I was attending Digwadekar Sir's class on Sanskrit Subhashitas.

At times, I tend overdo my exercise regimen, only because I want to develop my physical, mental and spiritual capabilities. I participate in marathons, play the guitar till my fingers bleed, suffer neck pain doing the Shirshasana for as long as I can to set a new personal record and hurt my spine bungee jumping. Although it is painful, it gives me the pleasure of learning something new. The pain lasts only a little while as nature heals every wound with time.

यौवनंधनसंपन्ति प्रभूत्वमविवेकिता |
एकैकमप्यनथाय किमु यत्रचतुष्टयम् ||

'Youth, abundance of wealth, power of lordship and lack of deliberation—each one of these are for calamities. What to say about their assemblage?' Taught by Digwadekar Sir, this Subhashita had a major impact on me at a young age. I resolved to never lose my patience while studying and even after becoming successful. I resolved never to allow myself to be tempted by wealth or power.

A master of wit and dramatic presentation, Digwadekar Sir would extensively explain Swami Vivekanand's vision of a youth icon to us. A youth icon, he would say, is one with a radiant face and an enthusiastic mind, a rational brain, a merciful heart, love for the motherland, self-control over the limbs and organs, unwavering confidence, unrelenting willpower, fearlessness like a lion, great ambition, dedication to the truth, lack of addictions, discipline in life, affection for others, respect for teachers, devotion to parents, compassion for the weak, a willingness to serve, devotion to God, abiding to the ethics of life and a spotless character.

I used to ask myself: Can I become a youth idol? Sure, I can! What's stopping me? Would I not be able to speak like Swami Vivekanand? Would I not be able to become glorious like him? Would I not be able to master anything in the first attempt? These questions and aspirations would crop up in my mind after listening to Digwadekar Sir's lectures. I would feel ashamed to ask such questions in the classroom. Therefore, I would gather the courage to step into the headmaster's office and plead, 'Sir, bless me! I want to find big dreams and make them a reality. Guide me. Tell me what I should do.' Digwadekar Sir would be delighted to find that a rural student was asking such a question. He would make me sit with him and explain the teachings of Swami Vivekanand to me. 'Select any idea and resolve to bring it to reality. Dedicate your life to that idea; dream of only that. Ensure that you spend every waking moment for that. This is the highway to success.' I found that his words contained a lot of wisdom. Thus, I resolved that I would never use brute force to fight with Kaustubh Wadekar. Instead, I would make use of Digwadekar Sir's teachings to reason with him.

Once, an elocution competition was declared. Prior to this, I had never heard the word 'elocution'. Even spelling it was difficult for me. Previously, I once had to deliver a speech in Kokrud at a function marking the birth anniversary of Lokmanya Tilak. I had learnt two paragraphs on Lokmanya Tilak's life and work. However, when I rose to speak, all I could say was, 'Honourable chairperson, respectable teachers and friends, today I am going to speak a few words to mark the birth anniversary of Lokmanya Tilak. I request you to hear me patiently . . .' I faltered and could not remember the rest of the speech. I awkwardly finished my speech by saying, 'With this, I conclude my speech.' This awful first experience made me believe that elocution competitions were not meant for me.

But I had the urge to debate principles with Kaustubh. He had a good memory and could recite many Sanskrit Subhashitas. On the day of the competition, we were to speak on the topic 'The dream I saw'. I had not prepared anything, having arrived that very morning from vacation in Kokrud. On Sunday night, I had watched a Hindi film entitled *Lal Pari* at Bapu's Talkies, about a poor boy who meets the Red Fairy, who magically solves all his problems. He finds himself able to attend school, eats as many chocolates as he likes and rides her back to see the entire world. I requested the judges to allow me to participate. When they granted me permission, I simply narrated the story of that film in my own language as my own dream. I was so engrossed that tears rolled down my cheeks as I spoke. When I concluded, thunderous applause rocked the auditorium. I stood first in the competition, winning a stainless-steel jug and bowl. That was when I realized that one should never hide one's abilities. Instead, one should stand up and fight back. Even if one is defeated, the fact that one fought back is bound to make one happy.

Every day that we spent at school, we would learn
something new. Rama Sir taught mathematics, explaining
the formulas of algebra, arithmetic and geometry with a
clarity that made them simple to solve. Navangul Sir taught
us history and would make us write a lot. I was Vedpathak
Sir's favourite student. Fair-complexioned and emerald-eyed
Vedpathak Sir, who taught us English, had recognized the
eager and bright student in me. His faith in me helped me
find my inner courage. I would go to his house in the evening
for English tuition. The path to his house stretched along
the stream. Having grown up, I was not as scared of ghosts
as I was when I was younger. I also started preparing for
the scholarship examination, which consumed me. Kulkarni
Sir would teach general aptitude and Marathi. This was
the first competitive examination I had appeared for, and
I passed it with flying colours. These small victories paved my
way to success.

My aunt was fond of me but neither she nor my uncle
ever pampered me. They had several codes of conduct that
they expected all of us to live by. I was expected to always
be punctual, to not waste money on unnecessary things or
time in watching television or movies, to not eat junk food
or oily foods served at hotels, to not wear flashy clothes and
finally, to always wash my hands and feet before entering the
house. They would implement these rules rigorously, and
we would abide by their rules even without being reminded.
In those days, children had no freedom. Whatever the elders
in the family said was the gospel truth. Arguing or expressing
one's views was not permissible. Uncle would spend the night
preparing the muster. As a result, the lights would remain on
throughout the night. Power would be supplied to us for only
two hours in the night. In its absence, I would read in the dim

light of a lantern. There was even a rule about maintaining
the most economical size of the lantern flame. I still have this
habit of saving money and living within my means. As a result,
my children taunt me and call me 'Miser Daddy'!

Sometimes, I shouldered the responsibility of repairing
and maintaining my uncle's big Atlas bicycle. When I sat on
it, my legs would not reach the pedals, but I learnt to pedal
by tucking my legs under the bar. It was tricky to maintain
balance this way. However, I would be delighted as the bicycle
moved along, quite smoothly. Once my uncle had gone out
of station, so I took his cycle and rode it to school. It was
my first time cycling such a long distance and I enjoyed it
immensely. However, I forgot the bicycle at school. When
I reached home, everybody was talking about the theft of the
bicycle. I panicked and ran back to school to get the bicycle.
Every such experience would teach me a new lesson, teach
me the value of things. Everything, big or small, had value
at my aunt's house. There were set rules about how to use
something, how to conserve it and how to dispose of it.

We would wear a striped pyjama and T-shirt to bed.
We would not use slippers at home. The floors of the house
were always spotlessly clean and plastered with cow dung,
protecting our feet. I see children nowadays gingerly stepping
on plush carpets with their shoes on.

Mutton delicacies would be cooked on the days of weekly
village market, that is, Wednesdays in Kokrud and Sundays
in Shirala. However, since I spent Saturdays and Sundays
in Kokrud, I would seldom eat non-vegetarian food. When
exams approached, I would spend Saturdays and Sundays
in Shirala instead of going to Kokrud. On such weekends,
my cousins and I would wait eagerly to feast on the mutton
curry cooked by my aunt using grated coconut. Vijay and

I would make plans to watch a movie on video in the afternoon. We would go for the 3–6 p.m. show, telling everybody at home that we were off to the library. We were afraid that our lies would be exposed, and we would get a beating. My uncle would visit the library at 7 p.m. After the show, we would go to the library and pretend that we had spent the afternoon there. Vijay could scarcely manage to sit still in the library for fifteen to twenty minutes. He would get bored and sneak out to join the game of volleyball being played outside the library. When Uncle would visit the library, he would find me reading and Vijay playing. As a result, Vijay would be beaten with a cane when we returned home.

In fact, in those days, sports competitions were not considered dignified. The importance of sports was limited to exercise. Sports, other than wrestling, were not openly accepted in rural areas. As a result, sportspersons were considered good-for-nothing students, and pursuing sports was not encouraged. On holidays, I would go to the talim enthusiastically. Seeing my body get plastered with red soil in the wrestling ring delighted me. The master would have high expectations from me because I was the son of a wrestler. Sanjay Mane, whom I would be paired with to wrestle, was a nimble player. He would defeat me easily in a few seconds. Watching me fail in wrestling made my father happy. My uncle had studied and become an engineer. Therefore, he expected me to study and succeed in life. He dreamed of the day when I would become someone affluent, maybe even a senior officer. When I looked at him, I could see the dream he nestled in his bosom through his eyes.

The atmosphere in the school was laid-back but as examinations approached, tensions would mount. There was a lot of competition between classes. However, this competition did not make much of difference to students who weren't interested in studies.

There were around ten to twelve girls in the class. Cold War-like relations prevailed between us. Conversation with girls was considered taboo. If we spotted a girl from the class anywhere outside school, we would turn our face the other way and walk away. When I was appearing for the SSC board examination, my seat number was in the Chhatrapati School. Our school, the New English School, and Chhatrapati School were rivals. My school bore the brand 'The School of Brahmins', while the Chhatrapati School was considered 'The School of the Masses (Bahujans)'. The atmosphere of the two schools varied greatly. Our school was academically inclined whereas the Chhatrapati School students would excel in sports and other extra-curricular activities. If one of our school's students was caught cheating during the examination, he would be rusticated. Moreover, word went around that some teachers made cheaters stand on the table and parrot, 'My school teaches me to cheat in the examination.' Besides, the Chhatrapati School was quite far from my uncle's house. Therefore, I was tense during the examination. As per the seating arrangement, the daughter of a country liquor shop owner in Shirala was to occupy the seat behind me. Her father was a well-known village goon, and her body language was like that of actress Sushama Shiromani in the popular Marathi film *Fatakadi*. Her two stout brothers would drop her to school in their jeep. All this had put me under pressure. Many a time, she would ask me the answers to questions during the exam. I would be tempted to help her but was prevented by the tales I had heard about her. One day, after the mathematics paper, she and her friends stopped me to ask how my paper went. I broke out in cold sweat. 'I have to reach home early,' I managed to say before bolting. That was the first time I had spoken to a girl who was a stranger to me.

In rural areas, biased and hateful attitudes towards the other gender are intentionally inculcated in the minds of young boys and girls. This results in them getting trapped in perverted attractions. Because of suppressed emotions, many a time, rural youths commit grave mistakes in their teenage years and spend the rest of their lives repenting. In fact, all adolescent boys who hold such a biased and negative attitude towards girls, spend a lot of time gossiping about girls. This manifests in the form of graffiti on the walls of public toilets and urinals. Suppression of one's sexuality in adolescent years is detrimental to their overall growth. Physical changes, the sexual feelings arising from them, and the gags imposed at home and school drive many children to explore their sexuality negatively. Such boys get lured by petty temptations and their life is ruined due to their becoming aggressive because of this inner sexual frustration and harassing other children of the same age or younger. We are in a quandary as to whether providing sex education will help the youth or frustrate them even further. Nonetheless, a healthy dialogue on good and bad touch, self-defence against sexual aggression, facing physical and psychological changes during puberty is rapidly becoming the need of the hour.

Moreover, the Internet has opened the doors to uncontrolled, savage and perverted pornography for children. According to a survey conducted in the USA, children spend 20,000 hours surfing the internet or watching television instead of studying. During this period, they watch approximately 15,000 murders, 12,000 rapes and more than one lakh clips related to pornography, drugs or alcohol. That is why American society deals with problems like teenage pregnancy,

AIDS, drug abuse and the use of deadly weapons like knives and automatic guns. Consumption of drugs and alcohol is considered 'trendy'. Today, Indian society faces relatively harmless problems such as taunting and harassing teachers in the classroom, unruly behaviour and lack of enthusiasm in studying. However, with the Internet making inroads, it is only a matter of time till the issues that plague American society crop up in our country. Addictions are becoming acceptable in our society too. Children are categorized on the basis of their cultural and economic background, which ultimately determines their tendencies. Therefore, it is difficult to provide the same education or inculcate the same values in all children. No doubt the younger generation behaves differently than the older ones, in accordance with the rapidly changing world around them. Not that everything that is old is good and all that is new is despicable. Therefore, value-based education has become the need of the hour. Teachers must attempt to teach children how to identify and accept good practices and values while rejecting bad ones. If we are to tackle the problems that arise due to the perverse and explicit content that young minds are exposed to through the internet effectively, we must provide equally effective and culturally relevant knowledge of anatomy to children at the right age. Parents must discipline themselves before disciplining their children. Inclusion of morality and values in the school curriculum must become a priority.

The structure of a society is not like an apple cart. Members of society come together like the seeds of a pomegranate. This process of coming together begins when the child is still in the mother's womb, and continues in schools and colleges. The economic, social, political and cultural environment that prevails around the child strengthens this fabric of values.

The relationships that children form with their parents, relatives and friends reinforce this structure. However, a lot of this is missing today. We have become 'Sunday Parents'. We go out with our children on Sundays and simply 'perform the duty' of talking to them. Even on weekends, we spend most of our free time scrolling through social media and chatting on WhatsApp. Similarly, children are trapped in the web of the Internet. They find their parents boring and annoying. This is because there is hardly any interaction between children and their parents. Whatever interaction happens takes place in the virtual world. The emotional world of our children has been reduced to fake friends on Facebook and other social media apps and the inner gratification one receives from likes and comments. Are there any playgrounds around? Do children bruise their knees while playing? Why is it that they never suffer cuts and scrapes on their arms and legs any more? If the robust energy of growing children is channelized through activities organized by the NCC, Scouts and Guides, Gramodyog, Shramdan and sports to inculcate the values of discipline and hard work in them, they would never stray. If some do stray, they would, in their own time, gain the wisdom required to correct their own course.

When I was promoted to Class VIII, I enrolled myself into the National Cadet Corps (NCC). I had been told that the holder of the 'B' certificate of NCC would not only get bonus marks for admission to the National Defence Academy but also a scholarship. On the very first day, we were told to choose our NCC uniform. The uniforms had been used by at least four previous batches and were worn out and stored in a sack. They included knee-length, broad-bottomed shorts that seldom fit at the waist. They tended to slide up when the breeze blew on the grounds. Wearing these khakis along with the striped boxer underwear posed the danger of facing embarrassment while doing front rolls or frog jumps. Lawate Sir, known for his short temper, oversaw the NCC practices. The NCC parade would be conducted on Sundays when I would long to return to Kokrud. Therefore, I would often bunk the parade. On Mondays, Lawate Sir would take a round of all the classrooms, looking for students who had been absent from the parade. He would enter the classroom, wielding a cane in hand. His very sight would make me uneasy to my stomach. He would make the absent students stand up and deliver blows of cane to their hands, in front of the whole class. He would hit the hands so hard that they would become red and swollen. Students would shudder, hearing the cries of the one receiving the caning. But these punishments taught me the lesson of punctuality, albeit out of that fear.

I still remember an incident. It was a cold day. My uniform, though altered, was still a poor fit. I had put my hands in the pockets of the shorts for two reasons—to protect myself from the cold and to prevent the shorts from sliding down. I saluted Lawate Sir during reporting but forgot to take my other hand out of the pocket. This led to the punishment of running ten rounds of the entire ground while holding the rifle in my hands. Today, giving such punishments has become a matter of much debate and discussion. Thanks to the influence of western culture, the trend of parents abstaining from scolding or punishing their children is setting in. But the fear of parents, teachers and punishments has played a major role in the upbringing of our generation. Of course, there were limits to that fear and discipline.

I had heard a lot about television from my friends when I was in school. There was a small cupboard which looked like a television set at the house of the Attar family in Kokrud.

We would loiter in their courtyard hoping that somebody would start it but never had the courage to enter the house or ask any questions. I saw a black-and-white television set for the first time in Shirala. That television set belonged to the Ubale family. The family head, Mr Ubale, worked as a head constable with Mumbai Police. Manoj, one of his three sons, was my classmate. His father would send fancy T-shirts and jeans for him from Mumbai, as well as toys, much to our envy. When we played cricket, no rules were applicable for Manoj because he owned the bat and ball. We had to ball at a slow pace for him. When he would bat, the other player would replace him only if he got out thrice in a row. It was not mandatory for him to do fielding. Several of us were friends with him out of sheer selfishness.

But Manoj and his mother had generous hearts indeed! Their house would be jampacked with people watching *Chitrahar* on the television set. For at least half an hour, someone would attempt to adjust the position of the antenna of the television set using a pole to get clear transmission. Once the programme started, pin-drop silence would prevail in the house. We wanted to watch dances to the tune of upbeat songs, but usually only sad songs would play, and we would return home with long faces. When the screening of the *Ramayan* serial started on television, the roads would be deserted on Sunday mornings. People would bathe early, light an incense stick before the television set and wait for the serial to start. Around this time, the Thorbole family bought a colour television set. This raised the status of the Thorboles in the neighbourhood. Mr Thorbole too was a police head constable. Besides, he had three daughters. One of them, Sangita, was our classmate. Therefore, we were not allowed entry inside the house to watch the television. The rule for us was to peep through the window and watch the serial. As a result, I feel a certain kinship with the crowds of people, with inhibitions written on their faces, that throng outside large showrooms to watch cricket matches on the displayed television sets. We used to be fascinated with colour television programmes which would be broadcasted once or twice a week. But we also loved to watch programmes on black-and-white television sets, from *Amachi Mati Amachi Mansa* to the news bulletin for impaired hearing on Sundays. I remember watching regional-language films even though I could scarcely understand what was being said.

Schools aimed to mould students into multifaceted personalities. Thus, there would be a fair combination of punishment and appreciation. Much as we feared punishment, we craved appreciation and approval. I was fascinated by the English language. I developed a keen interest in mathematics. Sanskrit lessons would ring in my mind long after they ended. My mind would be overcome by the feelings of love, hate, jealousy and attraction on different occasions.

I would go to Kokrud every Saturday. It was a welcome escape from the stern disciplined environment created by my aunt. In Shirala, I was unable to satisfy my only hobby of watching films. Whenever I would go to my native village, I would watch as many films as I could. In Kokrud, I was akin to a free bird and in Shirala, a caged animal. Kokrud meant unlimited, unrestrained freedom. Nobody ever questioned me there. I was free to bully my siblings and act arbitrarily at home. Since there were too many people in the house, nobody monitored what we did. Sometimes we would go to the Gavaloba hills to pluck and eat jamuns, berries and mangoes. Layers of silt would plaster our necks as we swam in turbid waters. We would catch crabs living in holes on the bank of the river, gathering a dozen in an hour, and cooking them there and then on the bank of the river using oil, spices, onion and salt. We ate this curry with stale bhakris. It made our noses runny, the tanginess of the red-hot chillies and the spices added in the curry.

Our wet shorts would dry up by the time we finished eating. We would then wear our trousers over the shorts and get ready for the 3–6 p.m. film show at the video centre. If a new film was not being screened, I would not waste time watching an old one. Instead, I would read *Chandoba* and *Champak*, the two popular children's magazines, which were sold for Rs 2 a copy. The moment I lay hands on the issues, I would rush to a secluded corner and read like a man possessed. Some of the issues contained ghost stories that would send a chill down my spine. To feel less scared, I would sit near the *choolah* in the kitchen, where my mother did her cooking. As my craze for reading kicked up, I began reading the Sunday supplements of newspapers too. During the summer and Diwali vacations, I craved to read books and that's how I read the entire Ramayana and Mahabharata. I experienced the thrill of reading Shivaji Sawant's novels. Reading the autobiographies of famous people boosted my self-confidence.

Much like the adage, 'An empty mind is a devil's workshop', if indolent, one tends to be attracted to dangerous things, making him a pervert. Adult videos had sneaked into villages too. Away from all prying eyes, I started watching such films on video player with friends, in the dead of the night. I developed an affinity for romance stories that were published in the Sunday supplements of newspapers. Adult magazines that belonged to my friends stirred my sexual instincts. Questions that I did not dare ask anybody started haunting me.

There was nobody at home or in school whom I could ask for an explanation of these crucial matters of adolescence. I was perplexed by the pimples that burst forth on my face and the bass in my voice. Wet dreams puzzled me endlessly. I was confused by the physical changes that my body was undergoing. Finally, I mustered the courage to visit our Doctor Uncle. I patiently waited until he had examined all the other patients and told him about the problems I was facing. He simply smiled, patted my back and said, 'Man! You have grown into a youth now.' I could not make much of it, but it was a relief to know that all that I was going through was a natural part of growing up. To properly channelize the energy in adolescents, you need someone experienced who can guide and instil good values in them. I was fortunate enough to meet Dr S.N. Patil when I was undergoing the transition from boyhood to manhood. He was fondly known as Doctor Uncle. After attaining his BAMS degree, he decided to set up his practice in an innocuous village like Kokrud, which was in the middle of nowhere.

Our village had two doctors: Ranga Doctor and Doctor Uncle. Dr Rangarao Patil had an MBBS degree but the way he treated his patients was unique. He would chase away patients from the dispensary saying, 'There is nothing wrong with you. Eat mutton, drink milk and you will feel better.' And lo and behold, the patients would actually recover if they heeded his advice, which had a positive aura about it. In sharp contrast, Doctor Uncle would give his patients a sermon, followed by a long prescription of pills and tablets. His treatment strategy comprised a combination of Ayurvedic and allopathic medicines and psychological counselling. Whenever I visited him, he would fondly pull my cheeks. It hurt so much that it would make me feel like pulling at his salt-and-pepper hair. There would be a long, serpentine queue of patients outside his clinic, but when he would see me, he would make me sit on the stool placed adjacent to his chair and chat with me for at least three to four hours. He adored children. He would enquire about my school and studies. He would lecture me on the importance of good habits that I should adopt to maintain my health. These lectures would bore me to death, but I absorbed his simple health tips; I continue to make a conscious effort to practise them in my daily life.

Doctor Uncle taught us simple yet important things about diet and exercise. The first thing he taught us was to have a sound breakfast comprising fruits, milk and curd, a nutritious meal in the afternoon and a light meal at night. He would insist that we should eat less spicy, nutritious food. He told us about the principle of Ayurveda wherein the stomach is divided into four compartments; two compartments should be filled with food, the third with water and the fourth should be kept empty. He would insist that one should drink water either before meals or half an hour after them.

He said that drinking too much water during a meal obstructed the digestion process and created the problem of gas. He advocated for drinking small quantities of water every now and then. In a day, he would say, one should drink at least 3 litres of water. He would insist that we eat slowly and chew every bite thoroughly, instead of gulping down the food. He advised me to savour raw fruits and vegetables. I started plucking guavas, mangoes and tamarind from trees to eat. The sourness of the tamarind would make my teeth sensitive. I would also eat a lot of carrots, cucumbers and tomatoes as a snack, whenever I felt hungry. I always thought that the secret behind Balu Mama's superhuman strength—he could lift a huge load of fodder—was his daily habit of drinking a jar of milk in the morning and eating rice with ghee.

Similarly, I developed a habit of eating bhakri with chutney or rice with curd. In fact, I used to bring rice and curd in my lunch box. Doctor Uncle believed that consuming a lot of cooked vegetables, mutton, wadas or sev chiwda made one feel drowsy. Therefore, I would try to eat eggs and fish more often, so much so that I used to eat raw eggs for several consecutive days.

Doctor Uncle would wake up early in the morning and take us out for a walk. We would happily accompany him as it gave us an opportunity to roam around and breathe in the crisp morning air. He religiously did pranayama and yoga for fifteen minutes every day. His daily yoga practice included breathing exercises like Bhasrika, Bhramari, Kapalbhati and Anulom-Vilom. He would also chant the Omkar to rejuvenate his brain.

Doing Surya Namaskars daily, facing the east and invoking the name of the Sun God, helped me develop a nimble body. Yoga, coupled with exercises that strengthen the back and core muscles, would make me feel fresh. Having studied Ayurveda, Doctor Uncle shared with me simple dietary tips in accordance with one's health conditions, age and the seasons. His advice on sleeping habits, breathing habits and the importance of introspection through meditation proved to be useful in my adult life too.

When I was a young boy, my mother would not allow me to eat papaya, fish and chicken due to the common yet false rural belief that these foods increase heat in the body. When I spoke to Doctor Uncle about it, he came home and gave my mother a detailed lesson on a balanced diet. He advised that excessive consumption of oily, sweet or spicy food causes heart problems, which caught everyone by surprise. The prevalent social norm was that the hostess would be considered discourteous to the guests if she served them tea which was not adequately sweet or mutton curry that was not oily enough.

Thanks to Doctor Uncle's wisdom, my family members changed their food habits. Bhakri, leafy vegetables, rice with ghee, curd and buttermilk were adequately introduced into our diet. My mother would hang curd overnight in a muslin cloth torn from an old dhoti. By morning, all excess water was wrung out of it and what remained was thick, rich curd. She would then mix it with sugar and cardamom and make delicious shrikhand. This simple dish, when eaten with chapati, was so delicious that we would consider it akin to a feast. While we would always make tea with jaggery to sweeten it, our domestic help would have tea without milk. Now, I realize how healthy it was to use jaggery. Tea prepared with too much milk and sugar causes acidity.

Doctor Uncle often said, 'People spend the first half of their lives ignoring their health in order to earn money. As a result, they end up spending the second half of it paying doctors like us to treat their deteriorating health. Instead of neglecting one's health, one should err on the side of caution and adopt healthy habits. The one who sees the greenery of nature never ends up needing spectacles. The one who does Shirshasana never loses the hair on his head. The one who washes their hands religiously before eating never gets sick. The one who eats freshly prepared food and appropriate portions of fruits and green leafy vegetables never feels tired.'

Doctor Uncle's approach to good health was at odds with the mentality of the villagers. He was a man of science and strongly opposed penance through fasting. He would reprimand people for believing in superstitions. He was against the tradition of abiding by an 'auspicious time' to perform any task or function. Many villagers opposed his point of view and the village god-men, in particular, did not refer patients to him. Often, victims of snake bite would be taken to the Maruti Temple wherein the god-man would chant mantras and sprinkle saffron or apply kumkum to the victim's forehead and tie a sacred thread around his neck or hand. But nature would do its job. If the snake was non-venomous, the victim would survive; if it was venomous, he would die instantly. However, most of the snakes are non-venomous so the victims would recover without any medical treatment but villagers would believe in the 'miracle' performed by the god-men. If the patient recovered, the family members would pay obeisance to the god-man, thanking him for the miraculous cure and if he died, the god-man would say that it was the outcome of the victim's sins in his previous life. I remember how our neighbour, Sutar Anna, had been taken to the Maruti Temple after he was bitten by a snake and died there. I strongly feel that Sutar Kaku would not have been widowed if he had been taken to Doctor Uncle in time. Because of this blind faith in god-men, she had to lead a lonely life and single-handedly shoulder all the responsibilities of the household.

Doctor Uncle warned our young fraternity against such baseless superstitions. He devoted much of his time to ensuring that a scientific and logical outlook was adopted by every man. Personality development programmes and body-building contests would be held on his birthday. Innovative programmes personally organized by him steered us in the right direction.

In fact, life in a village is akin to that in a university. The teachers you meet in life, who do not possess any formal training, have the prowess to explain the true meaning of life to you. People, despite their vocation, are treated with love and respect. Designations like Driver Nana, Doctor Mama, Postman Kaka, Peon Aba, Kotwal Bhai are considered more prestigious than the attainment of any formal degree. At night, when people gathered at the village square to catch up, discussions would revolve around relevant topics like guiding the youth, enterprise, market and agriculture. I do not recollect a single suicide or murder being committed in my village. The philosophy of the Warkari sect (the Warkari movement includes the worship of Vithoba and a duty-based approach towards life with an emphasis on moral behaviour) would give immense strength to the common man. At times, a few select bhajans would glorify idleness but many of them would inspire people to fight against adversities. The values and traditions made people so tolerant that committing suicide or exacting revenge through bodily harm or violence was not considered a solution to any problem.

When I was young, my grandmother narrated the tale of a murder, explaining how it ruined an entire family. The story went thus. One of my aunts was married to a schoolteacher in the neighbouring Chincholi village. Once, he had an argument with a local goon at the mutton shop in Kokrud which soon developed into an ugly brawl. The goon beat my uncle black and blue. Our family was humiliated. Therefore, a plot was hatched and on the village bazaar day, held the next week, our men reached the mutton shop. Dutta Dada and my cousin Tanaji Anna were at the forefront of the fight. The situation soon got out of hand. Tanaji Anna was just sixteen years old then. He wanted to even the score with the goon who had humiliated his father in public. In the ensuing brawl, the goon was killed. Everyone involved was sent to jail. Tanaji Anna, being an adolescent, escaped with a probation of two years in a reformatory school. The court case virtually brought the family to its knees. All my grandmother's jewellery and the family's farms had to be mortgaged in order to raise money to pay the legal fees. Just that one moment of anger resulted in not only a rivalry that carried on for generations but also forced several children of the family to drop out of school due to financial constraints. The girls of the family had to be married off at a very young age.

By the time I reached the tenth standard, I had heard several daunting stories about the SSC exam. Every day, I would hear a story detailing the formidableness of the SSC examination or about the distress of the students who were preparing for it. Newspapers would publish a report, after the SSC results were announced, on the front page. The news feature accompanying the report would contain details of the student who had stood first in the examination, along with an interview about his career plans and future goals. The student's parents too would be interviewed and a photograph of the SSC chairman feeding the rank-holder a sweetmeat would also be published. I used to be fascinated by these news reports. In 1987, the son of a mill worker scored 96 per cent and stood first in the state SSC exam. I cut the news clippings of his success story and photos printed in the newspaper and stashed them in my notebook. This inspired me, making me wonder, 'If he can achieve this, what's stopping me from doing so?'

My aunt's rented house, which comprised two rooms, had *kachcha* earthen walls. One room was an open bathroom as well as a kitchen while the other room, which had a cot and a radio set in one corner, was used as a living room-cum-bedroom. My three cousins and I would arrange two mattresses on the floor of this room and somehow make enough space to sleep. I would share a pillow and a bedcover with one of my cousins. I still remember the distinct scent of the 'Solapuri' bedcover that we wrapped ourselves in. Electricity consumption was minimal and therefore nobody would indulge in using a fan. We would suffer the nuisance of bedbugs, mosquitoes, fleas and other insects. Gradually, I got used to it. My aunt's brother-in-law worked in the army. He would bring the popular mosquito repellent cream Odomos from the military canteen, but my uncle was allergic to it. During the summers, it would be so hot that it would drive us to discard even the flimsy bedcovers. We would use the Odomos cream and sleep in the open courtyard, gazing at the stars and the moon. During winters, we would use *godhadis* (padded cotton blankets) which my aunt would sew herself using old, worn-out clothes. These homemade blankets kept us so warm that even the silk *razais* of five-star hotels pale in comparison.

It was evident to me that the space was too small to accommodate all of us but then who would address the issue and how? I needed a table and a chair to study, and I wished to use a table lamp too. Finally, I mustered up the courage to talk to my grandmother about my needs. After much persuasion, my aunt agreed to allow to me rent a room elsewhere but on the condition that I would have my meals at her house. Delighted, I started looking for a room. Gaikwad Sir, who taught us PT, lived in Bamanpada. I rented a room in a dilapidated building adjoining his house.

I moved to the rented room that was located on the first floor of the building. I took a mattress and a bedsheet along with my box of books there. Besides this, I brought a simple wooden table and chair from Kokrud. Tatya brought an old bicycle that had belonged to one of my cousins from Mumbai. With it, I could cycle to school in five minutes. As a rule, we wore striped boxers and sleeved *baniyans* at my aunt's house. All my friends would wear sando T-shirts and stylish shorts. I wanted to dress like them. I convinced Tatya and bought two pairs of sando T-shirts and stylish shorts. I also brought Tatya's lungi from Kokrud. Every year, I bought an earthen piggy bank and put loose change in it on a weekly basis. Guests who would visit Kokrud in the month of May would give me Rs 5 or Rs 10. Though I pretended to reject these small gifts, I secretly enjoyed getting them and they too went into my piggy bank. I excitedly looked forward to breaking the piggy bank open during the summer vacations and counting the collected sum. In the tenth standard, I used the piggy-bank savings, which had amounted to Rs 115, to buy a red alarm clock that I had been eyeing for a while. It allowed me to wake up early in the morning on my own, without my aunt's help. Tanaji Anna gifted me his HMT wristwatch which was old but in working condition. Having been provided with all the basic necessities, it was now my responsibility to study hard. What troubled me was that the landlord's son with mental health issues would keep on crying out all through the night. Though he was harmless, I was still scared of him and shuddered even when the gentle night breeze creaked the window open.

Gaikwad Sir was very cooperative. Stoutly built, he was a devotee of Bajrangbali. There was a Hanuman Temple of the Shivaji era built by Samarth Ramdas himself, which was adjacent to the *wada* where I lived. Gaikwad Sir would rise early in the morning, offer prayers at that temple and then proceed to do his daily exercise.

By the end of the first week at the new place, I had made myself at home. Somebody knocked on my door in the middle of the night. I woke up, trembling with fear, thinking that it must be the landlord's son, Girish. But, to my pleasant surprise,

it was Gaikwad Sir who was asking me to open the door.
I checked the time. It was 3 a.m. Sir had come to wake me up.
There was a public tap next to a nearby stream where Sir and
I took a bath. The silence of the wee hours, the gurgling sound of
the water flowing in the stream and the sound of chiming bells
in the temple . . . it was all so wonderful. I was shivering with
cold but got ready to study in half an hour. A strange energy
overcame my body. I opened my book and started reading.
Never before had I experienced such intense concentration.
My brain was able to absorb anything that I read. After that,
I got accustomed to setting the alarm to wake me up at 3 a.m.
I did not feel embarrassed to go out to freshen up because of
the early hour. Otherwise I would be embarrassed because
the State Transport buses would start plying the roads after
6 a.m. The bath water, though cold, was rejuvenating. I would
start craving tea around 5 a.m. There was a hotel at the ST
bus stand where I could have had tea, but I decided against
it for my aunt's sake. However, one time, I went there and
paid 30 paisa for a cuppa. That was the first time I had been
to a hotel. I started having tea there occasionally. Since my
bicycle was old, its chain would slip off every now and then.
Nevertheless, it helped cut down my commute from the school
to my room and back. I had understood the importance of time
management since childhood. I would pedal hard to reach
school before the bell rang. Even during the recess, I would
finish my lunch in a hurry and spend at least fifteen minutes
studying. I was competing with Milind Hirlekar in academics.
I started scoring 100 per cent marks in the school tests.

The girls' school was in the same premises as the boys'.
Our teachers would talk about the students who were favoured
to top the SSC examination at our centre and Milind, Seema
Jadhav and I would figure in their talks.

The year I prepared for the SSC shaped my academics and paved the path for me to do my studies in a systematic manner. I worked hard to improve everything, from my handwriting to my grammar. I planned my studies by dividing the syllabus into two parts—that which I needed to learn by heart and that which I needed to understand well. I collected old question papers and studied their formats. I concentrated on solving test papers without referring to the solutions. Scoring twenty out of twenty marks in the science practical was of utmost importance. Milind was the favourite student of our chemistry teacher. Therefore, I feared he would deduct my marks. As a result, I was extra cautious during the experiments to ensure that I would get an A-plus grade on every page of the journal. Since Marathi was our first language, we had higher Marathi, which was tough.

I would pay attention towards the introduction of the poet or writer while studying a story or poem, making my answers stand out from the others. I also started referring to maps while studying history. I drew flawless diagrams in my notebooks of science, geography and geometry. English was my favourite subject. Vedpathak Sir taught us English till the ninth standard and Vaidya Sir taught us the subject in the tenth standard. Initially, I found it hard to understand what he was teaching. But I was cautious and did not panic. I would read every lesson the night before he taught it in the class, finding the meanings of difficult words in the dictionary. As a result, it became easy for me to understand what Vaidya Sir was teaching. I would jot down my queries and doubts the night before the class and ask them the next day. I answered every question he asked. The student who stood first in the ninth standard would be given question banks and guides published by Navneet Publications free of cost. But I knew everybody would rely on these guides to write their answers, making them monotonous. I started making efforts to structure my answers in a unique way. Whenever I came across the adage, 'Winners don't do different things, they do things differently', I realized the importance of the strategy I had adopted for my studies.

As the end of academic year approached, the examination date loomed closer and tension mounted. However, I found it easy to cope with the examination stress because I had been studying hard. In fact, I was raring to take the examination. The examination forms had to be filled. I got a black-and-white passport size photograph clicked. That was the first time that I was ever photographed. I pasted the passport size photo on the hall ticket. My exam centre was Chhatrapati High School. Before the paper, I went to offer my prayers to Hanuman and to seek blessings from my aunt and uncle. I knew that I had studied well. I was confident that I had written my paper well too.

After the SSC examination was over, I was freed from the stress of studying. I returned to Kokrud. I longed to spend time with my friends and do things that I had never done before. I wanted to join politics and see Mumbai. I wanted to smoke cigarettes, drink beer, attend tamasha shows and whistle at the dancers. I wanted relief from the stress of studying. I wanted to relax and be a free bird. In short, I just wanted to let my hair down and behave exactly like a carefree, worthless vagabond.

I reunited with my friends in the village. I sported the red loincloth of wrestlers and began to visit the wrestling ring regularly. Instead of expending my energy on actual wrestling, I focused on exercising and building up my strength. I started doing dips and sit-ups. My forearms were so thin that I could not even produce a clap when I slapped them. Instead,

the slapping would turn my hands red. I would request
professional wrestlers to punch my ears so that they would
swell up, like any professional wrestler's. Their swollen ears
and muscular physiques would inspire me to do my exercises
with rigour. I became friends with the wrestlers, and we
formed a group of fourteen- to fifteen-year-olds. We
would tie saffron handkerchiefs around our shoulders, leave
the top two buttons of our shirts open and roam the streets
like Romeos.

Once, we decided to test our brawn at a hotel owned
by Ravi Shetty in the village. We rolled up our sleeves and
menacingly entered the hotel. Since Ravi did not take money
from cousins, we too intended to eat for free. We ate kanda
bhaji and missal pav to our hearts' content and drank tea.
The waiter gave us a bill for Rs 36. As planned, Tanya
smashed the cups and saucers. We were charged up. Tensions
mounted. We intended to thrash the waiter, followed by Ravi
Anna. Upon hearing the commotion, Ravi rushed to our table.
He gauged the situation and started apologizing with joined
hands for asking us to pay the bill, assuring us that the 'mistake'
would not be repeated. As we were leaving, he called me aside
and said, 'Brother, please stay away from these vagabonds.
The village has high hopes for you. You are a scholar. Please
concentrate on your studies and become someone important.
If you want, I'll serve you at your house every day but please
do not insult food like this again.' His words brought back to
me memories of Kadam Madam's scolding. But I was in no
age or mood to heed his advice.

When I was in the fourth standard, we had visited Uran
near Raigad, to attend my aunt Manda's wedding. On the
way, passed through Bhor Ghat at Lonavala and Khandala.
Travelling in a tempo, I sat adjacent to Tatya on the front

seat. I was fascinated with that road which led to Mumbai. I had seen a three-storied building for the first time when I went to Shirala. In Uran, I got the opportunity to see a five-storied building. I also got to see the sea. Standing on the seashore, I felt that I could almost see the faint outlines of Mumbai's skyscrapers on the other side of the shore. I had an opportunity to do some sightseeing in Mumbai, which I had seen only in films. Accompanied by Vikas and Vijay, I boarded a State Transport bus that ran between Chandoli and Mumbai to reach the Mumbai Central bus terminus. We stayed with our cousin.

My cousin had sold his room in a tenement and purchased a one-room flat in a tower. His flat was tiny and stacked with furniture. There was a small portable black and white television set too. People were living in overcrowded 10×15 feet cubbyholes. My cousin, his family members and relatives of my aunt were lying around all over the room and even in the tiny balcony but nobody complained. They were taking turns to use the only bathroom. The three of us were added to the crowd.

We stacked our luggage there and freshened up, donned our ironed clothes and ventured out to do some sightseeing. We walked around till our legs ached, seeing the Gateway of India, the Taj hotel, Marine Drive, Chowpatty and other tourist attractions. Our necks ached as we looked up at the looming skyscrapers. We spent a week in Mumbai. My cousin sister's son Neelesh accompanied us, acting as our tour guide. We were astonished at his knowledge of Mumbai. He took us to a screening of a film in the Minerva Theatre, which was one of Mumbai's most posh cinema halls. We were told that *Sholay* had been screened there for several weeks. I went to buy ice cream during the interval. I gave a Rs 100 note to the vendor and took four cups of ice cream. I waited for him to return the change, but he did not offer any. When I asked, he yelled, 'One scoop of ice cream costs Rs 25. How can you expect to get back change?' I had never eaten any ice cream other than the candy that cost less than one and a half rupees. Such shocking experiences jolted me out of the illusion that I would be able to enjoy life in Mumbai for more than a few days.

Deshmukh Saheb had become a cabinet minister by then. Hopeful, I boarded a bus and went to meet him at his Muktagiri bungalow early one day. His PA, Gandhi, was a native of our village. He asked us to wait in the drawing room. Deshmukh Saheb came to the drawing room at around 9 a.m. and met every visitor. He talked to everyone affectionately. When he saw me, he patted my back and said, 'Aren't you the son of the wrestler? I have been hearing a lot about you. You are doing very well at school. Let me give you a word of advice: dream big. Who knows? If you study well, one day you will become someone important and make your family proud.'

He took out a Rs 500 note from his pocket and tried to give it to me. His words instilled in me a feeling of pride and self-confidence. I politely returned the note to him, saying, 'Sir, your words give me a new strength and inspiration. I have appeared for the SSC examination and come here to seek your blessing for my future success. Please give me your blessings. Your blessing will give me strength to continue my journey.' There is a famous poem by the Marathi poet, Kusumagraj: '*Modun padla nahi sansar, tari modal nahi kana, pathivarti hat thevun nusta ladh mhana.*' (Even though I have lost everything, my spine will remain erect. Just remember to fight back, my son, with a pat on your back.) I had not read that poem, but my words reflected its spirit. Deshmukh Saheb admired my sense of pride. He took the three of us aside and offered us tea and poha. Later, he sent a jeep to drop us at Delight Road. Everybody scolded me for not accepting the money, but his words were ringing in my ears. I realized that I could get a similar bungalow, that vehicle, that lavish lifestyle but the pre-condition for that was I had to immerse myself in my studies, keep the fire in my belly ignited.

My holidays were about to end. The results were only a week away and I was anxiously waiting for them. The D-Day arrived. A long list was published in the newspaper. I went through the list, looking for my seat number. I had scored 616 out of 700 marks, and stood first in the exam centre, scoring 88 per cent. My hard work had paid off. I savoured my first success. Tatya's joy knew no bounds as he distributed sweets and pedhas to the entire village. My name was written on the display board of the school's most meritorious students. A felicitation was organized in the library. I touched the feet of the librarian at the function. I would cut the clippings of the SSC study column printed in the *Kesari* newspaper that the library subscribed to. The librarian was aware of this, but he never stopped me. I had tried every trick in the book to inspire myself to study, and I had been rewarded for that. However, I was facing a bigger challenge. The child's play was over.

Chapter 4

Junior College

After bagging the first position in the SSC Board examination in Battis Shirala, the million-dollar question was which junior college I would enrol into for the eleventh standard. The three options I had before me were Karad, Sangli and Kolhapur. I decided to explore Karad and boarded a State Transport bus to go there. As I got off the bus, I asked the bus conductor to return my Rs 5 change. He had the audacity to lie, saying that he had already returned it to me, and accused me of threatening him. Infuriated, I argued with the conductor and soon burst into tears. Seeing my anger, the other passengers were convinced of my honesty and rebuked the conductor. He was forced to return my money, but this foul experience propelled me to eliminate Karad as a viable option to pursue my studies. I visited Sangli next. I saw the sprawling campus of the prestigious Willingdon College, including the hostel. I liked the campus but decided not to take admission there for two reasons. Firstly, the college was on the outskirts of the town and secondly, the cinema was too far away.

However, when I visited the robust town of Kolhapur, it was love at first sight. Several students of the New College had found their place on the merit list. However, I did not like its hostel which used to be a horse stable. I opted to stay in the Commerce College hostel in the vicinity.

The New College was 1.5 kilometres from the hostel. I would cycle to and from the college and the hostel. The crowd in the college comprised scholarly students. This was unlike Shirala, where I was the only scholarly student and the others were quite ignorant. I was put in the 'Scholar Batch' of the New College, pursuing 'Science with Electronics as Vocational Subject'. However, the medium of instruction was English, something that I was not too comfortable with; I could not understand a lot of what was taught in class. Chemistry formulae went over my head. I joined two private coaching classes—Pethe and Patil. Thereafter, my schedule became even more strenuous. I was always found running from one class to another, then college, then hostel, then the mess and again back to the hostel. This constant back and forth, along with my increased academic load, made me tired and frustrated. Walking, cycling and travelling by bus drained all the energy out of me. Upon returning to the hostel in the evening, I would meet my friends from the commerce stream; their hobbies and tastes were different from mine. Since I was hanging out with different kinds of people in the hostel and the college, my studies were adversely affected. I realized I was straying from my chosen path.

My friends from the commerce stream took me to watch A-rated English films. I wasted my time in forbidden activities and mindless chatter. The hostel had two groups of students—one from the commerce stream and the other from the law stream. I looked up to Mankar, a law student, as my role model. He was a natural leader and would dominate others in the hostel. On the other hand, I started engaging more in extracurriculars which led to bunking classes. As a result, my grades nose-dived.

I did not like the food that was served in the mess. I would write letters to my mother, asking her to send a tiffin for me, through the State Transport bus. Once, I wrote to my mother, asking her to cook 'dry mutton', a dish she was excelled at, and asked my classmate and friend, Bharat Kambale, to post the letter. However, he forgot to post it. His mother found the letter in his pocket as she was doing the laundry. She was so moved that the following Sunday, she invited all of us hostel-residents for lunch at her home. We savoured her deliciously made tambda and pandhra rassa (red and white curry that is famous in Kolhapur). Bharat's mother hugged me and said, 'Son, consider me as your own mother in Kolhapur and do not hesitate to come for lunch with Bharat, anytime you feel like it.' I never took her up on this offer but even today, when I recall the incident, I can smell the aroma of her tasty dry mutton.

In college, relentless efforts would be made to prepare 'Fidayeen squads' to ensure that the students made it to the merit list in the HSC Board examination. The strategy was to ensure that students had learnt all answers by heart, by repeating them over and over again. I too found myself adhering to that routine. We would always be apprised of the number of alumni who made it to IITs, Walchand or the UDCT. Although I had been lax throughout the year, I studied diligently in the last leg of the academic year and scored an aggregate of 82 per cent and 94 per cent in the PCM group in the eleventh-standard examinations.

After I took admission in the twelfth standard, my level of study dropped further. Though my grandmother was against me having a moped, I pestered my father to buy me a second-hand Luna. This acquisition upset her so much that she passed away fifteen days after my father bought it. My grandmother and I shared a close bond; upon her demise, I cried like a baby and began spending time alone. My grandmother's memories haunted me—I remembered the warmth of the godhadi, the morsel of bhakri dipped in milk, the Re 1 coins that she would give me and the smell of snuff that she constantly sniffed. In the fairy tale, the life of a monster is in a parrot. It was akin to the bond shared by my grandmother and me. She was the binding force of the entire extended family and would take care of every visitor.

She would buy a saree and blouse for every daughter of our extended family, coming to visit her parents after marriage. We would fondly call our grandmother Mhatarey (old mother). For us, Mhatarai was the crème de la crème. Her loss was unbearable. I would bunk tuitions, every Saturday and Sunday, to return to our native village. I would sit alone, staring into the void. Tatya was puzzled with my behaviour. His relationship with Mhatarai had been full of friction. He had never returned the ornaments which he had borrowed from her and melted down to take care of the financial crisis that the family once faced. This used to bother me a lot. I wonder time and again how happy she would have been had she been given a new gold bead chain in lieu of the old one. The new generation, raised in the concrete jungle of cities, does not even know who lives in the adjoining flat. The 'in' thing is to sell the old *wada* in the village and invest that money into a two-room apartment in Mumbai or Pune. There is all the space in the world for materialistic pleasures and inanimate objects like the television set, refrigerator, microwave oven, and computer. But there is no space for aged grandparents.

Looking after them has become an onerous task. Therefore, they are sent to old-age homes. Youngsters on the cusp of adulthood become restless because they are lovelorn. When I was that age, I was grief-stricken because of my grandmother's demise. Gradually, I overcame that grief.

The lanky Mankar Dada of our hostel would often take my Luna moped without bothering to inform me. This irritated me but I did not possess the courage to confront him. One day, I happened to read the famous letter penned by Abraham Lincoln, which featured a sentence to the effect, 'Don't be afraid of goons; overpowering them is the easiest thing.' Inspired, I waited for the skinny Mankar, at the entrance gate of the hostel. I saw him ride my Luna Moped in style. After he had parked it, I removed the belt from around my waist and mercilessly thrashed him with it. Then I pulled him down and squatted on his chest. I did not even realize how quickly and easily I had overcome my fear of goons. Mankar looked like a deflated balloon, and I rose up to the challenge. Since I had showed Mankar Dada his place, I became famously known as Chotu Dada in the hostel.

I used the Luna to get to my private coaching classes, but its condition was so shoddy that I had to tug it along, more than ride it. Since I didn't possess a driving license, I was afraid of the traffic policemen standing at every signal. I would mostly get caught when I went to the State Transport bus terminus to get my tiffin, sent by my mother. Head Constable Fadtare, who would be on duty at the bus terminus, would demand Rs 10 every time he caught me. For almost a year, I didn't know that when you pay a fine for a traffic offence, you should ensure that you get a receipt.

My roommate Ravi Mohite was the son of the sarpanch of the village adjacent to ours. He studied in the twelfth standard in the commerce stream. He had also been elected as the CR of the college. He hardly ever studied and would insist on taking me to Rankala Lake every evening, saying, 'Come friend, let us go to Mahadwar Road and find some solace to the eyes.' He was obsessed with ogling at partially robed mannequins in garment showrooms. He had an awful dressing sense, though—once, he wore a formal suit with Kolhapuri slippers to a get-together. Keeping him company was bound to adversely affect my studies.

When I was promoted to the twelfth standard, Anand Patil and Abhinay Kumbhar took admission in the eleventh standard in Kolhapur. Both hailed from my village and had studied in my school. They resided in the same hostel as me. Anand was peace-loving and good-natured. He would never bother anyone. His father was a politician and his mother, a teacher. He was the youngest among eight siblings, but he was not pampered or spoilt. He was studious and would often keep to himself. Bespectacled Anand was charting new heights in education. Though he was my junior, he was concerned about me. Whenever we would go to the tea stall in the evening, he would anxiously ask, 'Vishwas Dada, the HSC examination is approaching. Are your prepared with your studies? Please revise everything you have studied. Avoid wasting your time with Ravi. If you wish, you may come and study with us in our room.' His concern was touching, and I was convinced that he was indeed my well-wisher. But I would stray again.

The world of hostelites is very different and attractive. Once you join a group of not-so-sincere students, you get accustomed to taunting sincere students and plotting to disrupt their studies. Anand would wake up early and walk into the dining hall, cleaning the lenses of his spectacles, to read newspapers. He would play tennis for half an hour in the morning and start studying at 7 a.m. sharp. Watching him go about his daily routine, I felt ashamed of myself and started studying. I prepared my timetable and sternly warned Ravi against insisting on me accompanying him to Mahadwar Road.

Abhinay had always been a multifaceted, all-rounder student. His father was the principal of Naik College and a celebrated speaker. His mother, who was a teacher, was related to Jagdish Khebudkar, a renowned poet. Therefore, Abhinay had been acting ever since he was a child. He was quite witty too. He had penned a satire based on the oath, '*Bharat kadhi kadhi maza desh ahe*' (India is sometimes my country). It had become popular in the entire college. However, he put a stop to his extracurricular activities for the sake of his studies. Anand and Abhinay came together to become study-buddies. Anand was following in my footsteps as far as education was concerned. We had been friends since childhood. While other members of our Ghode and Nangre clans would spend their energies bashing each other's heads, we became good friends. I went to Shirala to study and a year later Anand too landed up there. I took admission in Kolhapur and Anand followed me there. Later, I shifted from the science stream to arts and Anand too followed suit. I became an IPS officer and much to our joy, Anand went a step ahead of me and became an IAS officer. Sugandh Chaugule became an IFS officer and Abhinay Kumbhar became an IRS officer. It would be interesting to find out how all of us achieved success. But the seeds of our success stories were sown after we passed our HSC examination.

The twelfth standard was an especially tumultuous time for me. I struggled with the whirlpool of negative thoughts that haunted me incessantly. My maternal uncle from Mangrul village was admitted to a hospital in Kolhapur. Relatives attending to him stayed in my room, which affected my studies. My self-confidence shattered and I became anxious about my future, worrying that, 'What if I do not score good marks? How would that make my parents feel? I would lose face among my relatives. How would I face the world if I failed in a subject? I would become a laughing stock. Everybody would taunt me. My bubble is about to burst.' I had achieved tremendous success in the SSC examination. But I feared that the HSC examination would get the best of me. If I failed, my career dreams would come to an end. I felt as if I was trapped in a quagmire and though I was crying for help, help wasn't coming. I would wake up in a cold sweat due to these haunting nightmares.

Indeed, the SSC and the HSC examinations virtually puncture children during their teenage years. Young adolescents want to play and get together with their friends. They long to talk to their peers. At this time, studying for the HSC examination plays spoilsport. They cannot be carefree or entertain themselves. Their world is reduced to a study table, classes, tuitions, teachers and never-ending tests. They get crushed under pressure. Parents work hard, save money and dream that their child will become a doctor or engineer. The reality is far from this illusion. The child gets sick, eating the food cooked in the hostel mess. Sometimes, the child fails. There is no help available. Instead, the child is branded a failure. Once this branding sets in, the child either becomes frustrated or develops alligator skin. The latter are better off as they give up on their studies and waste their time in unwarranted activities. The former lot of frustrated children suffer from a hibernation of the nervous system. They become reclusive and turn to addiction. They force themselves to study hard due to parental pressure but find themselves unable to concentrate. They begin to despise books and feel like destroying their subject papers. Science formulas ring in their ears, as if they were hallucinating. They yearn to escape to the Himalayas or contemplate ending their life. Indeed, some budding youngsters do become victims of this deadly stress and commit suicide.

The million-dollar question is whether it is right to resort to such a drastic act due to the stress of preparing for the HSC or SSC examinations. Certainly, it is not right at all. Even an ordinary student can cope with studies, the pressure of which is negligible. Only one who cannot swim, drowns in the river. The one who can, rides the wave. Such people find studies enjoyable. Whatever one's goal may be, one must work hard to attain success, and learn the tricks of the trade. One cannot achieve success with a laid-back attitude. One should wake up from their slumber and persevere till one reaches one's goals.

God has gifted us all that we need to lead a healthy life. I have never heard of anyone who wore out or died because of studying. Then why should one opt for death over studies? Instead, one should overcome this monster and make strides in the field of academics. Everything is possible. In fact, it is easy. We need to be armed with self-confidence, realize our strength and taste the fruits of our success, earned with hard work. Depression is a temporary phase, though a delicate one. We need to defeat it by moving it out of our way, like Amitabh Bachchan did in the movie *Hum*. We must leap like a tiger, looking at books as if they were our prey and resolving to overpower them, by religiously finishing our daily homework. We need to solve all the questions in the tests and climb new heights every day. We can conquer new peaks and embrace new horizons. I used to be stricken by such emotional turmoil every day. When I felt like committing hara-kiri, I would think of my mother and Tatya. What will happen to them if I accept defeat? How would they be able to live after that? These thoughts would reinvigorate me, and I would get back to my studies with renewed vigour. I resolved to finish the race and give it my all, although I was trailing behind a little. In the last leg of my journey, I gave myself a boost by going all out with my preparation.

The SSC and HSC examinations are two of the most important stages of educational progress, akin to commas in a sentence. At different phases of life, we get attracted to different things and face new challenges. A baby likes to play with a rattle. A toddler takes to a ball, a teddy bear or a doll. An adolescent gets attracted to books, films or has a crush on a Bollywood heroine. She enters the imagination of a boy who is transitioning into a man. Middle-aged people yearn for money, reputation, honour and materialistic pleasures. As one grows older, one is attracted to spirituality. Time is Almighty. Our physical, mental and spiritual needs change with time. One whose needs do not change, one who chases only a single goal, is rejected by society for being selfish, eccentric or out of sync. To elaborate, if one continues to like toys in one's youthful years, it is considered unnatural.

The SSC and the HSC are milestones on the highway of education, the track of our career. Failure during these stages does not indicate the end of life. In fact, it is just the beginning.

The world is colourful and beautiful. God has created natural, serene beauty. We have magnificent flowers, birds, animals, the sky, hills, mountains, arctic landscapes, deserts and eye-catching oases. The people of this world are also an assorted lot. All cultures have created their own art forms, sports and traditions besides achieving social, economic and technological progress. There is an ocean of books to gain knowledge and information from. Tiny flowers bloom on plateaus. Children are as beautiful as those flowers. We have up to seven decades of life to watch all this splendour, play, dance and laugh. Indeed, life is very beautiful.

We should not allow failure in the SSC or the HSC examinations to take a toll on our body and mind. We must bring out everything within us to adorn our life like a garden of saffron, through our colourful and vast range of experiences. Each of our experiences must be attached with beautiful references. If we stumble along the way and get hurt, we must apply the balm of inspiration to treat the wound and resolve to take another giant leap ahead. Come what may, we must not humiliate the beautiful life granted us by God. We must certainly not end our own life. We must not display a negative attitude towards the world. This the real identity of youth.

Alexander did not collapse when he was faced with adversity. Several rivers run into the ocean, but the converse is not true. We must bear this in mind. We should not give up the struggle till we succeed. We should not fall asleep before we succeed. Dreams are not what we see when we fall asleep. Dreams are those which do not allow us to sleep. One never becomes successful without hard work and the one who tries is never the one who fails. Labour always bears fruit. The key to success lies in perseverance, hard work and vision.

Helen Keller was physically challenged and visually impaired. Despite her physical limitations, she achieved miraculous success. You might sometimes think, 'My limbs are working and my body is strong, but my brain is a little rusted.

I'm unable to concentrate. I'm unable to study.' Remember, this is just an inferiority complex. All one needs to do is to cure themselves of it by acting determinedly. I don't need anyone's permission to make such a resolve. All I need to do is make an agreement with destiny, to prove my mettle with hard work, persistence and relentless effort, until destiny accepts defeat and asks me what I want my future to be.

Indeed, when I was preparing for my competitive examination with dogged determination for twelve months, success followed in 1996–97. My friends would jokingly say, 'Even Madhuri Dixit or Angelina Jolie would not turn down a proposal from you.' This success was not the result of Lady Luck's influence. Had I not been able to overcome my depression in the twelfth standard and taken my own decisions, I would've remained in a well of confusion regarding my career and future. It is important to make your own choices. If one takes a back seat, one is bound to get those opportunities that have been rejected by others.

Life is like a bicycle with ten gears. Most people struggle because they use only one gear. Make use of all ten gears and take a giant stride to conquer the heights of success. The SSC and HSC examinations are a relatively negligible challenge. Tell yourself, 'I am here to conquer the highest peak of Mount Everest. I will not get tired during this onerous journey. My body will remain energetic and my mind will remain fresh. What I need to do is extend the day and shorten the night. Those who want to only dream extend nights and those who want to make their dreams a reality need to extend their days. I shall use every waking minute of my life to achieve my goal.' Make this resolve and watch your inferiority complex, laziness, distractions, and bad habits vanish. With this resolve, you will experience a new dawn. Every day would be full of new opportunities and every step would be in the right direction. Let us make such a resolve!

The academic year of my HSC examination was about to conclude. Bhushan Gagrani was the chief guest at the annual day of our college. He had chosen the Marathi medium for the UPSC written examination and had stood third in the national merit list of the IAS examination. The biggest revelation of his speech was that he became an IAS by opting for Marathi literature as a subject and choosing Marathi as the medium of instruction. Indeed, Bhushan Gagrani is the personification of success. He is a Marwari youth, born in Kolhapur and having remarkable knowledge of the Marathi language and literature. In fact, he is the first successful IAS officer from Maharashtra. His success inspired several candidates, whom he taught his method of studying, to sit for the UPSC examination. Reading his notes is the key to achieving success in Marathi literature, the winning formula for studying when we were aspiring UPSC candidates.

The fair-complexioned and slender young officer had an attractive personality. Expressive eyes, clarity of thought and approach, a heart-winning smile and infectious enthusiasm were an integral part of his personality. His speech left us spellbound. It fired me up, and Anand too, seated beside me. We made a firm resolution to do something as spectacular as Gagrani.

I was not interested in pursuing science. Chitnis Sir, who taught us electronics, would hurl pieces of chalk at those who were being inattentive. Every student in the scholar batch was like the character of Chatur Lingam in the movie *3 Idiots*. I found the pungent, chemical odours of the chemistry lab to be suffocating. Once, I found a bullet in our village. Back then, it was fashionable to attach these bullets to a chain and wear it around the neck. As I had opted for electronics, I had a soldering gun to connect PCB. I fail to understand what made me solder a hook on to the bullet's triggering point. A blast occurred within a few seconds. Thankfully, I was holding the bullet with a pair of tongs and had kept it away from my body, with the 'lead' in the opposite direction. The lead shattered the glass windowpane and zoomed away. I narrowly escaped disaster and realized that I would not achieve anything by studying science. Such knowledge was dangerous and if I ever strayed from my path, I could commit some self-destructive scientific misadventures. Therefore, I decided that come what may, I would not pursue a career in science and engineering.

I had been suffering for two years, having chosen the science stream. I appeared for the examination in a restless frame of mind, due to the Gagrani factor. When the results were declared, my score had nosedived to 78 per cent from the previous score of 90-plus per cent. Twenty-four of the twenty-five students in our scholar batch took admission in electronic engineering at Walchand Engineering College. I had hit a new low. I had scored 91 per cent in the PCM group, the lowest score in the entire batch. Nobody in the village realized this, yet I felt discouraged. I was paranoid and thought that everyone was staring at me and gossiping about me. I was not in a mood to meet or talk to anyone.

While travelling from Kolhapur to my village, I would often board the State Transport bus that went to Shittur. It stopped two kilometres away from my village, across the river. I would sneak home, unnoticed, walking down the trail in the fields. I had not scored as much as I had expected, but I felt guilty as if I had committed a crime. Such guilt can prove to be very dangerous. Had I failed, someone would have insulted me or my parents would have expressed dissatisfaction over my result, and that would have helped me overcome my guilt.

The development of the pre-frontal cortex of the brain occurs during adolescence and therefore adolescents often cannot digest psychological shocks. Several of them sink into depression because of cruel treatment or due to shattered beliefs. But failure is never constant. The one who faces the situation bravely becomes successful. I got admission for BE Civil and BE Electrical at the Government Engineering College, but my mind was preoccupied with pursuing BE Mechanical or BE Electronics. I did not want to study in a private engineering college, though. Gagrani's speech had opened another avenue for me. Therefore, I took a firm decision and enrolled myself in the BA class at Rajaram College. The dream of becoming an IAS officer, triggered by Gagrani's speech, had become my magnificent obsession.

Chapter 5

Mission IAS

When one scores sufficiently high marks in the HSC Board examination, one generally opts for the science stream. My approach was beyond this conventional mindset. Despite having scored 91 per cent (in the group of three subjects) and 78 per cent aggregate, I decided to pursue a BA. This decision shocked everyone I knew. My professors summoned me, trying to make me see 'sense'. Everybody was wondering why I was taking such a foolish decision and why I was so hell-bent on ruining my life. However, I believe that the ship is the safest while it is ashore. Its purpose is only fulfilled when the navigator sails it through the choppy waters of the raging sea and successfully and safely completes the journey. Should a ship be allowed to gather dust on the shore, just because it is safe? I was ready to sail the ship of my life into risky waters, where uncertainty reigns supreme. I yearned to free fall into the vortex of the unknown. Engineering would have ensured that I found meaningful employment and job security. It would have guaranteed that I never starved. However, if

I completed my BA, I would have only two options left—I would either become an IAS officer by cracking the UPSC examination or I would be compelled to do menial work on the ancestral farms of our village.

I had taken my decision after carefully considering the pros and cons of both situations. Therefore, I was never in two minds, though my relatives and professors were against it. Thankfully, my father did not comprehend the implications. Such was his faith in me that he was confident that his son would be taking the right step. He offered me his unwavering support after I took him into confidence and convinced him of my decision.

The onus was on me to sail the ship of my life in the right direction. If I sailed in the wrong direction, I might get lost. I dedicated myself to the fulfilment of 'Mission Gagrani'. If he could do it, why can't I? Words of wisdom from Rabindranath Tagore, which made a lot of sense to me, went something like this—'Wherever you find yourself presently, do not give up on what you have undertaken. Do not laze, dreaming that you will explore new horizons.' These lines repeated in my head over and over again.

My college was in the vicinity of a pre-IAS training centre and the Shivaji University, my *karmabhumi*. I was ready to sow the seeds of hard work and reap the harvest of knowledge and success. I don't have to nurture an inferiority complex, I thought. I shall develop my personality, ensure that I do not become redundant in any way and fight to win. If I lose, I shall get back up and fight with renewed ferocity. I shall not grumble or complain, I shall keep the struggle on. My head was filled with such thoughts but my age and surroundings presented a colourful kaleidoscope of college life for me.

Many of the students of Rajaram College hailed from well-to-do families. This manifested in the buzz of four-wheelers on the campus. Shyam's tea stall, a popular watering hole, would attract students more than college lectures. Hostel life had adversely affected me in junior college. This time around, I was more cautious. Hostel life is known for wasting time and indulging in dangerous activities. It is inevitable to make mistakes at that age. Good as well as bad experiences impact the mind equally. Many stray from their chosen paths. Some are smart enough to pass all the tests and ultimately become successful.

Madhavan, who would later become a Bollywood superstar, was allotted as my room partner in the hostel. He would only speak in English, and was quite unkempt. His socks would stink so much that I would not feel like entering my hostel room. However, soon the hearty, confident and charming Madhavan became my good friend. Groups of English-speaking girls in college would chase him. Even when surrounded by hordes of girls, he never failed to be a gentleman. He was chivalrous, and never talked to anyone rudely or misbehaved. He would talk to girls, crack jokes with them, spend time with them in the canteen but still appear like a radiant yogi. He was engaged in several extracurriculars and would always try to implement innovative initiatives in college. Both of us had volunteered for National Cadet Corps (NCC). He was sent to England through the NCC's Youth Exchange Programme. His skill in elocution and debate was par excellence, and would teach hostel students the basics of phonetics. He would teach us how to pronounce the silent 'K' while saying 'thank you', but we were never able to pronounce it like him.

We would go to college together, riding double seat on a cycle. Along the way, I hoped to hear him speak in English, so I could improve my diction. Vikas Dhas would often taunt him, saying, 'Madhya, did a flight carrying the British fly over your house when you were born?' But Madhavan remained unperturbed—he showed tremendous self-restraint. Not because he was wary of Vikas but because his ideas of life were different. He dreamt big, knew his purpose. His thoughts and actions aligned with each other. He also had tremendous physical and mental abilities. Such was his physical prowess that that none of us were able to defeat him in arm-wrestling contests; it hardly took him a few seconds to put us in our place. Nothing could ever make him angry. Therefore, he was the teacher's favourite.

Madhavan was responsible for organizing the 'Just A Minute' competition on the college campus. The idea was that each contestant would speak for a minute on a given topic, without fumbling. Subsequently, Madhavan went on to host the television show *Tol Mol Ke Bol* and became a well-known Bollywood and Tollywood star.

I still remember, in our final year of college, Madhavan, five girls and I were in the running for the 'Best Rajaramiyan Award'. Madhavan, who excelled in extracurricular activities, was miles ahead of us. But he had not cleared the exam of one subject, due to the distraction of the NCC camp in England, and had an ATKT (Allowed to Keep Terms). As a result, I won the 'Best Rajaramiyan Trophy'. Even as I received the award, I was aware that Madhavan deserved it more. When I look back, I think that the criteria to award the 'Best Rajaramiyan Trophy' was like denying Sachin Tendulkar an excellence award in cricket because he did not clear his SSC examination. Madhavan went on to famously play Farhan

Qureshi in the film *Three Idiots*. Presently, he is trying his luck in Hollywood too. We would meet often when I was posted in Mumbai. He continues to have his feet planted firmly on the ground and his willingness to take giant leaps ahead and fly high with the desire to work hard for success is still intact.

In my college years, I was too naïve to recognize his worth. I got bored of Madhavan's high-flying English and stinky socks. I gave my bed to Colonel Sable's son and moved to the adjacent room with my rural friends. Sable didn't know how to behave. Once, he removed the iron bars from the library chairs and sold them in scrap to buy cigarettes. His behaviour made me so angry that I was forced to give him the Mankar treatment. I demanded that he explain himself. We got in a heated argument and an exchange of blows followed. I beat up Sable. The episode was reported to the rector. At that point of time, soccer matches were going on in the college. The rector gave me my first Yellow Card as a warning and threatened to rusticate me from the hostel if I faltered again. That marked the beginning of my 'dabang-giri' (showmanship of one's rowdiness).

On campus, lobbying and politics were common. When it came to rowdiness, the 'G' gang and hostel group would compete. The 'G' gang was a group of city boys, led by Hemant Nimbalkar, while the hostel group comprised rural students. Their leader was Vikas Dhas. Hemant was a unique character. Though notorious for his pranks, he was brilliant and innovative. He had defeated the hostel group's candidate in the university representative elections. Hemya, as he was fondly called, would always be surrounded by girls and boys. He was an excellent orator and had given several insightful speeches. He skilfully organized all college cultural programmes. But when it came to confrontations, he would pull a vanishing act. Such was his skill in politics that this strategy would prove useful, and he would always maintain the upper hand. Hemant possessed extraordinary presence of mind and knew when to withdraw. However, he would not miss exacting revenge when the time was right. He had beautiful handwriting; his writing style was excellent too. Hemant achieved glorious success and became an IPS officer. During training, we put our college rivalry behind us and became fast friends. During our training in Hyderabad, when I stood second in the marathon, and our batchmate, who stood third, accused me of taking a short cut, Hemant grabbed him by the neck, saying, 'My brother would never take a short cut in his life,' in front of the academy director.

In the initial days of our training in Mussoorie, Hemant had penned a mind-blowing skit on all the Marathi candidates, entitled 'Aajki Mahabharat' (Mahabharat in Today's Era). Its hero was Duryodhan. Slimly built, Davale Dada enacted the role of Bheem, staging his entry, pulling out his bludgeon. Arjun slayed Karna while the latter was repairing the flat tyre of his bicycle. A young French woman who taught us played the role of Draupadi. I was cast as Duryodhan. The skit concluded with Draupadi eloping with Duryodhan. Officers from north India hurled rotten eggs at us when we performed the climax. The skit resulted in a discussion on freedom of expression in the academy. Hemant, the 'Chocolate Hero' of our college, was a genuinely charismatic man. The rural students would watch this fair-complexioned, cat-eyed ladies' man mingling with the female students on campus with jealousy.

Vikas Dhas, the hero of the hostel group, was a robust man. He could be found crossing swords with someone or the other every day. Once, a group of fifteen to twenty students had gone to threaten Papya, who lived near the hostel. Vikas had also summoned Uttya Pawar, a goon from Dombarwada. Uttya was slated to beat up Papya. Vilya and I had become a part of the group as onlookers-cum-associates. Uttya knocked on Papya's door and shouted, 'Papya, step out. I'm not going to leave you alive today.' Papya and his three brothers were waiting inside the house, fully prepared to take us on, but we had no knowledge of it. The foursome stepped out of the house, wielding sickles and shouting, 'Wait, Uttya. We are going to rip you apart.' As the situation got out of hand, Vilya and I ran away, stopping only after putting a couple of kilometres between us and the house. We halted, speculating that the foursome may have slain either Uttya or Vikya. However, a breathless Uttya soon joined us. Seeing the ire of Papya, he too had fled. He was clearly embarrassed to see us and started picking up twigs and talking about teaching Papya and his brothers a lesson. But we realized what a loudmouth he was. We told him to return to his house instead and went to the hostel.

A police team had already reached the hostel and the situation turned ugly. We hid Vikas in an overhead water storage tank. The rector assembled us in front of the hostel building. The sub-inspector was angry. Speaking in English, he said, 'I know who is in how much water.' We were puzzled, wondering how he had found out where Vikas was. We breathed a sigh of relief when the sub-inspector went away after a brief search.

Soon, the first-year examinations were looming over us, and we were not prepared. Papya's father worked as the driver of a corporator, who was said to be a dangerous man. He had broken someone's hand in a scuffle.

The hostelites were worried that he would break Vikas's limbs. Vikas and I would ride double seat on my bicycle to go to Nana's mess. We changed our timings. However, one day, the corporator's gang members accosted us. Bhagwan Jadhav, the son of a notorious goon from Rajarampuri area, alighted from the jeep.

He was followed by three people wearing gold chains, wielding hockey sticks. I was convinced that not only Vikas's bones but mine too were about to be broken. Vikas was about to remove the bicycle chain to defend himself. Bhagwan called out, 'Which one of you is Vikas?' Putting up a brave face, Vikas stepped forward. Bhagwan Dada unclenched his left fist to reveal three revolver bullets. He said, 'One of these was destined to make a hole in you but you are saved. I would have killed you had Hemant Patil not intervened.' Hemant was Vikas's friend. His father was an MLA. I had no clue that this set-up had been worked out. Bhagwan took a rose out of his jeep and said, 'Let bygones be bygones. We will shower petals on you even if you stone us.' Vikas and I were shocked, but we realized that he was simply being witty. He took us in his jeep to a rundown hotel in the red-light area of Dombarwada where he treated us to misal, and strong tea from broken cups. Thanks to Vikas, I would get to experience more of such situations. Later, Vikas was recruited as a police sub-inspector and made headlines when he gunned down a stray leopard in Karad, trying to save a child's life.

The moment one entered the hostel building, one started acting like a vagabond or a spoilt brat. Every hostel student received a crash course in eve-teasing and bullying. If one taunted a girl and she looked back angrily or threatened to beat one up, it was an accomplishment. Rural students in the hostel were not as savvy as the city lads. Their chances of seducing a girl were slim to none. They would be looked upon with contempt for being 'low class'. As a result, some indulged in perversions. I frowned upon such incidents but did not have the courage to raise my voice. I had already got a 'Yellow Card' due to the Sable episode and any more trouble might've resulted in a 'Red Card'. Therefore, I concentrated on my studies. I made several friends in the hostel, all of whom had different talents. Vilya was the 'Master of Taunts'. Once, he taunted some NCC girls by remarking, 'Attention, at ease, left–right.' One of the girls said to her friend, 'Look at that monkey.' The incident embarrassed Vilya, but he managed to impress a good-looking girl and the couple started romancing in the campus. People in love forget about the world around them and Vilya was no different. I realized that I was wasting my time gossiping about girls being teased, having love affairs or indulging in meaningless chatting sessions. I decided to turn my attention to the Pre-IAS Training Centre and the college library.

My first year BA classes had commenced. In the New College, I was mingling with the intellectual crème de la crème of Kolhapur. But this college had students who were not as intellectually gifted, who were pursuing BA for the sake of it. Besides this, goons with a PhD in laziness had also taken admission. This intellectually unstimulating environment led me to lose interest in attending lectures. However, the college, established in 1880, had a state-of-the-art library. I started browsing through books, magazines and journals, and visiting the government-run Pre-IAS Training Centre. I met my seniors Vikas Kharge and Prakash Pote who were preparing for their exam there. The centre did not have a lot of candidates, so I was permitted to attend lectures because of my keen interest. I would sit at the back of the class and observe the aspirants, make an effort to hang out with them. Initially, they were hesitant because of my young age and immaturity. Gradually, I got acclimatized to being in their company. I met Gholkar Sir and a clear vision of the road ahead formed in my head. All I needed to do was continue my journey down that road, without any accidents.

I would return to my village on the weekend and during holidays. Since childhood, I was intrigued by those youngsters who would spend their time chit-chatting in the village square. I would idolize those who danced during a public figure's birth anniversary celebrations or festivals. As a child, the beats of the *dhol-tashas* in the Lezim troupes would thrill me and I craved to dance to those beats. However, I would never join a Lezim troupe because I did not have the talent for it. The village youngsters enjoyed festivities like Ganesh Chaturthi, Shiv Jayanti, Ambedkar Jayanti and *dahi handi* during Janmashtami. The wrestling arenas would be filled with youngsters and the sound of wrestlers beating their chests would resonate in the entire village during the annual festival. Processions of victorious wrestlers would move through the village. However, my attraction to such events was dormant.

Though I primarily lived in Kolhapur, I started making friends with various young folks from my village. My subconscious intention was to organize them into some sort of social welfare work in case I failed to crack the UPSC. I made friends with Mujafya, Hanafya, Tanya and Pakya. The Ghode and Nangre brethren dominated the entire village. Youngsters belonging to these two families had the privilege of watching movies at the video centre free of cost. They bullied people who gathered at paan stalls and ate at the Udupi hotel without paying the bill, as if it was their birth right. Frustrated with this hooliganism, several village traders began migrating to Shetkwadi Phata. The village market, once alive with trade and commerce, became deserted. These young hooligans could be found stumbling on the road, evidently intoxicated. Without the advantage of an education, they were unfit even for farming. They would brawl over petty matters during festivals and sour the mood of the entire village. Elections were marked by the distribution of free liquor, mutton delicacies and drunk folks with perverse aggression. Our village was listed as a 'sensitive' place in the police records. The politics of division and jealousy between brethren was ruining the next generation.

The division in the village made me deeply uncomfortable. I despised the open display of jealousy during festivals. I looked at the lathi-wielding youth as people gone astray. I was convinced that such drunkards and Gutka chewers could not do anything constructive for society. By pursuing a college degree in the city, I had chosen a different life, but I still wanted my village to thrive. I had heard about Ralegan Siddhi and the work done by Anna Hazare. I took my village friends to Ralegan Siddhi in a jeep to meet him. Anna Hazare had transformed his village for the better by banning the sale of liquor, deforestation, over-grazing by cattle as well as by encouraging the contribution of labour to the betterment of the village by every villager. He had started a school for students who didn't do well in normal school. Mass felicitation of women were organized there. For the last twenty-five years, no elections have been organized in the village, saving it from their ugly aftermath. All festivals are celebrated in a simple manner. I found his achievements extremely impressive.

Anna met us for hardly five minutes but in that brief span, he connected with each one of us. He said, 'Young men, I had nothing to lose and therefore I had little to sacrifice.

But you have an entire life ahead of you that you can dedicate to the fulfilment of a cause. Today, you are all preparing for competitive examinations. I wish that you become successful men one day. But once you make it in your chosen careers, learn to make sacrifices. Sacrifice your comforts for the sake of the country. Stay away from corruption. To love, to serve and to help are the three actions to live by—make them your mission. We seldom forget our rights but conveniently fail to remember our duties. Respect national symbols and those who sacrificed their lives for this nation. Do not hesitate to contribute your bit for the good of the nation. Think beyond regional, religious and caste barriers and inculcate the values of tolerance and integrity. Be proud of our diverse culture and rich traditions and do your best to conserve and protect our natural resources. Hone your skills. Always speak the truth. If you embrace humanity, rationality, and intellectualism, you will never be embarrassed. If you dedicate your lives for the transformation of society, it will never cease to respect you.' Anna's precious and gentle guidance and four lines from Kusumagraj's poem 'Swatantryadevatechi Vinavani' have influenced me deeply. The lines are:

वेतन खाऊन काम टाळणे हा देशाचा द्रोह असे,
करतील दुसरे बघतील तिसरे, असे सांगुनी सुटू नका |
जनसेवेस्वव असे कचेरी ती डाकूंची गुहा नसे,
मेजाखालून, मेजावरतून द्व्य कुणाचे लुटू नका |

(Avoiding the work for which one is paid is akin to treason. Do not shrug off your responsibilities onto someone else's shoulders. The offices are meant for service; they are not caves inhabited by dacoits. Do not strip anyone of his wealth by accepting bribes, either from under the table or across it.)

I started organizing the village youngsters; the Ganesh Festival was a good platform. Ever since our visit to Ralegan Siddhi, we had been contemplating doing something constructive in the village. We visited Gavaloba Hill and took an oath that that if one failed to crack the UPSC examination or become a collector or a commissioner, he would strive to at least become a police sub-inspector or a tehsildar. However, the biggest challenge was to find a way of acquiring the books we needed. Since none of us had taken formal admission in the Pre-IAS Training Centre in Kolhapur, we could not procure books from its library. The voluminous books of general studies and history, published by Delhi-based publishing houses, and other study material were costly. A candidate could not afford to buy them on his own. An idea struck me. The Ganesh Festival was round the corner. We established a study centre, to set up a library through it. We organized a book exhibition to mark the festival. Bhaskar Bhau, Dilip, Vikas, everyone came together to set up a lecture series that would be held during the festival. We planned that every day we would host a different chief guest and chairperson. One would have to contribute Rs 1000 to become a chairperson and Rs 500 to be the chief guest. It was a ten-day lecture programme and the response was overwhelming. We had invited reputed speakers from Sangli and Kolhapur, which drew in a sizeable crowd. The villagers showed their appreciation for our efforts. A surplus amount of Rs 25,000, raised through contributions, was now in our kitty. The Mandal workers came together to decide how to spend it. Suggestions like building a new *kalas* (the pinnacle of a temple), a new wrestling ring or a new gym were put forth. However, I came forward and said, 'We need money to buy books for the library of our study centre.

We don't need these books for our enjoyment. We want books to prepare for entrance exams of MPSC, UPSC, railway and bank recruitment boards, police, army, navy, IIT and NDA. I, or the son of any farmer, would not be able to afford these books. We implore you to use this money to provide us with the books we need. We will study hard and become successful. This is my promise.' I made an emotional appeal to the villagers, as planned. Four to five others supported our idea. Finally, the villagers agreed to our plan.

We hopped on a State Transport bus and reached Pune. We had a list of books that were recommended for the UPSC examination, published in *Competition Success Review*. However, we could not find NCERT books anywhere in Pune. Finally, someone told us that the Central School in Viman Nagar stocked these books. When we reached, we found the entire store stacked with NCERT books. We had no clue as to which books we needed, so we bought them all, from standard VIII to XII, like the mythological story of Lord Hanuman who, instead of bringing just the Sanjivani herb, had brought the whole mountain. We bought volumes on general studies as well as some to improve our English. Bhaskar Bhau had decided to choose psychology as an optional subject. However, in the lists, he had written 'Phiscology' instead of psychology. After many efforts, the shop owner finally understood what Bhaskar Bhau wanted. He bought several volumes written by various psychology scholars, from Sigmund Freud to William James. I had painstakingly prepared the list of general studies and history books. Most of them were available. Dilip bought all the books for MPSC as well as those on personality development.

We returned to the village with five large boxes full of books. These books would help us get government jobs and unveil the mystery of how to become an officer. The villagers looked at us with pride. We arranged all the books in the cupboards of a room at the Gram Panchayat office. When Deshmukh Saheb visited our village, we enthusiastically told him all about this initiative and showed him photographs of the lecture series event. He was proud of us and asked us to meet him in Mumbai in the coming week to accept a cheque of Rs 50,000. He delivered on his word and our study centre received an aid of Rs 50,000 from the Chief Minister's Relief Fund. Our joy knew no bounds. We built a modest building near the Gram Panchayat office. We bought tables, chairs and bookshelves, ready to prepare for the UPSC.

I had spent my entire first year of college in deciding my line of education and training in politics and hooliganism. In the second year, I saw an advertisement for Jagdale Sir's one-to-one classes. He started training me for personality development. He would make me recite 'Manache Shlok' when I went for coaching.

He was impressed by the marks I had scored in the SSC and the HSC examinations and had enormous confidence in me. He had analysed my capabilities accurately and started training me in time management. He advised, 'Good handwriting, excellent structuring, clear thinking and a positive attitude will make you succeed in competitive examinations.' However, he warned, 'You must complement your abilities with hard work and perseverance.' He would recite inspiring poems for me every day. He made me write on the first page of my diary: 'The heights great men reached and kept, were not attained by sudden flight, but they, while their companions slept, were toiling upward in the night.'

Every day he would motivate me, saying, 'You will compete against students preparing in JNU, SIAC, Jaykar Library,

Agricultural College and Old Rajinder Nagar in Delhi. They spend sleepless nights preparing for the UPSC. They stay rooted to their study table for twelve hours a day. This is how they achieve their goals, one step at a time. Nobody becomes successful by fluke. Those who dream of becoming successful, spend every waking moment toiling to achieve their goals. To them, food, sleep, rest, and recreation hold no value. Hordes of such candidates are preparing for competitive examinations. It is a constant, ongoing war. What are you doing? You must plan for every day, every month, every six months and prepare yourself for the battle ahead. This time is crucial, it will decide whether you will become successful or not. You cannot wake up at the eleventh hour. You will have to put in the work. You must inculcate important values in yourself. Be confident. There are a million sparks in you, a whole world of potential. You must steer them in the right direction with discipline and through your thought processes and lifestyle. Don't be afraid of failure or your own weaknesses. Don't let other people's negativity bring you down. Your identity is not limited to your outer self. Your identity is defined by the books you read, your words, your mannerisms, the extent of your knowledge and your dreams. Identify your strengths and weaknesses. Resolve to transform yourself. Think of yourself as a winner and strive to become one. Work hard, harder!'

I quit the hostel and rented a room on a cot basis in a colony near the Pre-IAS Training Centre. My cousin Bheema Bapu too had come to Kolhapur to pursue his studies. His elder brother Anna wanted Bapu to become a PSI. Bapu, a famous wrestler, became my room partner. He had an MA in Hindi but could barely speak it. He would go to the wrestling ring, eat mutton cooked in ghee and sleep soundly during the day as well as the night. All he wanted to know was how and when the PSI examination paper would get leaked. He would ride to the university on a Bullet motorcycle. He had the patience for sitting or studying in the library for not more than twenty minutes. He would then take a stroll in the garden. He soon met his girlfriend in the garden. After that, Bapu gave up on his studies and started preparing for his wedding.

I started visiting the Pre-IAS Training Centre regularly. My close friends who were also very sincere, Vikas Kharge and Prakash Pote, studied at the centre. Vikas Sir was decent, reserved and brilliant. He was a man of few words. He used novel methods to study. I often sat with him and tried to understand his deep, meaningful thoughts. When I read a book, first I would simply skim through it. I would underline important passages in the second reading and prepare micro-notes in the third reading. I would methodologically jot down these micro-notes in small boxes on a page. When I revised, just browsing through these notes would refresh my memory and understanding of the subject. Sir had a concise method even for reading newspapers. When he sat down to read the newspaper, his first thought was about the questions that would be asked in the preliminary examination, the main examination and finally, the interview. No wonder he became an IAS topper and earned repute across Maharashtra as a respectful, honest and dedicated officer. I made attempts to get close to him and he, in turn, responded positively. He appreciated the fact that I had chosen the arts stream despite securing good marks in the HSC examination from the science stream. But gradually, the vagabonds from college started coming to the Pre-IAS Training Centre to meet me. We behaved wildly on the college campus, which Vikas and Prakash Sir were aware of. My friends and I dined at the same mess as them, gossiping about the campus. My group respected Vikas Sir. If he was at the mess, our gossiping would stop. However, to embarrass me, some of them would continue to gossip loudly.

Once, after we had dinner at the mess, Vikas Sir called me and reprimanded me, saying, 'Vishwas, you will have to stretch yourself out, and stay away from such rowdy and negative friends. You will have to face frustration and failure if you do not get out of this comfort zone.'

He told me a story, 'Once upon a time, a king bought two eagles and appointed a man to teach them how to fly. After some days, one of the eagles started flying high but the other one could not even take off. The king was worried. He made a public announcement, issuing an open challenge to all to make the other eagle fly. Early next day, the king went to the garden and found out that the eagle, who could not even take off, was flying higher than the other eagle. He was astonished and wanted to know how it happened. An ordinary farmer stepped ahead and respectfully told the king that he had simply cut off the branch on which the eagle was sitting to prompt the eagle into taking off into the sky.'

He said, 'Vishwas, you need to get out of your comfort zone and see what lies ahead. Do not live a happy, complacent life in a shell. Step out, and you will find a world that is freer, richer and full of constructive challenges. Change your attitude and your life too will change.' His words put me in deep thought. Indeed, students living at the hostel spent 80 per cent of their time pursuing useless activities and the remaining 20 per cent, blaming others for their academic failures. I resolved to suffer to any extent but to stay away from negativity and allurements.

I had chosen history, political science and English literature as my optional subjects in the second year of my

BA course. Ekonde Sir taught us history. I was his blue-eyed boy. He came to meet me when I was the district superintendent of police at Ahmednagar. He brought with him the answer sheets I had written during the internal assessment tests in college. So impressed was he by my handwriting and writing style that he had preserved the answer sheets. Kapase Sir taught us political science. He also taught at the Pre-IAS Training Centre. He would explain the concepts of fundamental rights and republic, lucidly and in flawless English no less. He was in charge of 5 Maharashtra Battalion of NCC at the college. He encouraged me to participate in the shooting and elocution competitions at the annual training camp in Rukadi. Those participating in the competitions were permitted to remain absent for the evening parade during the three-day long camp. The competition was held only in English and Hindi medium. I had carried with me *CSR*, a magazine read by candidates preparing for competitive exams. In two days, I managed to memorize an essay on 'National Integration' featured in the magazine. Though I hadn't understood it completely, I recited it in over seven minutes. Satish Gurav was my biggest competitor but I bagged the first prize. Even in the shooting competition, my grouping was 3 inches, winning me the first prize. This means that four of the five bullets fired by me from a .22 rifle had struck within 3 inches of the bull's eye. I also got certificates from the district collector. My photograph was published in the newspaper the next day. Gradually, I was gaining self-confidence.

I attended all the lectures organized in Kolhapur, including those given by stalwarts like Narendra Dabholkar, Shivajirao Bhosale, Vivek Ghalsasi, Narendra Jadhav and Nirmalkumar Phadkule. I watched several movies and dramas. Cinema was a source of not only entertainment but also knowledge.

Since I was a student of literature, the story presented through the audio-visual medium impressed me immensely. I reflected on the cathartic power of cinema in my answers too. Ultimately, movies and examinations are performances that last for three hours. Those who perform well become successful.

I started building up my general studies. I made a diary to paste clippings of useful information and pictures related to political, economic, social, cultural news and events. I used another diary for writing informative snippets like 'today in the history'. I jotted down the dates of as well as notes on international, national and state-level historic incidents on a calendar. I discovered the atlas, because of which I was able to understand the geographical and political borders of countries. I could make out the exact location of nations, states and places of importance. I was learning new words and their usage every day. Economics was one subject which mostly went over my head. D.D. Basu's book on the Constitution of India or Maurya and Sundaram's volume on economics were of no use to me. A treasury of knowledge lay ahead of me, but opening it remained a struggle. Nevertheless, I put in the work.

BA examinations were not a cause of much stress. My study of English literature and its criticism proved useful in Marathi literature too. George Orwell's *Animal Farm* was a part of the syllabus. It is an aptly worded satire. It depicts the chaos and mediocrity that prevailed in Stalin's Soviet Russia, through the characters of two pigs: Snowball and Napoleon. I understood the correlation between literature and social situations because of this novel. 'Methods of Writing History' was included in the history syllabus. Studying that topic gave me an inkling of how to refer to sources from ancient carvings to middle-age documents while writing history. I benefited from this when I gave the UPSC exam.

I regularly visited the Khardekar Library or the Pre-IAS Training Centre for studying. My college campus was on the way to the university. I would often meet my old friends on the way. They would say, 'Vishvya, why are you spending all of your time studying? Spend some time with us too.' We all would occasionally get together at the hostel at night. Some seniors would drink beer and start jabbering. Since the ladies' hostel was nearby, boys would loudly call out the names of girls living in the hostel. Frequently, it would result in complaints and subsequent identification parades. It is very difficult to overcome one's bad habits. Once, some boys started talking about Sharlin, a girl from Bengaluru, in a perverse manner. I was respected in the hostel for being decent and studious, but some did not like it. To put me down, somebody pushed Sharlin against me, saying that I was among those who were disrespecting her. The next day, she accosted me and rebuked me in fluent English. I had no idea why she was angry, and was unable to give her a fitting reply. My ego was hurt. I was publicly humiliated. I decided to seek my revenge. I memorized an English paragraph on personality development that had appeared in the CSR, and let everyone in the hostel know that I was going to give Sharlin a fitting reply. I accosted Sharlin in the college building and before she could understand what was happening, recited that paragraph, pretending that I was angry. She was stunned. The words were inspiring but angry. I walked away. Several students had seen the incident. My rural friends did not understand what I had said. As a result, everyone started talking about how I rebuked Sharlin in English. This trick boosted my ego. This incident impressed other students and thankfully, Sharlin was also not mad at me anymore. Such funny incidents add spice to college life.

Get-togethers and festivals add colour to life. The enthusiasm of youngsters, their passion and budding feelings alike are expressed through dancing, singing, taunting or sometimes giving each other a rosebud on Rose Day. Messages are exchanged, eyes meet and at times hearts too meet.

Preparations for the gathering begin a month in advance. Hrushikesh Joshi, who is a Marathi star, looked like royalty. Hemant Nimbalkar led the drama troupes. We, the ignorant, didn't fit in but since it was the last year of college, we decided to prepare a musical and dance performance. Satish Kambale, the son of a senior government officer, lived in the hostel with us. He was always loaded with money. Sanjay Dutt's song 'Rahne Ko Ghar Nahi, Sone Ko Bistar Nahi' was popular those days. We decided to perform a group dance on it. Satya brought a TV, a VCR and a skinny choreographer on the condition that he would be the lead dancer. We rehearsed the dance well. Satya's steps were not in sync with the others. In alignment with the lyrics of the song, we were all paupers. Since we did not have good shirts, we decided to wear Sando T-shirts as the dance costume. But that would showcase our ribs and armpit hair. Satya had expensive clothes and a jacket. Vikas Dhas and Satya had an argument, and I was chosen as the lead dancer instead of Satya.

My experience of dancing to Bollywood songs was limited to dancing at wedding processions or dahi handi celebrations. However, I danced enthusiastically to the beats of the halgi in a Lezim performance. I knew how to coordinate my steps with the rhythm. The dance practice continued. Every group member was in sync. I quickly learnt the steps as the lead dancer. Our dance performance was ready.

I also wanted to perform a song at the gathering. I was a bathroom singer and knew nothing about the technicalities of singing. But if Sant Dnyaneshwar could get a buffalo to recite the Vedas, why shouldn't I be able to sing? I knew I was overconfident, but I was eager to try new things. What's the worst that could happen? At the most, people would laugh. If I could learn and win, it would help with my personality development. If I lost, I would learn a lesson. Inferiority complex is the biggest enemy of rural students. With hard work, I overcame this complex. When we crush the phobia, we set off on the journey to success. When I revisit the past, I am happy that I didn't shy away from leaving my comfort zone. However, it doesn't mean that I forgot my old friends. I am as confident and relaxed with foreign officers I meet during training as I am with my SSC-failed friend Shivjya Kadam from Nerle village. I can chat with Javed Akhtar or Amitabh Bachchan with the same confidence as I do with the nine-yard saree-clad Paru Kaku from Kokrud. So what if I come from a village? I can manage everything as well as any city lad.

After I joined the police service, I intentionally tried to improve my elocution and debate skills. Today, I am often requested to give lectures as a reputed speaker; seniors ask me to participate in talk shows on national TV channels. In short, we should never hide our ignorance. I decided to perform a song at the gathering. Whether my voice was good or not was for the audience to decide. Back then, Rishi Kapoor's film *Diwana* had been a blockbuster. Its song 'Sochenge Tumhe Pyar Kare Ki Nahi' was a super hit. I started practising, using Vilya's tape recorder. Orchestra artists came to campus three days before the event, selected the songs and singers and began conducting their rehearsals. I went for my first ever 'screen test' with my hostel friends. I found out that as many as eleven people had started their tests with the same song. I was the twelfth candidate but my college mate, G.S. Dipak Jamenis, warned the orchestra artists that only I would sing this song. Thus, my song was selected on account of the recommendation. I drank milk with turmeric to ensure that my throat was in good condition. Finally, it was the day of the gathering.

Kolhapur is an orthodox city. To avoid chaos, the gallery was reserved for girls. Students from the hostel sat in the first four rows to cheer us for our dance and my song. Of course, the song was romantic and I performed it while looking at the gallery, my lyrics aimed at the girls. I did not falter during the performance and the tuning was good. As my song ended, the students demanded that I sing again. Once the performance was over, the hostel students gave me 'bumps' for not looking at them while singing. The dance performance was towards the end of the event. I had bought a pair of jeans especially for the performance, but our hostel was on a grazing land. I washed the jeans and spread them on the barbed wire fencing to dry. A grazing cow chewed up its seat. Finally, I found a tailor and got the damaged part fixed with a patch. In those days, such experiments on jeans were common. Anyway, the song was about streetside vagabonds so my attire was fitting. Our dance was well received, and our troupe won the prize, that too at the hands of TV star Mahesh. I have preserved the photo of that prize-giving ceremony.

I gained a lot of popularity on campus because of my song and dance performances. Now I wanted to set my third record—presenting a rose to at least one girl on Rose Day. But I worried about what I would do if some girl accepted the rose from me. I could not afford to spend my time running behind someone, reiterating my love for her. The idea also did not appeal to me. Still, I decided to give it a try. Traditional Day and the Rose Day were celebrated on the same day. I polished my Kolhapuri chappal. After watching the movie *Parinda*, starring Nana Patekar, I had stitched an 'Anna Dress' for myself. So transparent was the cloth of the shirt that one could have counted my ribs when I wore it. I borrowed an innerwear T-shirt from Vilya. I also wore a pair of fake Ray-Ban goggles which I had bought near the ST bus terminus to look impressive, like Dagadu Parab's character in the movie *Timepass*.

I reached the college to find a girl to give a rose to. Several city girls came to college riding a Luna moped. Rarely did they become friends with rural students living in the hostel. A look of love from one of these girls was not in the destiny of the rural students. If they sought to become friends, they would be given a look of contempt. Conventionally, a pink rose meant friendship and a red rose, love. I had decided that it would be better to give someone a pink rose. Some recent couples came to campus on motorcycles. I was worried about how to take a girl double seat on my Atlas bicycle. Finally, I mustered some courage and zeroed in on a group of three girls who were pursuing a BSc degree. I resolved to give the rose to at least one of them to mark the beginning of our friendship. Satya Thombare was the only student living in the hostel who would mix with girls. I loitered near the girls with Satya throughout the day but could not gather up the courage to give the rose to one of them.

I realized that they were mocking us. Finally, as the college hours were nearing their end, Satya got frustrated and said, 'Come with me. I will speak to them.' We rode our bicycles and accosted the girls near the parking lot. Satya said,

'Hello! Can you spare a minute? This is Vishwas. He wants to talk to you.' The three girls halted and looked at me with contempt. In a pleading tone, I managed to utter, 'Will one of you accept this rose? I would like to be your friend.' Satya was furious. He said, 'Whom do you want to give the rose? Address her directly and give the rose.' I started approaching the girls from the left side. The first one bluntly refused to accept the rose. The second said, 'I am sorry.' The third girl was more polite. She simply walked away without saying anything. At the end of the day, the rose had wilted. I chewed its petals, thinking, 'Forget about falling in love, I cannot even become friends with a girl. My life is rotten.' Pretending to be heartbroken, I drank beer with Raja, Vikas and Satya that night. They had the 'he is still new to the game' look on their faces and sympathized with me. Suddenly, I remembered Kharge Sir's rebuking words and decided that there would be no more friendship, love affairs, roses or girls for me. I would start studying hard. I made a resolve and immersed myself in my studies.

I have never understood the changes that one undergoes when they are eighteen years old. The body grows. Psychological and physiological needs increase. The blood runs hot. Allurements are tempting. Even before the train of dedication towards studies catches speed, somebody pulls the chain. We feel as if everything that glitters is gold. It could be a sharp piece of shattered glass too, piercing the leg. The wound could end up getting infected and ruining your entire life. It is more dangerous for boys living in hostels or on a cot basis. Their condition is like that of a batsman facing a fast bowler without using a guard, helmet or pads. They don't have anyone who could guide them or teach them the good from the bad. Once they are lured, they sink. One never knows where the energy and zest of this age will take him. In my third year of BA, I started ignoring my studies, inching towards village politics, rowdy behaviour and acting like a smart aleck.

I insisted that Tatya buy a motorcycle for me. My sister's marriage had been finalized. Since the groom was a police sub-inspector, Tatya planned the wedding with much pomp. I was aware that Tatya was facing financial problems because he had asked me to visit a few relatives to borrow money. The ones he had helped had turned their backs on him when he needed their help. Finally, Tatya's friends came to the rescue. As many as twenty friends, right from Tukaram, who was a shoeshine boy, to Shamu, who ran a tea stall, took out a loan of Rs 25,000 each from the bank and gave the money to Tatya. The bank had one Gaikwad Saheb as an agriculture officer. He lived on rent in our old home. Though they were not related to us by blood nor was there any guarantee of return, his wife gave her own fifteen-tola gold to my sister Seema Tai.

In fact, Seema Tai had received two marriage proposals on the same day. One was a senior officer with Bharat Petroleum. He was a tall, handsome young officer with a plush salary and a well-off lifestyle. Everybody had liked him, but Daji (my brother-in-law) came to see Seema Tai in the afternoon. He looked impressive in his *pheta*. Since his father was a farmer and his family was from a village smaller than ours, we chose his proposal, in the hopes that Tai would find it easier to adjust with his family.

The wedding took place with much pomp and show. Despite his loans, Tatya took an advance from the commission agent and bought a motorcycle for me after the wedding. I fail to understand the nature of the relationship between a father and his son. This is the only bond between two men devoid of jealousy or hate. A father blesses his son, wishing from the bottom of his heart that the other man becomes someone better than him. The father's chest swells with the achievements of the son. When I was selected as the Best Student, I had taken Tatya and my mother for the prize distribution ceremony. Tatya's confidence had grown upon hearing my teachers praise me. I had insisted that Tatya buy a motorcycle for me, pretending that I needed to travel a substantial distance to the university and the bicycle consumed a lot of time. Tatya bought a second-hand Kawasaki Bajaj motorbike for me. My stature at the college increased. Even the snobbish girls and boys started greeting me because I had the bike. I relished the attention. As my college days were coming to an end, I spent a good deal of time riding my bike, from the college to the university to the canteen, meeting groups of friends.

Zilla Parishad elections were to be held in our village. We were confident that this time Tatya would get the party ticket and started campaigning for him. One night, we painted Tatya's name on the village temple's wall, announcing his candidature. That backfired and Tatya was refused candidature. This was an insult. My father filed his nomination form as an independent candidate. I was in my early twenties. I resolved to enter politics at the village level and avenge Tatya. Entering politics in the village was impossible without asserting muscle power, so I brought together local youths. The elections were approaching. There were some brawls over the selection of candidates. A complaint was filed against me at the police station. Sub-Inspector Sanjay Nikam summoned me to the police station. Arrogantly, I swaggered into the police station with a dozen youths. Nikam roared to the head constable, 'Drive away everyone except for Bhavdya. What do they think a police station is? Is it a marketplace that anyone can simply walk into?' Hearing the roar, everybody fled.

I was taken to Nikam Saheb's cabin. We had been acquaintances. He had helped us organize the lecture series. He appreciated that we had used the money collected to set up a library. He had even praised and congratulated us. I was worried if he was going to 'honour' me differently today. He offered me a chair and called for tea. He showed me the complaint that had been filed against me. He said, 'Bhavdya, listen to me carefully. Instead of summoning you here, I could have filed a case and arrested you on the basis of this complaint. And what did you do? You brought a dozen youths from the village here to pressurize me? Who are you trying to intimidate?' I kept quiet. I couldn't look him in the eye.

He continued, 'The entire village sees you as a symbol of hope. Your father is a saintly figure. He has suffered every pain for you to succeed. This is a turning point in your life. If I file a case against you, it will end the possibility of you studying further and living an honest life. Your only option then would be to become a goon. You are a good organizer. No doubt you have the potential to become a notorious goon, a leader. But then you will not lead a life of security. Today, you must make your choice. It is your father's dream to see you become a government officer. What would happen to that dream once a case is filed against you? It would get crushed. I have summoned you before summoning the other party and recording their statement. I will convince them that you were not directly involved in the fight. The condition is that you will return to Kolhapur today itself and will not show your face in the village during the election period. You will not return even for voting. I understand that you are angry because your father's candidature was rejected. You should vent your feelings by studying hard. Why don't you dedicate yourself to studying and show the entire village what you can do? If you become a district collector someday, you would supervise thousands of such elections. Now be smart and tell me what decision I should take.' Nikam Saheb rebuke reminded of the way Kadam Madam had slapped and reprimanded me when I was in the sixth standard.

Nikam Saheb's words stung me to my core. I was playing with fire and knew that, at some point, I would get burnt. I got up, folded my hands to Nikam Saheb and, without a word, left. Nikam Saheb understood what my decision was. I returned to Kolhapur and immersed myself in my studies. The final BA examinations were three months away. My room partner Khandekar was studying hard. He had resolved to score better than me. One day, after I went to sleep, I suddenly heard Vikas Dhas and Khandekar talking to each other, 'Vishwas is straying. He is preoccupied with the village politics. He will not be able to take the MPSC now. He will spend time riding his motorcycle around the university campus. I will stand first in the college and show him his place.'

That statement rattled me. It was a moment of rude awakening. I had given up admission in an engineering college and opted for the arts stream to chase my dream of becoming an IAS officer and here ordinary students of the arts stream were boasting of defeating me. I was angry. One must face insults and failures in life. This reignites your inner fire and makes you aware of your self-respect and confidence, making you unbreakable. Pretending to be asleep, I resolved, 'I will not rest till I become successful. I will dedicate myself only to my studies. I will do my best.' I found myself re-energized. The motorbike was a distraction. I sent it back to the village, asking my father to sell it. For three months, I studied like a madman. I finished the entire syllabus, revised it and appeared for the BA final. The papers were average, not challenging at all. But I did not write routine answers. I ensured that my answers were different from those written by others. I stood first in the university in the subject.

I was satisfied with the results of my BA examinations. The Gram Panchayat at my village praised and congratulated me. The Nangre brethren were so proud of me that it believed, 'Bhavdya is now slated to become a district collector.' Madhu Lad, an illiterate leader from the neighbouring village, came to extend his congratulations. Some people had advised him that now that Deshmukh Saheb was a cabinet minister, he should insist on being made the chancellor of Shivaji University. The chancellor gets a car with a red beacon, a bungalow as well as influence and money. Madhu Lad was convinced that it was more desirable to become a chancellor than the president of a corporation. He went to Deshmukh Saheb and made the demand. Deshmukh Saheb convinced him that a university is a temple of education and that one needs to be highly educated to become the chancellor. Madhu Lad remembered it well. Therefore, he spoke as if I had already become a senior officer by standing first in the college. He explained the importance of my achievement to Tatya. This elevated Tatya's expectations from me. He decided to sell half an acre of land to ensure that I had everything that I needed. This embarrassed me. My responsibilities had increased. People were already treating me like I was a district collector.

There are three categories of candidates preparing for competitive examinations: self-proclaimed, accepted by people and selected by the commission. Only one among a hundred candidates from the first two categories can make it to the third category. He becomes an officer. He is celebrated in his village. He marries the daughter of an MLA or MP. If such a 'boss' ever returns to the village, he needs bottled water and air conditioning. His children speak fluent English. His wife wears imported sarees. But what about the other candidates? As they grow old, their hopes shatter. Their responsibilities towards their parents and village haunt them. Frustrated, they give up and return home. Such a candidate, despite having studied every topic in the world, proves useless even for agricultural work. I was well aware that I only had a BA degree and that too in history. Even though I had stood first in the university, I would not even be offered a peon's job. I had heard about the State Institute for Administrative Careers (SIAC) in Mumbai. At least thirty to forty candidates from there made it to the final selection list of the UPSC every year. I resolved to seek admission in Mumbai University for MA and prepare myself for the UPSC examination with the SIAC. I was gearing up for Mumbai.

Chapter 6

Tryst with Mumbai

The dream city of Mumbai attracts not only job seekers from all over the country but also teenagers with Bollywood aspirations. Mumbai is a sea of opportunities where anyone with fire in his belly can make his dreams a reality. I wanted this city to be my destination as I picked up the gauntlet to appear for the toughest examination in the world. The Maximum City fulfils the dreams of a myriad of aspirants, whether they want to join underworld gangs or white-collar criminals aspiring to become billionaires. Many advised me to go to Delhi or Pune, but I was mesmerized by Mumbai, to chase my dream of getting a Union Public Service Commission job. I had visited Mumbai twice earlier, during my summer vacations. This meant a two-day-long travel in a State Transport bus or a truck from my native village. The biggest nightmare was the mind-boggling traffic jam at the Khambataki Ghat pass, where one would get stuck for the entire night. I would be repulsed by the snoring of the co-passengers crammed into the bus. We had several relatives residing in chawls in Mumbai. Our sojourn would be with them, and the schedule of the 10–12-day-long holiday would be the same—shopping for new clothes and sightseeing till you dropped dead with exhaustion.

My post-degree-examination vacations concluded. I paid obeisance to Ninabai, our village deity, and sought blessings from my mother and Tatya before packing my books and clothes for Mumbai. I took the Chandoli-Mumbai State Transport bus and the entire village descended upon the bus stop to see me off. Seated on a seat that was stained with paan and resting my head on the handle of the seat in front of mine, I dozed off. I reached Mumbai and found my way to my cousin's (paternal aunt's daughter) house at Bhandup. My cousin, Gangu Akka, was better off than all our relatives in Mumbai. I felt awkward as I stashed my luggage in her pigeon-hole-sized house rented in a chawl. My arrival there was an additional burden but she never treated me like one. On the contrary, she cleared the dining table so that I could use it as a study table.

I had already decided that I would take admission at Bombay University for my MA. The last two times I had visited Mumbai, somebody had accompanied me. For the first time, I was moving on my own. Clutching the bag containing my certificates, I took the train to Bombay University. Getting on and off Mumbai's local trains requires a special skillset. The locals are used to it but non-natives and tourists get pushed back in the jostle. I tried to board a couple of times but failed miserably. Finally, I boarded a bogie which was less crowded. It was packed with women who stared at me angrily. I realized that it was the ladies' coach. I panicked and got off at the next station. Incidentally, a policeman caught me. Terrified, I broke into a cold sweat and started stammering.

He understood my plight and realized that I was not an eve teaser. He too had come to Mumbai from a village. He said, 'Why didn't you tell me right away that you're new here? It's only natural that you're so confused. Have you come here to find a job?'

He was kind enough to help me board a general bogie. I was still trying to find space in the crammed general bogie when the train reached the Kurla railway station. I got off there and hopped on a bus to the Kalina campus of Bombay University. I enquired my way to the History Department where young boys and girls had flocked for admissions. I found it difficult to even communicate with the clerk who spoke in fluent English. Somehow, I filled my admission form. The displayed name plates of professors like Mariam Dossal, Ruby Melanie and George Cameroon made feel like I was in a foreign country. Elite boys and girls, also seeking admission, looked at me with disdain. I went to the canteen by myself, had a half-cooked vada pav and returned home. Four days later, I undertook the same arduous journey to reach the university campus. The merit list was displayed on the notice board and my name figured right at the top. My chest swelled with pride. I could hear students whispering about me, wondering who this Nangre Patil could be, who had scored 74 per cent marks in history from Shivaji University. Some pointed towards me. In Bombay University, a B-plus grade, which meant more than 55 per cent marks, was considered a big achievement. I had secured first class with distinction. In ancient history, I had scored 90 out of 100. It was difficult for them to digest that I had scored such a high percentage. I felt that the Mumbai students were making fun of me.

Mariam Dossal Ma'am conducted our first lecture. All of us were asked to introduce ourselves, with our names, the marks we had scored and the university we hailed from. Everyone in the class did so in fluent English. I did the same in my mofussil English accent. The class burst out laughing. For the first time, I felt embarrassed about my marks. I consoled myself, thinking, 'I'm not going to hang out with these people. My destination is different. I am not going to lose myself in this crowd of people, whose greatest aspiration is to be a teacher.' Feeling humiliated, I stepped out of the classroom. It was raining. I waited outside, under the porch, for the rain to stop. It was then that someone called from behind, 'Hi, you are Vishwas, right? Myself Sucheta!' She offered to share her umbrella with me till the canteen. I politely declined the offer, fearing I'd have to talk to her in English. Just then, Avinash called out to her and the two walked away to the canteen under the same umbrella, laughing and brushing against each other. I stood there, watching them. The realization that English was my biggest enemy sunk into my mind.

I wanted admission to the hostel but was disappointed to find out that the Jagannath Shankarsheth Hostel was not on campus but in the Churchgate area on B Road. I breathed a sigh of relief when I found out that my destination, the state government-run Pre-IAS Training Centre, SIAC, was a stone's throw away from this hostel.

I gathered my things and reached the university hostel at Churchgate. Both of my room partners were north Indians—Dungwal from Odisha and Punit Chaturvedi from Bhopal. Both had come to Mumbai to pursue law. Both were very talkative. I kept my luggage in the room and went to have a cup of tea at a stall opposite the Sydneham College with Dungwal. Churchgate, I discovered, was a posh locality. Bespectacled Dungwal was staring at the fashionable girls walking down the road. He had stepped out of Odisha for the first time and landed in Mumbai. For him, every girl was a Madhuri Dixit lookalike. When I asked him to mind his behaviour, he talked about how the Constitution of India gives us the fundamental right to look at anyone, anywhere and at any time.

I countered by explaining to him that the fundamental rights have some moral restrictions, but to no avail: his main goal was to enjoy himself in Mumbai and break free of all restrictions. I figured it would be better if I maintained my distance from him. Punit was, however, the polar opposite of Dungwal. He would converse with even the homeless street children and offer them tea and biscuits. Like a true intellectual, he would talk about topics like democracy, law, society and corruption for hours on end. If Dungwal was like the hedonist Charvak, Punit was the wise Vishwamitra and the two would indulge in exhaustive debates. Though I tried, I could not concentrate on my studies due to their constant jabbering. Finally, I met the hostel superintendent and submitted an application for a single room. In it, I mentioned that I was preparing for my UPSC examination.

He summoned me and talked to me for a while. I realized that he was unhappy with the fact that I was preparing for the UPSC examination. He wrote a letter to the head of my department and, in my presence, handed it to the peon for delivery. I sweet-talked him into giving me the letter, saying that since I was going to the university, I would deliver the letter myself. I opened the letter and saved myself from losing my room. The letter recommended allotment to a single room on the grounds that I was preparing for the UPSC examination instead of pursuing my MA. I had almost jumped out of the frying pan into the fire. I got rid of the letter. In a bid for a single room, I was about to lose the room equipped with a fan, never mind if I had to live with the two idiots. The hostel even had a shower in the common bathroom. It was the first time I was enjoying such luxuries. A cold shower followed by sleeping under the fan was the ultimate relief from Mumbai's heat.

I started looking for a library because I could not study with two eccentric room partners. I became a member of the British Council Library at the Maker Tower Building, located near the hostel, by paying the fee of Rs 150. The next day, I went to study in the spick and span library. The moment I entered the library, the chill air inside hit me. After a while, I started shivering. I couldn't understand why I was feeling so cold. Somehow, I managed to sit there for thirty to forty-minutes, rubbing my hands together to keep warm. The moment I stepped out of the library, I felt hot. The contrasting temperatures surprised me greatly. I asked a Marathi-speaking peon, who was chewing tobacco, about the cool library. He explained, 'The library has an air conditioner. It's a machine that blows out cool air. This village boy knows nothing.' By then, I was used to such contemptuous remarks.

As I walked back to the hostel, I could hear sounds of the Sai Baba aarti coming from the adjacent building. I followed the sound and reached the Sai Baba Temple which was in the garage of the building. I sat through the whole aarti with great devotion in my heart. It was Thursday so sweet rice was served as prasad. I asked for an extra serving of prasad. It had been a while since I had eaten something so delicious. Otherwise I was subsisting on the bland, watery aamti (tuvar dal) and burnt rotis served in the hostel mess.

Gradually, I realized that my preparation so far had been negligible. When I started reading V.K. Agnihotri's history book for the prelims, I did not know the meaning of several

English words in it. Till then, I had been reading history books written by authors like Deshmukh and Pawar which emphasized war stories and strategies and the tales of kings. I was now required to learn history from a different perspective, understanding contemporary history from the point of view of farmers, workers, trade, economics, and society at the grassroots level with reference to the prevalent socio-economic conditions. Though it was difficult to understand, I continued to read. There were at least ten to twelve English words which I couldn't recognize on a single page but I would find their meaning in the dictionary and jot them down in the book, using a pencil. As a result, my books would be full of scribblings and notes, lending the impression that I was studying hard. My vocabulary rapidly improved. The British Library was cold and unfriendly, so I found admission in the university library located in front of the hostel. I settled down in a corner of this library and began my studies in earnest.

I would catch a local train in the morning to reach the university campus and attend my MA classes. Then, I would alight from the train at Wakola and board a Kalina-bound bus. The level of history taught at the university was tough. I struggled to make friends as the elite Mumbai crowd did not approve of my mofussil mentality. Or perhaps my inferiority complex prevented me from freely mingling with them. I used to apply coconut oil generously on my hair and its smell would offend others. Finally, I made friends with Jayendra Bhosale. He was the son of a retired assistant commissioner of police (ACP). He started counselling me on life in Mumbai, how to converse and behave with people. Once, he took me to his house and introduced me to his father, who asked me, 'What will you have—tea or soft drink?' Seeing his stern disposition,

I preferred to have only a glass of water. Sonali Bendre, who had just begun her career as a model in advertisements, also lived on the first floor of the same building. I had seen hoardings of her advertisements displayed at the railway station. When I saw them, I would stop for a while and stare at them. We would often halt on the first floor hoping to catch a glimpse of Sonali Bendre but unfortunately for us, and fortunately for her, we never crossed paths.

The schedule of the Maharashtra Public Service Commission (MPSC) examinations for police sub-inspector (PSI) and the sales tax department (STI) was announced. I dreamt of becoming an IAS officer. But my dream was akin to hunting a tiger; I wanted to test myself to see if I was at least capable of snatching up a rabbit. Therefore, I applied for the examination. I bought a couple of books in the market. I read them and sat for the examination.

Climbing the staircase of the MPSC office building in the Fort area and checking the result displayed on the notice board proved to be a Herculean task. My heart was ready to jump out of my chest even when I saw the Bank of India signboard on the ground floor. When I spotted my number in the list of selected candidates, I was overjoyed. I had passed the prelims for the post of PSI in the first attempt. This was my first taste of success in relation to competitive examinations. This small achievement went a long way in giving my self-confidence a much-needed boost.

The main examination was in two months. It comprised papers of general studies and language in the multiple-choice-questions (MCQ) format. I already had books for general studies. I bought Leela Govilkar's Marathi grammar book and Wren and Martin's English grammar and memorized every word in them. I memorized the dates of important events in the history of Maharashtra as well as the birth and death anniversaries of social reformers, along with the causes they fought for. The IQ tests were akin to those conducted as part of the fourth- and seventh-standard scholarship exams. I finished studying for every subject.

Studying for a competitive examination is like training at the gym. Very often, we start liking a particular exercise or get used to it. If you like doing cardio, you tend to neglect weight training or if you do weight training, you may not like legs or triceps exercises. Confining yourself to a particular set of exercises prevents you from attaining a wholly fit physique. Thus, the exercise regimen becomes meaningless. MPSC had changed the monotonous pattern of the main examination for the PSI rank and included boring and difficult subjects like engineering, agriculture and commerce. Understanding the concepts of these subjects in Marathi proved troublesome. I too had gone through this grind. I did not study commerce, economics or agriculture while preparing for the subject of general studies.

When you lay emphasis only on the subjects you like, the subjects you ignore fail you. Moreover, the main examination of the PSI/STI and the main entrance exam of SIAC were scheduled on alternate days. Of course, my priority was the SIAC entrance test. I read the kit of the general studies subject for the UPSC examination for the SIAC entrance test. One had to choose two optional subjects for the main UPSC examination. One had to solve a paper with essay-type answers for a subject other than the one chosen for the SIAC entrance test. I had prepared well for the Marathi paper, thanks to Gagrani Sir's notes. Because of the confusion in the schedule of the two examinations, I could not prepare thoroughly for the MPSC examination. As anticipated, I failed by three marks in the main examination of the MPSC for the PSI rank. The cut-off in the merit list was 210 marks and I had scored 207 marks. However, I passed the SIAC entrance test. Selection in SIAC is done on the basis of two categories—day scholar and resident. I was selected in the resident category. I was allotted a tiny room in the hostel on the SIAC campus.

Chapter 7

The SIAC Campus

SIAC stands for the State Institute for Administrative Careers. This seemingly innocuous yet significant institute was established when Vasantdada Patil was the chief minister of Maharashtra. It is tucked behind the Zunka Bhakar Centre, opposite the Chhatrapati Shivaji Terminus in Mumbai. The primary objective of setting up this institute was to prepare candidates from all over Maharashtra for the UPSC examination and help them join the civil services as IAS, IPS and IFS officers.

I secured admission in this renowned institute right after my graduation in 1994. I bid adieu to the spacious room at the university hostel and my eccentric room partners, and shifted to the SIAC hostel with my belongings. My room partner was called Langhi. He was short and a man of few words. Like me, he hailed from a village. We made ourselves comfortable in the inadequate 10×10 ft room. The tiny room housed two study tables, chairs, bookshelves, a noisy fan and a large window that looked upon the lawns outside.

The environment was conducive for studying. Initially, though, I felt awkward sitting in the corridor outside the room or in the library to study. Several stalwarts who had successfully passed the main examination and faced the interview as well as those who had got selected would camp there. Piyush resided in the adjacent room. His father was the then chief secretary and his brother-in-law too was an IAS officer. Therefore, he would receive visitors and relatives who came to the hostel to encourage him. They would pamper him with coffee and lavish foods. As for us, we had to content with the 'cutting tea' and vada pav that we bought from the stall opposite the gate. Our brothers-in-law too were police sub-inspectors (PSI). Therefore, we would use the logic that if Piyush became an IAS officer, we could at least become PSIs.

Half the prospective candidates studying there had obsessions of various kinds—some were passionate about achieving their goals; some were obsessed with studying; some were foodies; some liked alcoholic beverages while others, chasing women. Several were deceptively gentlemanly on the surface. However, they would indulge in unruly behaviour, disturbing those who studied throughout the day, then burn the midnight oil within the four walls of their rooms and study hard.

I was the youngest among all the candidates. Therefore, I felt that I was the object of everyone's scrutiny, though there was no reason for me to feel this way. I met all kinds of people there, each of them a unique specimen. Bapu, for example, had taken an oath that he would not put on his footwear until he became an IPS officer. He had also printed his own visiting cards, leaving an empty space in front of his name. While handing over the card, he would mention that it would be subsequently filled up with the title of 'IPS'. He struggled round the clock to realize his dream of sporting the uniform and brown shoes of an IPS officer. He hailed from a well-to-do family. Therefore, he would often take us to posh hotels for lunch. However, he lived and dressed shabbily. Once, after having lunch at a hotel, we were standing outside when a good Samaritan took pity on him and gave him Rs 2. Bapu went on to become a regional transport officer (RTO) and gained eligibility for the interview stage of the UPSC.

Avinash was my other friend. He was a merit holder in the SSC and HSC examinations. We would often stroll after dinner in the Azad Maidan behind the SIAC building. Streetwalkers and eunuchs stood there soliciting people. Pawaskar would tease them though warily. Once Pawaskar was not with us. Some eunuchs accosted us and hurled a string of abuses at us. They got physical with Avinash, saying, 'Hey, Shah Rukh Khan, now show us your *nakhras*.' Avinash was boiling with rage. We approached a police head constable standing nearby. Instead of taking action against the eunuchs, he threatened us. He even humiliated us by saying, 'Roll your degrees and shove it up your butt.'

We were not in the mood for insults and mockery. We decided to raise the issue of indiscipline in the public space and our humiliation with senior officers. Avinash and I went to the office of the deputy commissioner of police (DCP), Zone I, and found streetwalkers queued outside his office too. Convinced that we would not find justice there, we kept quiet, resolving to discipline such rowdy behaviour on the streets and other public spaces when we occupied those offices in the future. Later, in 2007, when I took charge as DCP for South Mumbai, the first thing I did was to ensure that the streets in the Fort area were free of streetwalkers.

SIAC was a tiny and peaceful campus in contrast to the hustle and bustle of the CST nearby. It is a barracks-like

structure comprising ten to twelve rooms that were adjacent
to the Azad Maidan. One could always find three or four
candidates either sleeping or studying in every room. Now and
then, one would find unfamiliar faces, thanks to the number
of 'parasites' who accounted for more than the number of
candidates. The hostel warden was Bagade. Dressed in a
shirt and trousers with a tilak on his forehead, a full-grown
beard and a booming voice, he looked less like a government
employee and more like a goon-turned-politico of Mumbai.

But he was a good-natured man. Even if the hostel was
swarmed with parasites, he would turn a Nelson's eye. There
were a number of good libraries in the vicinity but candidates
would flock to the SIAC to study. One could see lungi–
baniyan-clad candidates sitting under noisy fans that barely
stirred the hot and humid Mumbai air, some translating the
notes of Delhi-based Wajiram Rao to Marathi under the
dim lights. Hot-headed intellectuals from meagre economic
backgrounds could be seen conducting experiments. Several
of these experiments were revolutionary. Ravi Gaikwad felt
a review of Constitution of India was the need of the hour
and had undertaken the task of writing a new draft himself.
There was a lot of gossip on the scams in the MPSC. Several
candidates had given up studying and had started preparations
to file writs in the high court. Nobody knew the whereabouts
of Hemant during the day but when he returned to the campus
at night, he would boast about his romantic expeditions.
We tried our best to digest his bombastic talk.

While studying Marathi literature, I read that inspiration
is the sister of a brainwave. To sum up, a number of inspired
newcomers congregate at the SIAC every year. Some of
them start off strong but give up eventually. Some rely on
memorizing the study material. Some have negative thinking.

Some are hard-working. Several of them make it to the SIAC, after struggling against all adversity, but are clueless about their future. I too was one such candidate—compared to the others, I hadn't studied as much, was younger than most and rather inexperienced. Therefore, I would feel restless among these intellectuals, and feared I might go insane.

When one learns to play a new instrument, it makes sounds that wouldn't be called melodic. I was facing a similar situation. I was unable to find the right line and length. I was trying to study but could not comprehend what I read. Shah Sir and Gholkar Sir taught history but I found it difficult to understand. Vijaya Rajadhyaksha and Ramesh Tendulkar taught Marathi, which was music to my ears, but I found it hard to pen it down. Kamlesh would appreciate literature as he puffed on his cigarettes. Though Peshwe did not understand much, he would pretend to be a scholar and debated vehemently. This resulted in increased tension for me. On such occasions, I would retire to my room and discuss the same topics with my room partner Langhi. He chewed well on his thoughts before giving his opinion, making me feel more confident.

Our batch had around half a dozen girls who were senior to us and were stoutly built. Most of them were distracted. They could be seen lined up outside the telephone booth in the evening. For them, getting out of this mire successfully required not only hard work but also luck. Girls hailing from middle-class families had to work hard to convince their parents about studying for the UPSC examination. Arguments like 'You are growing too old to find a suitable match' and 'If you become a smart officer, who would marry you?' would ensue at their homes. Already harassed by this familial struggle, these sisters looked older than they were when they came to the SIAC.

Occasionally, there would be a candidate like Damayanti whose father was a senior administrative officer in Mumbai.

She had studied in an English-medium school and had an upper-class background. She would drive her own Maruti 800 and alight from it in style in the SIAC parking lot. The fragrance of her perfume would make the cramped campus feel pleasant. She, like a lotus blooming in a swamp, would transform the atmosphere of the campus. We were village boys; we resembled the character played by Aamir Khan in the movie *Rangeela*. We tried to attract her attention in the library by wearing crisply ironed, colourful shirts but she only had eyes for her notes. She attended lectures, studied in the library for three or four hours and left, unwittingly splashing water over several boys' hard work, done over a period of three to four days.

Candidates who had stolen glimpses at her would spend time gossiping about her elite lifestyle. We were sure that the beauty queen would not find any of us worthy but still held hope. Sipping 'cutting tea', we would dream of sitting in the passenger seat of her red Maruti 800 and going on long drives with her. Once a large, decayed tree branch fell on her vehicle. Several of us got wicked pleasure in seeing her car in a mangled condition but she was unbothered. A car with a red beacon came to pick her up, leaving behind her driver whose lifestyle resembled ours, and the Maruti 800 which was as mangled as our luck.

Chapter 8

Preparing for UPSC Prelim

My round-the-clock struggle with NCERT textbooks, the voluminous Tata McGraw Hill's general studies kit (GSK) and history books with leftist leanings began in right earnest. Though I found them difficult, I read them persistently. After going through them twice or thrice, I would understand them a little better. Gradually, my studies started falling in line.

The preliminary examination of the UPSC has long, wordy, multiple-choice questions. When I appeared for it, we had to solve 150 questions of general studies in 120 minutes. My optional subject for the prelim examination was history in which we had to solve 120 questions in 120 minutes. The question paper is set in either English or Hindi. Therefore, understanding the question quickly and correctly and choosing the right option for the answer is the three-point key to success—a strategy I meticulously followed. Even the options would be in the form of long paragraphs. Therefore, solving the entire paper in time was a real challenge. At that time, there was no system of negative marking. One who could score at least 85 out of 120 in history and 100 out of 150 in general studies could be assured of success.

I finished studying Agnihotri's history book. I could barely comprehend the subaltern history scripted in Marx's method by the Jawaharlal Nehru University (JNU). History books written by Romila Thapar, Bipin Chandra and A.L. Basham gave me an insight into the milestones which shaped the history of India in the ancient, medieval and modern eras. When one prepares for the UPSC examination, it is more important for one to understand what one should not read in a book, rather than what one should read. For example, one needs to read only three chapters of Basham's *The Wonder That Was India*, which covers the topics of society, religion and day-to-day life. When it comes to the Mauryan Era, questions are normally asked on the stone carvings of Ashoka. Therefore, it is important to study the appendix of edicts at the end of *Ashoka and the Decline of the Mauryas* carefully. Keeping these tips in mind, I started studying systematically. The SIAC began conducting tests for the prelim exam. I scored 65 out of 70 marks in the history test. Gholkar Sir assured me, 'You may pass the prelim examination this year itself if you study harder.'

Gholkar Sir always wore a smile on his face. He was reserved, calm and encouraging. I had made his acquaintance in Kolhapur. Whenever I felt depressed, I would visit his residence in Kandivali. He never displayed any lack of enthusiasm when it came to spending his precious time with me. He would always explain the concepts in detail, patiently. Sometimes, he offered me poha and tea. We were not in a position to offer him *gurudakshina* (fees) nor did he ever utter a word about it. Though he had grown old and found it difficult to come to campus, he would make it a point to be there. Admirably, when a student approached this dedicated teacher with a doubt, he would ensure that the student left with all his doubts cleared. His teaching method focused on making students understand—straight to the point and with utmost clarity. Gholkar Sir's class was a breeze compared to Shah Sir's, who taught in such a scholarly way that it would leave students confused.

When I visited Sir at Kandivali, I would stay at my sister's house in the Sahyadrinagar area near Charkop. This neighbourhood consisted of migrants who hailed form Satara and Sangli. The complex of around seventy-five buildings, had tiny blocks of 10×10 ft size, giving it an aura of a village. Young rural women who had migrated to Mumbai after marriage would move around in nightgowns, which was seen as a sign of modernity.

When I was a child, men who were employed in Mumbai looked modish. Dressed in spotless white shirts and trousers with a pair of matching sandals, they would carry a black Murphy radio which almost matched the colour of their skin. Many a time, a rose sticker would be pasted on their stark white shirt. They would imitate the gait of Bollywood stars like Dev Anand, Jitendra or Mithun Chakraborty. Women of all ages—older ones draped in nine-yard sarees or the younger ones dressed in skirts—would stare at them. I would be impressed by their stylish persona. However, when I came to Mumbai and saw the same people toiling and moving around in shorts in the 10×15 ft room of the chawl, the illusion shattered. Tired from pulling handcarts all day or blackened with the smoke of the mills, these heroes, wearing striped boxer shorts, slept huddled together in the crammed rooms of the chawl. Every time I studied, the image would send a chill down my spine. I feared that I would have to join this brigade if I failed. This propelled me to study even harder.

As the exam approached, tests were conducted frequently. In one of the tests, I scored less than fifty marks. I was shocked. How could I have performed so poorly when the exam was only one and a half months away? Confident that I could not have done so badly, I requested a recheck of my answer sheets, which revealed that I had actually scored 72 marks. Candidates would be given the responsibility of checking each other's answer sheets. My answer sheets had been checked by Kothikar, who had deliberately reduced my marks. When I confronted him, he was dumbfounded. I longed to teach him a lesson but, on the advice of my seniors, I reined in my anger, bursting into tears instead. During my preparation, I would constantly oscillate between hope and hopelessness. My self-confidence had been shattered. Regaining it was a big challenge. The only way to do it was to study even harder.

The results of the previous year's examination were announced. With all the candidates gearing up for their interviews, the hustle and bustle that ensued on campus could be aptly compared to the hubbub that preceded the tying of the marriage knot during a wedding. Those who had passed the examination shifted from the corridors to the library for serious studies. Several candidates from Pune and Nagpur flocked to the SIAC to prepare for the interviews. The atmosphere was charged with the energy of mock interviews being conducted by panellists seated in every room.

All around, students could be heard discussing national and international current affairs. Personality development experts were invited to groom the students. Candidates got new suits tailored to match their personality and demos on how to properly tie a tie were conducted. We, the freshers, would watch the preparations with awe. We were waiting expectantly for our turn to make similar preparations in the coming year. Avinash too had passed the main examination. I accompanied him everywhere—right from shopping for new clothes to visiting senior civil services officers to seek their guidance. His mock interview was conducted in my room and I insisted on being a part of the interviewing panel. Amused at my insistence, Pote remarked, 'Vishwas, you serve us tea and water. You can join us on this side of the table after you have experienced giving an interview at least once.' His words stung but rang true. Such incidents not only kept me aware of the reality but also kept me rooted.

Along with the UPSC, I was contemplating appearing for the Maharashtra Public Service Commission (MPSC) examination too. According to the advertisements released in newspapers, there were vacancies for eighteen posts of deputy collector and 250 posts of finance and audit officers. I submitted my application for the MPSC examination, in the hopes of selection. In the SIAC, if you were appearing for the MPSC examination, it had to be done clandestinely. As per the standard norms, those who took admission in the SIAC aimed only for the UPSC examination. Stealing glances at others' books was common among candidates and it would indeed be embarrassing to be caught reading MPSC examination books. One would either cover the books or hide them in the bulky UPSC examination kits.

Since I had appeared for the main examination for the post of police sub-inspector (PSI) just four months ago, I found the MPSC prelim exam relatively easy although I did not prepare for it in earnest.

The real test was round the corner, but the preparation for the prelim examination of the UPSC was still far from finished. This examination tests the real mettle of the candidate. I was studying for up to twelve hours every day but still found the syllabus difficult to cover. To prepare for my general studies paper, I had read NCERT books up to the tenth standard. Besides, I was trying to read D.D. Basu's book on political science and volumes of Datta and Sundaram for economics. I read NCERT books on ancient, medieval and modern India up to the twelfth standard to lay the foundation for my studies in the optional subject. These books were of a very high standard and formed a solid foundation for my study, as they covered more than the syllabus for the university examination.

I read Bipin Chandra's *India's Struggle for Independence*, which enabled me to experience society during the independence struggle. Romila Thapar's *History of India* was an important book that provided in-depth knowledge of India's rich past. However, I did not dare buy it as it cost Rs 300. By a stroke of luck, I stumbled upon a second-hand copy at the street book market in the Fort area and bought it for only Rs 35! I remember how overjoyed I was when I spotted it amid a heap of old books. Several other candidates would spend hours scavenging through heaps of old books strewn in the roadside market, stumbling upon such precious books at times.

After I became deputy commissioner of police (DCP) of South Mumbai Zone, I never permitted taking action against such roadside book vendors. I was well aware that the sale of books in this manner was an offence but paradoxically that very offence provides access to knowledge to several needy and poor students. Similarly, begging is an offence, but I never permit police action against young children who are forced to beg as a consequence of being the victims of a merciless system. No doubt, the law must be enforced in letter and spirit, but one must be conscientious of protecting the interests of the needy and aware of the impact of law enforcement on them.

Rock climbing at Sardar Vallabhbhai Patel National Police Academy, Hyderabad, 1999.

Receiving the Student of the Year award, Rajaram College, Kolhapur, 1993.

Jungle tactics at the academy.

Delivering a speech to the youth in Kolhapur, 28 February 2016.

Post-blast investigation training: Receiving a token of appreciation as the leader of ATA 8199 in Moyock, North Carolina, USA, December 2011.

Finishing the
21 km Mumbai
Marathon.

Leading the
ceremonial parade.

Celebrating
India's secularism.

At the Taj hotel in
Mumbai, on the
night of 26/11.

A battle with terrorists,
with police constable
Amit Khetle.

During the
counterterrorism
operation at
the Taj.

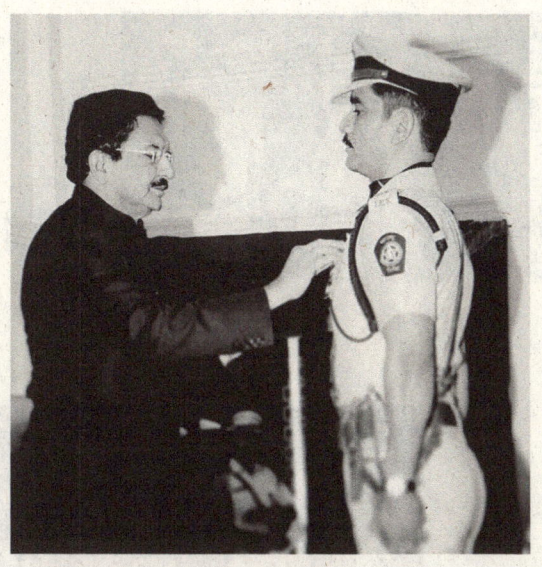

Receiving the President's Police Medal for Gallantry from the governor of Maharashtra, C. Vidyasagar Rao.

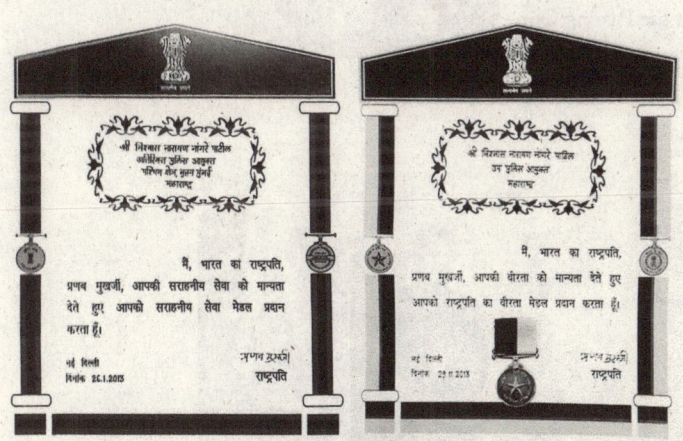

Certificates for Meritorious Service Medal and President's Police Medal for Gallantry.

Bandobast supervision for law and order.

With my parents and the guest of honour on the day of the Passing Out Parade.

With the President of India, Ram Nath Kovind.

At a police welfare event, with Amitabh Bachchan, Sachin Tendulkar, Asha Bhosle, Karan Johar and others.

Cricket for Peace Tournament, 2014, with Dilip Vengsarkar and Julio Ribeiro.

Saluting the martyrs at the 26/11 memorial.

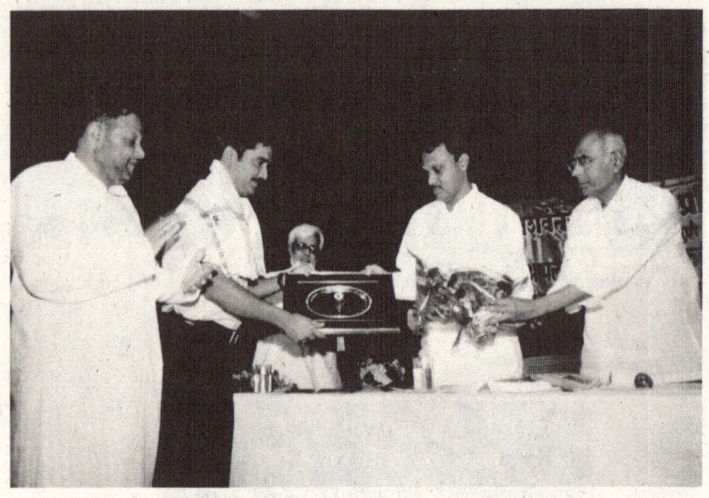

Felicitation for the successful investigation of rave parties and the drug mafia. [*Left to right*] Ankush Kakde, Vishwas Nangre Patil, Anil Awchat, Ajit Pawar and Narendra Dabholkar.

Mann Mein Hai Vishwas.

Often, I wonder whether it is possible for starving, orphaned beggar children who face hate and contempt and bear the curse of the world every day, to ever become honest, trustworthy and patriotic citizens. What is the future of someone who has been subjected to sexual exploitation at a tender age and introduced to brown sugar, when he should be suckling? When such a child grows up, he will either become a beggar or a delinquent. He will be branded a beggar, a junkie, a scum from the gutter. No matter the attempts, the concepts of freedom and equality of rank and opportunity would go over his head. He would never garner recognition in society or experience these principles being practised.

These would be bogus, vain and misleading terms from his perspective. His psyche would be totally different from my middle-class mindset. My haphazard love and half-hearted efforts would fail to win over his anger with the system and his frustration and depression. Therefore, I look at beggar children with sympathy. Child labour is another serious issue in society where there has been negligence. The worst kind of crime, though, takes place when young girls are forced into prostitution and live in the most cruel, merciless and painful conditions. During my studies, all these oppressed human beings would attract my attention. I felt I had a duty towards them. What does reform and transformation mean? It simply means sharing a part of whatever we have with those who have nothing. Why couldn't I start such a reform with my own initiative? The feeling that we owe something to those who belong to the lowest rungs of society lends a moral strength to those who are preparing to join the civil services. This moral strength, which motivates us to study, will automatically manifest through the words of reason and mercy, which we write in the examination. Today, UPSC has now a 250 marks, worth subject of 'Ethics, Integrity and Aptitude' in its main examination.

The roadside book market in the Fort area was an intellectual feast for us. I found several pictorial books on world history. Although these books were not relevant to the syllabus of the UPSC examination, reading them would help me visualize world history. I found Norman Lewis's *Word Power Made Easy* in this market and could build my English vocabulary systematically. Dale Carnegie's books on personality development helped me in maintaining a positive attitude. I found Nani Palkhiwala's *We, the People* and *We, the Nation*. They helped me understand concepts in contemporary history in elaborate detail. Gandhiji's *My Experiments with Truth* gave me tremendous strength. It made me realize that even the greatest of men made mistakes more colossal than the ones made by common folk. It enabled me to learn from my own mistakes to avoid repeating them. I stopped repenting my mistakes and started living in the present.

In *Vijayache Manas Shastra* (Psychology of Triumph) written by Bhishmaraj Bam Sir, I read that, 'One who does not plan his success well, plans for his failure.' I learnt the skill of time management and the importance of reading from Bam Sir's *Mental Strategies to Gain Victory in Sports*. I tried to inculcate the winning habits elaborated in his book by working out a schedule. I would study in three slots—four hours each in the morning, afternoon and evening. Dharmadhikari Sir, in his book *Vijaypath*, has explained the graph of study. When one studies for a period of four hours, the understanding of the study material is the best in the first hour, remains stable for the next two hours and then starts to decline.

I understood this very well. I would take a tea break after every four hours of studying. We set up this schedule with precision. Our tea breaks would align perfectly with the opening of the offices, during the lunch hour and the closing of the offices, at which time a group of girls and boys studying in the colleges nearby would come to the SIAC canteen for tea or snacks. The youthful atmosphere that they would bring with them refreshed us. An anonymous author once wrote that watching beautiful girls is good for your eyes, like an oasis in the desert. However, we ensured that these breaks did not extend beyond twenty minutes and didn't adversely affect our studies. I was in the habit of waking up early in the morning. With a fresh mind and body, I studied complex and tough subjects early in the morning. Since I felt drowsy in the afternoons, I studied easy subjects at that time. I prepared a chart of all the subjects in the syllabus along with the units they included. When one exercises in the gym, one ensures that exercises are done in a manner that they shape one's entire body. I did the same with my studies.

I also started cultivating hobbies that would add to my knowledge and give me new inspiration. I attended good public lectures, watched good Marathi plays and English films. I attended Nana Palkhiwala's lecture on the annual budget organized at Brabourne Stadium. Chief Election Commissioner T.N. Seshan had made reforms in the election process to make it corruption-free and transparent. I attended his speech in the university but did not like his complex, pompous language which used too much Sanskrit. In the conclusion of his speech, he said that IAS stood for 'I Am Sorry'. I am still experiencing that myself. I remember his rumbling voice very clearly.

I read *The Hindu* and *Frontline* every day to keep abreast of current affairs. In short, I was to absorb as much knowledge as I could although my brain had not matured enough to grasp it. As a result, my efforts to fly higher proved to be in vain. I would have been able to prepare better had I started when I was still in college. But my plight was like that of an underweight wrestler who had accepted the challenge of wrestling with a champion. Since I was trying to get ahead without adequate preparation, I was bound to suffer.

My exam centre was the spacious hall on the eighth floor of the Sales Tax Bhavan building in Mazgaon. Almost all the UPSC exams would be conducted in the same hall. Candidates from the SIAC would travel to the centre in groups on the train. On the day of the examination, I offered prayers at the Lord Shiva temple in the Fort area, trying to woo God with offerings of bel leaves, flowers, coconuts and fragrances if I found the paper easy. After that, I went to the mess where I had kanda poha with a cup of tea. Then I carried my kit consisting of two pens, two pencils and a writing pad and set out for the examination centre. I took the train to Mazgaon. My heart was pounding with excitement. I had not slept well the previous night, and my eyes were red and stinging, which perhaps gave a hint as to my performance in the exam.

The first paper was history. When I read the paper, I found the questions heavily worded and complex. I ticked the questions which I felt I could answer and finished the 120 marks paper. My restlessness was building. There was a gap of two hours between the two papers. I went out, ate a vada pav and drank Thums Up. Ever since I was a child, I believed that drinking Thums Up makes you burp and gives relief to your stomach. But the exact opposite happened. I started feeling nauseated. My condition was no better when I solved the general studies paper. It clearly prioritized current affairs. Even the questions related to economics, science and technology, political science and history were asked in the context of current affairs.

The question paper was unlike the ones for previous examinations. My performance was average. I instinctively felt that my wicket was out. I lost my composure and enthusiasm, and returned to the SIAC with a heavy heart. I knew I would not be able stay there for long, as only those who pass in the prelim examination can continue to stay in the hostel for the next six months to prepare for the main examination. The results of the prelim examination were two and a half months away. Till then, candidates were allowed to keep their luggage in their rooms. I had already given up claim for a room in the University Hostel.

I returned to my village to rejuvenate myself. I spent a week loitering in the lush green farms and ate mutton delicacies and bhakris cooked by my mother. I dozed off during the afternoons. The one-week sojourn at the village worked miracles for my depression. I found comfort in the knowledge that other candidates spent five years preparing for this examination while I had sweated it out for only one year. Thus, my frustration with failure lessened. I resolved to pull myself together and try more vigorously to reinforce my preparations. While preparing for the prelims, I had experienced how my grip on studies became stronger as I continued studying. If by any chance I passed the prelim examination, I would appear for the main examination within three to four months, which would be a major challenge as I had not studied adequately. I made another resolution, overcame the depression and negative thoughts that were haunting me and took to studying with renewed vigour.

I decided to opt for Marathi literature as the second optional subject for the main examination. I had never formally studied Marathi literature, Marathi grammar and criticism of Marathi literature, nor did I want to. I had to study in a professional manner for two papers in Marathi and I had only three months to do so. While I was at the SIAC, I had come to know about the capsule course in Marathi literature offered by Soman in Sadashiv Peth in Pune. Those classes were to begin in a week's time. I boarded a State Transport bus to Pune. Soman Sir's tuitions were near Kala Haud in Pune. I rented a 10×10 ft room in Sadashiv Peth for two months. Sir would conduct his class in a small room on the ground floor of his three-storey ancestral wada.

We would accommodate ourselves in the crammed room and listen to the lecture. The old wada had been divided among twenty-five families over five generations. Therefore, the great grandchildren were forced to live in spaces that were too small when compared to the one unified space occupied by their great grandfather. But when Sonam Sir taught, he was possessed by the character in the book, just like the actor Prashant Damle. He completed the criticism of H.N. Apte's voluminous historic novel *Pan Lakshat Kon Gheto* in two hours. It was a critique par excellence and would help the students to write a 600-word-long answer to any question posed on this novel.

In Maharashtra, there is no better place than Sadashiv Peth to learn about the language, critique and quality of literature. Walking on the asphalt roads that run along the ancient wadas and new concrete buildings, I observed many people who resembled the characters from many works of Marathi literature. I would have silent interactions with those characters. When I noticed a pious, simple yet beautiful woman cleaning utensils, I could see the character of Sindhu from the play *Ekach Pyala* in her. At night, I could spot the character of Taliram from the same play, in several drunkards who could be seen stumbling on the roads.

Many Marathi plays and cultural events were organized in Pune. I used to watch movies at the cinema and watch plays to gain a better understanding of concepts like story, poetry, drama and the novel. Films are works of art. The characters in them become close to us, as if they were real. The joy of movies makes one's eyes well with tears. When I read a novel I get completely lost in it, visualizing the plot and making an imaginary film. In my mind, I would assign roles in that story to my favourite actors, and understand them.

The characters thumb-sketched by Madgulkar in his *Mandeshi Manase* came to life. Reading, and more importantly, understanding Marathi literature, from *Leela Charitra* to the writings of authors belonging to Sant, Pant and Tant (Warkari, scholarly, ballard) schools, became easy. Marathi literature was interesting, but I found the grammar difficult. Leela Govilkar's collectible on Marathi grammar did not prove useful. The examination pattern allowed one the option of excluding the entire section of grammar. However, this meant that the candidate had to be prepared to answer any question on the criticism of Marathi literature. I worked hard on the criticism of Marathi literature, linking it with society, looking for real-life references of traditions and novelty.

The result of the MPSC prelim examination, for which I had appeared in March, was declared. I had qualified. There were several vacancies for Class I posts. Since I had a flair for writing, I was confident that if I could pass the main examination of the MPSC, I would become a saheb of sorts. I left Sadashiv Peth and returned to Mumbai. A week after that, the results of the UPSC prelim examination were announced. As expected, I had failed. The promises of bel leaves and flowers to appease God had made no difference.

My foolishness had cost me an attempt. What was more hurtful was vacating the room in the SIAC. However, the pleasant outcome of the MPSC exam had given me a lease on life. My self-confidence and ambition remained intact. Deshmukh Saheb was the public works department (PWD) minister. I met him at the Mantralaya and apprised him of the problem I was facing. He provided me with accommodation in the PWD rest house adjacent to the SIAC, till the examination was over. I picked up my things from the SIAC and walked to the rest house. Two deputy collectors, Jitendra Yadav and Deepak Patil, occupied the adjacent room and were preparing for the main examination of UPSC.

I established a rapport with Yadav Saheb, hoping to get some guidance from him for my MPSC examination. He had studied well, and his company became my line of preparing for the main MPSC examination. He told me the mantra that had worked for him, 'Recruit six employees. They will teach you how to write answers. These six employees are: What, Why, When, Where, Who and How.' I started applying these six references to each question. My assessments and explanations started improving. My answers became comprehensive. He told me to lay an emphasis on writing. He would say: 'Writing brings in accuracy, discussion brings promptness and wit. This is the key to success in the prelim, the main examination and the interview.'

Several friends and relatives from my village would visit me. Being a social animal, I would receive them and chat, pretending that I was soon to become a big boss. On several occasions, four or five visitors would live in my room, many of them coming to Mumbai for sightseeing. I would study at the Petit Library throughout the day. Bored in the evening, I would take a stroll at the Gateway of India or Marine Drive with my friends. We would return to the rest house late, our jokes and chatting disturbing others.

Yadav Saheb, observing this behaviour, once summoned me and rebuked me, saying, 'Vishwas, let me tell you some words of wisdom by Swami Vivekananda on the company a man keeps. If a raindrop falls on a hot iron plate, it will vanish in a moment. If it falls on a lotus flower, it will glitter like a pearl and if it falls into an oyster shell, it transforms into a pearl. The raindrop is the same; its value depends on the company it keeps. Vishwas, your main examination is approaching. If you want to fly high like an eagle, do not waste your time swimming with ducks. Every moment is precious. Every hour of leisure will cost you a mark in the exam. Keep this in mind. If you lose a mark, five other candidates will supersede you in rank, in this cutthroat competition. Like in the race between the hare and the tortoise, speed and continuity are important in your race too. If you want to win the race, give up frivolous, aimless enjoyment. I have observed that you study throughout the day, but it all goes to waste at night. Stick to your chair like iron particles stick to a magnet. There is a saying, "When the going gets tough, the tough get going." Your test is when you are tired, when your pen stops working, your brain stops functioning. Have you heard about Muhammad Ali, the boxer? He would only start counting his dips when he started feeling pain in his arms. This is the nature of a real fighter. When he gets exhausted, practice and penance give him the strength he needs. Like a phoenix rising from the ashes, you will have to find your hidden energies. Thousands of candidates will sit for this competition. If you fail to bring out your hidden weapons and fight tooth and nail, you will be defeated again. You must study round the clock. Wake up! This time is crucial. Realize this and stay alert. Work out your tactics, and don't let others find them out. An opportunity is like a sunrise; if you wait too long, you'll miss it. The iron is hot now, strike it.'

Yadav Saheb spoke to me too earnestly. I was fortunate to meet such people who loved me, protected me, helped me and taught me the important lessons of life when I faced hurdles. Every now and then, some messiah would bring me back to reality. With Yadav Saheb's sermon, I awoke from my slumber and geared up for the race of the main examination.

Chapter 9

My Tryst with the MPSC

The main examination of the MPSC was only a month and a half away. Short nights and endless study matter became the norm. I was all set to fill out my form of candidature. However, there was one hurdle. I had studied Marathi literature as the optional subject for the Union Public Service Commission examination, but everybody advised it as the optional subject for the MPSC examination. According to them, I would not score well since there was a sea of difference between the pattern of questions of the UPSC and MPSC examinations. These inputs confused me and wasted my time.

The SIAC was packed with candidates who were appearing for the main examination of UPSC. It was demoralizing to prepare for the MPSC examination there, so candidates would study at the Petit Library in Fort. The spacious study room on the third floor was full of candidates preparing for high-profile examinations like MBA, chartered accountancy, NET, GRE and GATE. All newspapers and magazines were available for reading, free of cost. When we got bored of studies, we would pass time with titillating photographs in magazines like *Femina*, *Filmfare* or *Stardust*.

Next to the library, a rice plate was available for Rs 12 at the Anandashram, a south Indian mess. People who worked in Fort would throng to this mess in the afternoon. We went for the bonanza of a spoonful of ghee served with the rice. We would eat to our hearts' content and get back to studies in the library. Women working in corporate offices in the vicinity would visit this Parsi library during their lunch break. Stealing a glimpse at them would be a treat to our sleepless eyes. My friend Sanjay Deshmukh had passed the prelim examination and studied at Petit Library for the main examination.

This was his third attempt and he suggested that I choose sociology as my optional subject. Having graduated with an MPhil in sociology, he promised to help me prepare for this subject. His earlier score was not the best but time was precious. I filled out the form with sociology and history as my optional subjects. I prepared a comprehensive schedule to complete my revision over a period of forty-five days. As per the schedule, I could spare only nine days for sociology. I went to the book market and chose the thinnest book which had only 175 pages. This was a general book on sociology meant for the main examination. I requested Sanjay to teach me for two hours every day. He came to my room with three volumes of sociology. He had learnt the definitions of more than 300 sociological terms scripted by renowned sociologists. His explanations and teaching method was well structured but I found it difficult to understand. I became apprehensive about having chosen sociology as the optional subject. But I have always been a risk-taker; I knew that the bigger the risk, the greater the success.

Since sociology was new to me, it was like starting with a clean state. I started self-studying, relating my own life experiences to a sociological point of view. This allowed me to study it thoroughly in a shorter amount of time; I virtually romanced with the subject for nine days. I didn't dilly-dally, I didn't allow myself to get frustrated because it wasn't an option. I simply studied day and night, nursing my ambition like a child nurses a toy. On the day of the exam, I solved the sociology paper, writing detailed answers in lucid handwriting.

When the results were declared, everyone was shocked. Sanjay, an MPhil in sociology who knew nearly 300 definitions of the basic concepts, had scored 85 marks out of 200 whereas I had scored 150. I achieved in nine days what Sanjay could not in nine years.

In fact, the question paper for sociology was not too difficult. The marks are granted on the basis of how well the answers are written. Each of my answers was based on common sense. I made use of the six elements explained by Yadav Saheb to formulate my answers. One of the questions was on the 'Balutedari' system (an occupation-based caste system which evolved around the fifteenth century). Since I had grown up in a village and had interacted with twelve Balutedars, eighteen Alutedars and Kunbis, I did not find it necessary to read about the Balutedari system. For the examination, I wrote about my experiences with the system during my childhood. Another question was to critique the concept of secularism. I went beyond the sociological analysis of the topic and touched upon the fact that Europe had witnessed the Thirty Years' War—the Peace of Westphalia came after the war between Catholics and Protestants, resulting in the concept of secularism. This reference made the answer unique. I also did a critical comparison between India's religious tolerance and secularism. I had studied the Constitution of India. I explained how this concept, integral to the Constitution of India, is linked with national integrity. Thus, my answer sheet appropriately reflected several issues of humanities. The examiner liked my unconventional approach and therefore I scored excellent marks.

The MPSC examination comprises compulsory papers of English and Marathi as well. Just as I had studied sociology, I used special tricks to study English. The English essay on 'National Integration' which I had memorized for the annual NCC Camp at Rukadi came to my aid. I had memorized this award-winning essay which had secured the first place in the national-level CSR competition. I had not understood the wordy language of the essay. Regardless, I realized that the language of the essay itself was free-flowing, meaningful and effective. The words, however, were complex. I had memorized the essay without grasping its meaning or relevance. I had meticulously preserved all that I had prepared while studying in school or college in a separate file. This came in handy during the 100-mark paper on the compulsory subject of English language. We were asked to write a 40-mark essay on 'If I Were to Become the Prime Minister'. Thanks to my study of the English language, I could now fully comprehend the meaning of the speech that I had memorized on the topic of 'National Integration'. I tweaked it suitably to fit my essay.

My speech on 'National Integration' began with the sentence, 'The strength of the nation lies not in its loud claims and salivating directive principles of state policy but in the spirit of service and of the relentless dedication of one's body and soul to the cause of unity and integrity of the nation.' To make it relevant to the topic at hand, I wrote: 'The strength of the nation lies not in its loud claims and salivating directive principles of state policy, but in the prime minister's spirit of service and that of complete dedication to the unity and integrity of the nation.' In fact, even students who study in English-medium schools found it difficult to score more than 70 marks, but I was able to score more than 90 marks thanks to my presence of mind. In the end, studying is mostly about using one's common sense. One needs to realize when and how to use it. Everyone should develop their own study technique. If one tries to replicate someone else's technique blindly, he will fall flat on his face. P.R. Patil tried to copy my trick of essay writing blindly and failed. We must devise our own plans, methods of study and preparation formulas.

My second optional subject, history, was my domain of expertise. Its syllabus comprised 'The Modern History of the World and India'. One of the questions was on the uprising of 1857. I wrote an elaborate and analytical answer delving into whether it was an uprising, a mutiny or a struggle for independence. While writing on the issue of 'United Italy', I drew a map showing the contemporary situation of Europe. I also discussed the policy and constructive programme that were laid down by Gandhiji during the independence struggle. I detailed his multifaceted approach to social reforms and individual satyagraha after every agitation. In short, I wrote high-quality, thought-provoking and analytical answers.

We had to solve two papers in the general studies segment. One consisted of questions related to Maharashtra and the other was along the lines of the UPSC papers. Since I had studied well, I found the second paper easier than the first one. In short, I solved all the papers to my satisfaction. I could not afford to camp at the PWD rest house for long. Not only was I required to seek an extension every week, but the clerks would harass me for bribes. I vacated the rest house and there was no question of being admitted into the hostel as I had not appeared for the university examination. I was frustrated as I had to figure out a way to stay in Mumbai. Out of this frustration, I packed my books, boarded a bus at the Kurla terminus and returned to my village. I contemplated continuing my studies in Kolhapur.

When I reached my village, I found that campaigning for the state assembly elections was in full swing. I considered the option of joining politics if I failed again. My younger brother was in his second year of BA in Kolhapur. I went to his room with my belongings and decided to stay there. He had a second-hand Bullet motorcycle, which I would take to the Khardekar Library of Shivaji University, where I used to study. I was considered the wisest among the lot, though I disagreed. Here, the crowd was mainly made up of rustic village wrestlers. I met friends who aspired to become police sub-inspectors (PSI). I had an edge over all the other candidates because I was 'SIAC returned' and had appeared for the main MPSC examination. Several candidates would approach me to seek guidance. My standard of living had improved after returning from Mumbai. I wore jeans and T-shirts, and was considered stylish. This new look helped me get acquainted with girls from rural areas who lived in the ladies' hostel of the university and were pursuing their post-graduation. This obviously affected my studies. I began wasting time again, chatting with old and new friends in the canteen.

That was the time when Kharge Sir got selected for the IAS with top ranking. I called him to congratulate him. He asked me to pay him a visit in Ichalkaranji. When I visited him, he asked me about my studies and exam preparation. Nervousness overpowered me and I started stuttering.

He rebuked me but I knew he was right. His wife served shira and pohe but I could not eat, humiliated as I was. Sir said, 'Vishwas, you have returned to Kolhapur from Mumbai. Do not waste time indulging in fun in college, otherwise you will end up spending your youthful years making mistakes, your matured years struggling to make a living and repenting when you're grey and old. Remember, a word to the wise is sufficient.'

His words kept ringing in my years. Kharge Sir is a role model for candidates struggling in the arena of competitive examinations. I find him to be peaceful, nonchalant and restrained just like Lord Ramachandra. His smile and wise words reflect his mature and pleasant personality. He had opened my eyes. After giving me a piece of his mind, he talked to me cordially and guided me. He explained how one should read an English newspaper. He showed me how to prepare micro notes and use them for revision just before the examination. As a result, I learnt how to have a last-minute glance at several topics on a single sheet of paper. Besides this, he lay emphasis on writing grammatically correct answers in a neat handwriting.

The results of the MPSC main examination were declared; I had passed with flying colours. My joy knew no bounds. Bursting with enthusiasm, I called everybody. Everyone celebrated as if I had already become a deputy collector. I was just twenty-one years old then and everybody knew that I was about to become a 'boss'. The final stage, that is, the interview was left but I was under the impression that the interview was a mere formality. I returned to my village, bragging about my achievement. I would soon be disillusioned.

I returned to Kolhapur to prepare for the interview. I prepared my biodata as well as charts of information on history of my native place, district, powers and duties of various posts in accordance with the preferences and especially the current affairs related to Maharashtra. I visited current and retired officers for tips on how to face the interview. However, despite all this, I was not able to make enough preparations. I decided to return to Mumbai. I shifted my base to the PWD rest house near the SIAC. Several candidates studying at Petit Library as well as the SIAC had received the call for the interview and were preparing for it. I gave mock interviews, but the experienced panellists ripped my inexperienced and superficial answers apart. They would remark that I still had a long way to go. The date of the interview was getting close. I went to the Study Circle. Dr Anand Patil asked thirty-five questions in thirty-five minutes. Most of the questions were about the economic policies of Maharashtra. He too expressed dissatisfaction with my preparation.

The night before the interview, some of my cousins and friends came to boost my morale, as if I were about to fill out my nomination for an election. As a result, we all had to sleep in the tiny 10×10 ft room. Two of them snored all night. I had nightmares too. I was only twenty-one and a stubble would grow on my face and chin, which I would shave once a month. I needed to be clean-shaven for the interview. That happened to be a Sunday. I walked all over in Fort area in search of a barbershop in the morning but to no avail. Finally, I found one in the Churchgate area. I walked inside, got a shave and got my moustache trimmed. The bill was Rs 100. I was taken aback. The amount was what I paid at the mess in a week. I argued with the owner as to why he had not displayed the rates or cautioned me about them. I was running late, and my mood was spoiled. The owner was embarrassed because the other customers were watching. He reduced the bill by Rs 10.

I was left with only one Rs 100 note. I took the discount because I needed to travel in a taxi to return to the Chhatrapati Shivaji Terminus.

Sporting a brand-new white shirt and grey trousers, I reached the MPSC building. Earlier, I would try to peep behind the reception counter. A stoutly built peon stood near the wooden partition. If we loitered there for long, he would raise his eyebrows. That day I showed him my hall ticket, and he allowed me to cross the mysterious door. I crossed a corridor filled with heaps of files to reach the waiting room. The clerk mumbled something about my being late and handed over the forms. I filled out the forms in a hurry. My number had come, and my name was announced.

The chairman of the MPSC welcomed me and offered me a chair. I had prepared myself as per the instructions of my seniors. Those who had coached me for the interview said that I should wish good morning, first to the female interviewers and then to the men. There were no women there. Accustomed to that way of wishing the panellists, I started with, 'Good Morning, madam. Good morning, sir!' It was my first mistake. The chairman asked me to sit down. Flustered due to the mistake I had already made, I again said, 'Thank you, madam!'

The panel members probably thought that I was confused about their genders and started smiling mischievously. I broke out in a cold sweat even though the room was air-conditioned. It is of utmost importance to overcome such inadvertent mistakes and regain composure quickly, but I was so ruffled that I could not speak clearly or logically after that. The interviewers saw my date of birth and congratulated me for making it to the last stage at such a young age. I made the mistake of informing them that I was preparing for the

UPSC even though it was not required. Over enthusiastically, I started attaching wrong references to my answers. I failed to give a satisfactory answer to a question on the Employment Guarantee Scheme. My interview was over in ten minutes. I walked out of the interview room and went straight to the Marine Drive in the afternoon heat, for a long walk. The walk miraculously rejuvenated me. Whenever I would get stressed, I would go for a walk on the Marine Drive. The cool sea breeze would comfort me and pull me out of depression. The waves crashing against the boulders on the shore would rid me of feelings of insecurity. The sunset would cleanse my mind. Whenever I felt uncertain about the future, I would go to the Marine Drive, sit on the retaining wall and cry, staring at the sun on the horizon. This would purify my body and mind and give me new hope and optimism to latch onto.

Psychologically, I felt the same way I had after my underperformance in the HSC examination. Somehow, I consoled myself and returned to my village. There everybody was ready to celebrate, sure that I would return from Mumbai a 'saheb'. I alighted at the State Transport bus stop. Everybody, from the goons to the local leaders, were waiting to welcome me. The jeep of the gambling den owner Jafar was ready to take me home. A chain of firecrackers was burst as soon as I got down from the bus. The booming sounds of the firecrackers made me feel numb. The welcome party showered me in gulal and flowers. I did not react. My success was being celebrated even before the battle was over.

When I reached home, my mother welcomed me with aarti. I touched her feet and tried to make her see the harsh reality of my dismal performance. She did not accept that her Vishwas might get beaten in this battle. She firmly believed that the blessings of Goddess Ninabai would make a miracle happen. My house was to witness some good fortune after a long time. People were to throng to the house of Aaba, who had got sidelined again. Tatya too was looking forward to better days. He had been elbowed out of active politics and elections because of his adamant approach. He had not experienced success in the last fifteen years. I did not want to disappoint anyone. If I failed, their expectations would be shattered and my entire house would plunge into darkness.

The next day, villagers clad in dhotis and lungis arrived early in the morning. Somebody wanted to get his son recruited in the police force, while someone else wanted me to call the PSI at the local police station to sort out the matter of his fight. They were all pleading for help. Wearing crisply ironed clothes, the gambling den owner Jafar arrived in his new Qualis jeep. Sipping a cup of tea served by my mother, he was telling me, 'Bhausaheb, if you need to go to Kolhapur or Sangli, my vehicle is at your service. Just send me a message and the vehicle will be here with the driver within five minutes.' I was angry at his illegal, immoral and daring attempt. I wanted to become a public servant to not only to avoid such allurements but also to curb them. My head was spinning with this dilemma. I shouted, 'I have not become an officer and if at all I do, I will not spare you and your business.' Jafar fled.

I went to Gawaloba Hill with Bhaskar Bhau and Pakya Sutar and told them that I had tanked my interview. Bhaskar Bhau tried to console me in his fluent English. Bhaskar Bhau was a dreamer ahead of his times, like Mohammed Tughlak. He was the first one to buy anything new that arrived in the market and once he had had his fill of it, he would sell it at half the price. When he was in a good mood, he would play the tabla and sing in his screeching voice. We would be forced to praise his tabla playing and singing. He was the first one in the village to buy a treadmill, a computer, cable TV, a tabla and a helmet. When he rode his Rajdoot motorcycle wearing the helmet, he would look like an astronaut alighting from a spacecraft. Barely 5 feet tall, Bhaskar Bhau had a pointed chin and incomparable intelligence, but he was also stubborn. He would always go against the wishes of his brethren. He had taken a lead in forming a study circle in the village, to make preparations for the UPSC examination from the donations received by it.

He had convinced me to work with him and bought all the books needed for his study. He vowed that, 'Learning English is my birthright, and I will attain mastery over it.' Therefore, wherever he went he would speak in English, notwithstanding whether whom he spoke to understood the language or not. As a result, the villagers avoided him. Once, his father Bapu, who used to wear a *langot*, was driving a bullock cart and Bhaskar Bhau, sitting atop a haystack in the cart, was reciting, 'To be or not to be, that is the question.'

Bapu had to bring him back to his senses, cracking the whip on him and subjecting him to the choicest of abuses. He had selected psychology as an optional subject, making him more aggressive. He started psychoanalysing everyone he met. He did not even spare his mother from his eccentricities, subjecting her to his psychology experiments. She was as stubborn as he was and, after his father's demise, the mother-son duo was always at each other's throats. The mother summoned her five daughters and handed over the family land to them. This enraged Bhaskar Bhau but, influenced by the renowned thinkers of the world, he remained silent and devoted himself to his studies. Back then, people found it very difficult to clear the NET in English as a subject. He cleared that examination. However, he needed to address his situation. He gave up his preparations for the UPSC examination, working as a college professor at the taluka. As a result, the Indian Administrative Services lost an exceptional man.

Bhaskar Bhau was a great influence on me. Though the entire village called him 'Bhaskya', I respectfully addressed him as 'Bhau' or 'Sir'. We would talk in English for hours. I was smart, I would talk to him in English only after reaching Gawloba Hill. Nobody except for a few stray dogs would be around to listen to our conversation. He would explain to me the various schools of English literature, right from Shakespeare to Milton. He taught using several examples and made even the most difficult topic seem easy. Everything about him was different. He advised me to get back to my studies. I couldn't return to Mumbai as I had nowhere to stay. I decided to return to Kolhapur. I packed my bags again and took admission at the government-run Pre-IAS Training Centre in Kolhapur.

The conditions at the centre were not up to the mark. Ninety per cent of the candidates at the centre, run in the name of UPSC preparation, were preparing for the examinations for the posts of police sub-inspector (PSI) or sales tax inspector (STI). It was a sister institute of the SIAC but there was a sea of difference in the environment of the two centres. I was the only candidate there preparing for the UPSC. Ganesh Kulkarni and Pandurang Patil became my room partners. They were poles apart, not only in their complexion but also in their attitudes.

Ganesh Kulkarni was simple, straightforward and pious. His Solapuri dialect was like music to my ears. He would worship Gurudev Dutt for half an hour every morning and recite several mantras. I teased him a lot. His father had died

when he was young and he and his siblings had been raised by
their mother. His elder brother was an officer with the Bombay
Municipal Corporation and Ganeshrao too was preparing to
follow suit. He studied with admirable dedication. I liked his
company. We would go to the university together to study.
I was the centre of attraction as I had appeared for the MPSC
interview. Though my performance at the interview had been
sub-par, I was sure that I would be selected for the Class II
post of section officer or pay and accounts officer. The UPSC
examination was approaching but my preparation was not
complete. I was in a predicament over whether to appear for
the examination or not.

I had taken a fancy to a girl who visited the library to study
for the MPSC examination. She looked like Meenakshi in the
film *Hero*. I found it hard to concentrate on my studies when
she was there. Finally, I mustered up courage to ask her name.
I took Ganesh Kulkarni with me. He got nervous when I told
him about my intentions. We waited for her at the bus stop.
I had memorized the English sentence, 'If I am not mistaken,
are you Miss Paranjape?' to start a conversation with her.

She came to the bus stop with three friends. Ganesh
was insisting that we leave but I bravely stepped ahead and
uttered the memorized sentence as naturally as possible. Quite
unexpectedly, she replied, 'Yes, I am Miss Paranjape.' 'Does your
father work with the PWD?' Things were taking a different
turn. She, on her part, asked me, 'Aren't you Vishwas Nangre?
Aren't you preparing for the MPSC examination? You should
concentrate on your studies. Many Vishwamitras come here
and end up becoming Majanus.' I was convinced that seducing
someone or falling in love was not my cup of tea.

Pandu Patil's personality was the exact opposite of
Ganeshrao's. His complexion was like Lord Vitthal. He had

a muscular body, a robust face and a mischievous way of speaking. Though he looked like a typical villain of Marathi movies, he was actually sensitive and emotional. Since his brother was a policeman, he had come to Kolhapur with a resolution that he would return home only after becoming a PSI. His mother would send his tiffin from his village on a State Transport bus. Pandurang would cycle to the bus stop to get the tiffin.

He would eat half of it in the morning and the remaining half in the evening without any complaint. He would do 100 dips reciting the name of Bajrangbali. The odour of his sweat during his daily exercise would bother Ganesh and me no end. We would burn incense sticks to mask the odour and continue with our studies. Every now and then Pandurang would measure his chest to see if it was at par with the standards for recruitment of PSI. The results of the prelim examination for the post of PSI were announced and Pandurang had failed. Ganeshrao had passed the examination. A dejected Pandurang was contemplating returning home but I insisted that he appear for the prelim of the MPSC. Pandurang's handwriting was neat and clean. He had a lively style of writing. He had chosen the science stream since eleventh standard but wasn't interested in it, preferring literature and the humanities. Finally, he relented. Thus, the three of us decided to appear for the prelim exam of MPSC.

The results of the main examination for the post of PSI were announced. Ganeshrao cleared the examination and started preparing for the physical examination on the Shivaji University grounds. However, he only had one month to build up his physique, was unable to build his chest to the required standards for the physical examination and returned with a long face. Our common concerns and goals strengthened our friendship. Such was the enormity of our struggle that we would not have been able to face the hardships without each other's help. It is said that one should sweat more in a time of peace to ensure that the loss of blood is minimal during war. We were burning the midnight oil to study.

Meanwhile, the results of the MPSC examination were delayed. Newspapers published articles about scams in the MPSC recruitment every day. This made us more anxious and restless. I did not appear for the UPSC prelim exam due to this confusion and because I was of two minds. However, I appeared for the MPSC prelim exam. But the year 1995 witnessed the paper leak scam. I was afraid that I would have to start afresh in this game of snakes and ladders. My fears came to pass. The results of the interview round were announced. Leave alone the post of deputy collector, my name was not even in the list of candidates selected for any Class II post. I was shell-shocked. My dreams were shattered. Fate had brought me back to square one.

Frustrated, I wanted to run away from this maze of competitive examinations. Ganeshrao tried to convince me otherwise, saying, 'God willing, everything will be okay. Whatever happens, happens for the good.' He insisted that I visit Narsoba Wadi to offer prayers. That day we boarded the State Transport bus to the Nrusinh Saraswati Temple, located along the Krishna River. We reached there during the evening aarti. We took darshan of Nrusinh Saraswati. Though I was not much of a believer, I would always ask God for something. This time, I thought I should give up something. Being a son of a Patil who had grown up in Kolhapur, I loved to eat fried mutton and tamdarassa (red mutton curry). In the presence of Ganesh Kulkarni, I pledged in the temple that I would not eat non-vegetarian food till I achieved success in the

UPSC examination. We boarded a truck on the highway to return to my village.

Everyone in the neighbourhood had found out about my failure. Some of my relatives hurled abuses at Deshmukh Saheb, though he was not at fault. My father though kept his disappointment to himself. He had visited Ninai goddess early in the morning and prayed that she would give me the strength to continue my struggle. He took me aside and gave me his blessings, saying, 'Do not lose hope, keep going.'

Several villagers visited our house in the morning in a show of solidarity. Some even wept, saying, 'Bhavdya, how did this happen?' It was as if everybody was offering condolences to a grieving family after the death of a family member. The elders reassured me that I would overcome this failure. Some mischievously tried to convince my father than no one could become a saheb without paying bribes and using 'influence'.

On the surface, I was calm, but a volcano was churning in my head. I felt as if I was on fire; I needed to steer my fiery spirit in the right direction and charge headfirst into the battle with renewed vigour. I was in a mire of failure and defeat. Many villagers were rejoicing over my failure. I thought to myself, 'The real satisfaction of victory comes when others want to see you fail.'

I kept a framed photo of my parents on my study table and resolved to channel the burning fire within me to speed up my studies. I did not want to harbour any confusion. Till then, I was in the category of self-declared or people-declared candidates. I resolved that come what may, I would top the third category of selected candidates. I may be forced to suffer humiliation or pain, but I vowed to never let depression or exhaustion get the better of me. Life is a race. Horses participating in a race do not know their purpose of running.

They go faster because of the whips that they suffer. In my case, the cracking of the whip of adversities would increase my speed. Thus, with renewed hope and self-confidence, I resolved that, 'God is riding on my back. He will decide whether I will win this race or not. I should run as fast as I can.' Just like victory, failure is not the end. Your courage and willpower lend a direction to your efforts. I told myself to continue my struggle without any apprehension and set out for the final race of the examination conducted in 1995–96, which would take my life in a new direction.

Over the last one and a half years, I had become well versed in the pattern of the examination. I had also realized the scope of the subjects and had an inkling as to how studies should be conducted. I had collected the books needed to pursue these studies. I had tasted failure and learnt what I should not be doing. I chalked out a plan for success. I needed to arrange for a library for studying, a mentor to guide me and a place to sleep at night in Mumbai.

I returned to Mumbai.

I kept my things in Deshmukh Saheb's room in the MLA hostel and patronized Petit Library where I had earlier started my studies. Just like a book of accounts, I maintained a book which detailed the schedule of my studies. I prepared a chart of my study schedule for the prelim and main exam for each day, each week, each month for the six months I had left. I analysed the question papers and the syllabus and resolved that I would study for a total of twelve hours daily, breaking them into four hours in the morning, afternoon and evening. I stuck to my schedule for the first two shifts. However, after the library closed at 7 p.m., I faced the problem of where to study as, at that time, political workers from rural areas would flock to the MLA hostel, inebriated and spitting paan in the corners of the rooms. The toilets would become unbearably filthy. The kitchen of the canteen was located on the ground floor, and the slab would absorb its heat.

Deshmukh Saheb's was the only air-conditioned room. I could concentrate on my studies in the pleasantly cool atmosphere of the air-conditioned room when it was empty, but when I had to sleep in the room, jampacked with potbellied leaders and the various stinks that emanated from them, I felt claustrophobic. I would try and sleep on a mattress in the corridor, but hordes of mosquitoes would bite me, even after applying the mosquito-repellent cream.

Lack of sleep would affect my studies the next day. I would try to compensate for my sleep by napping in Petit Library but inadvertently I would fall into a deep sleep, snoring within minutes. When this became a frequent occurrence, the peon warned me to stop being a nuisance to others. Fearing that I would be thrown out of the library, I began searching for a room in the posh localities of Mumbai. I had heard that senior officers of the Public Works Department (PWD) let out vacant rooms of their servants' quarters on rent. I even went to look for a room in the Yashodhan building, where I would later be allotted a 2200-square-foot official accommodation. Finally, I shifted to my cousin's vacant room at Ambivali beyond Kalyan. My plight was like that of the Marathi *manoos* migrating from South Mumbai to distant suburbs.

I would walk across the Irani settlement in Ambivali to reach the room. The police would frequently conduct raids there as it was the residence of several robbers. I once again got into the habit of waking up at 3 a.m. which I had inculcated when I was studying for the SSC. My mother often sent shira (sweet dish made of rawa) cooked in pure ghee for me from our village. I would cook it on the stove, mix it with hot milk and savour it. I studied in my room for an hour early in the morning, boarded the train that departed at 4.30 a.m. and reached Petit Library in an hour.

There would be plenty of vacant seats in the local train at Ambivali during the early morning hours. I studied during the train journey too. My schedule was steadily building up. Subsequently, I had the luxury of reducing the frequency of my visits to Petit Library. A rural couple lived in the neighbourhood. I ordered my tiffin from them. I had virtually turned my cousin's room into a treasure trove. Books lay scattered all over. If the shira fell on the floor, it would attract red ants. I had to fight the bite of red ants and the nuisance of flies when I went to sleep.

Mutton was served on Sundays and, although I had made a resolution to give up non-veg, I was in two minds. But I did not waver from my oath, despite the temptation. Like a voracious tiger, I charged on my studies. My manner of studying was going on in a 'SMART' manner. SMART stands for Specific, Measurable, Achievable, Realistic and Time-bound. By then I had learnt how to do accurate, final, required, achievable, objective and time-bound studies. I would employ smart tricks wherever possible. For answering map-based questions in history, we needed to write about the importance of various places. I prepared maps on the basis of time periods and put them up in the room, some of them in the toilet too. Thus, I could study for this sixty-mark question even while answering nature's call. I jotted down the important points in every chapter so that I could easily memorize it. I related some of them to obscene terms so that such perverse words would get fixed permanently in my brain and, sure enough, I could recollect them easily during the examination. I always wonder why it's easy to forget good things while the opposite is true for bad things. Maybe it is an inherent quality of human beings.

Titwala is two stations away from Ambivali. To rejuvenate myself, I would visit it once a week and pay obeisance to Lord Ganesha. Since I had no friends, I considered God to be my friend. I would have conversations with Him. Every morning, I would tell Him everything, discuss my daily happenings and plans for the next day. It helped me as I started looking at God as my saviour. I would make imaginary calls to Him to update Him about my results of the prelim and the main examinations, interviews and allotment of cadre from the telephone booth opposite the Siddhivinayak Temple. It may seem like superstition but the penance of studying and the consumption of simple food gave me spiritual energy. I may not have blind faith, but it has been impressed on my mind since childhood that God is the symbol of goodness, generosity, love and mercy. I firmly believed that He would ensure that my hard work bore fruit. Once I was assured that He was there to support me, I didn't stray from my path even when I was depressed and frustrated.

It rained cats and dogs during the monsoon. The building in which I lived was deserted. There was a dense growth of bushes behind my room. Gangs of motorcycle-riding Irani goons would loiter outside the building, but this didn't scare me in the least. However, when dogs whimpered in the wee hours of the night, I would be terrified of ghosts. However, just like Bapu came to the rescue of Munnabhai whenever he was in trouble, I would find my saviour in God. Even on the fateful night of 26/11, as I was staring death in the face, fighting AK-47-wielding terrorists with my pistol, my hands did not tremble even once. It was God who was giving me the courage and strength to fight. I wasn't even wearing a bullet-proof vest, but I felt God's presence in every nook and cranny of the Taj hotel. He was my bullet-proof vest. Faith in a higher power can help us overcome the problems we face. On that night, terrorists who had strayed in the name of religion and hypnotized by the wrong ideals were present in that iconic building. As a result, their bodies rotted in the JJ Hospital morgue. But the names of those who faced them with a sense of duty and patriotism and performed the supreme sacrifice are scripted in golden letters in the annals of history.

When one's spiritual strength comes from one's sense of justice and mercy, one finds oneself doing humanitarian work. The abuse of power for pleasure and selfish reasons, devoid of the sense of giving, gives rise to satanic strength and leads to the commitment of brutal acts. The prayer, 'God, grant us the serenity to accept the things we cannot change, the courage to change the things we can, and the wisdom to know the difference,' summarizes the wisdom of life.

Having resolved to not stop or succumb to any doubt during my battle, I continued to conquer new subjects of study every day. I had adopted a well-known battle technique while studying the famous Chinese general Sun Tzu's book *Art of War*, which is all about military tactics in 511 BC. He has summarized it accurately. He says if you know yourself and your enemy well, you emerge victorious in every war. If you know yourself but not the foe, you face defeat after every victory and if you have no knowledge about yourself or your foe, you will be defeated in every war. The battle for UPSC becomes easy when one considers the UPSC examination as a challenging foe and implements this war tactic. One should study one's strengths well and use them appropriately when it comes to the battle, that is, the examination of UPSC. One should also identify one's weaknesses and try to overcome them.

One must look out for the opportunities and risks involved, in full measure, before appearing for the examination.

How must Shivaji Maharaj have planned his career? How did he achieve miraculous success? Planning is nothing but being meticulous and systematic in everything that we do. Shivaji Maharaj set a goal for himself. His biggest strength was his mindboggling self-confidence. He put forth the concept of the welfare state. He developed military tactics to suit his needs. For communication, he used sound, smoke, fire and light. He used weapons like tiger claws, spears and swords innovatively. He augmented his cavalry, strengthened his navy and, most importantly, created the passion of love and dedication towards 'Swarajya' in the mind of the common man. He studied geographical conditions and developed guerrilla warfare tactics. Success can become a reality if we overcome our weaknesses and nurture our strengths. I would chant the mantra 'Shivaji, Shivaji, Shivaji' whenever I felt stressed. I would spend several hours just planning how to win those battles which were six months and a year away. I was already sweating and toiling hard to ensure my victory.

There were several distractions and allurements in my path. Sporting a stubble on my face, I used to wear a round necked t-shirt, jeans and slippers, making my disposition akin to that of an educated beggar. When I visited relatives during the evening, they would grumble that my arrival had disturbed their supper time. I looked like a prodigal son. Once, on a holiday, I went to pay a visit to my cousin sister whose husband worked as a peon at the dockyard. Seeing me in my shabby avatar, he gave me a long lecture and advised me to start earning and settle down. I tried explaining to him that I had given the interview of the MPSC for the officer's post. For him, all these examinations were a gamble with selections through unfair means and that hardly a handful made it due to their hard work and luck. I challenged him, saying, "I will ensure that I am among those handful of candidates," and returned home, resolving never to visit any relative again.

Study and loneliness became my companions. Occasionally, my childhood friend Balya Kadam would visit me. He was unemployed but remained a happy man. He would roam around aimlessly. Whenever he visited, we would catch a bus and go to watch a movie. The bus used to be jampacked and we would hardly get any space to stand. Balya would pretend to be lame and occupy the seat reserved for the physically impaired. At times, he would come riding a friend's motorbike. Then he would deliberately brush against a vehicle and get in an argument. If the owner of the other vehicle spoke aggressively, he would run away but if he sounded apologetic, he would take on a stern tone. He was not serious in life, his only goal was to have fun. He worked in a footwear mart for a while in Mumbai and tried to seduce the shop owner's daughter. This resulted in an ugly brawl wherein the shopkeeper bit off flesh from Balya's cheek. He vowed that he would not remove the bandage until he bit off flesh from the shop owner's daughter's cheek. He was aware of the smallest of things happening in every nook and corner of Mumbai. He took us to a factory that made duplicate branded jeans in Dharavi, promising us to get original jeans at an affordable price. We bought rugged jeans with the labels of the brands of our choice. He also knew where one could get food at affordable prices. He would escort us to wedding receptions, birthdays and other functions held in posh halls, so that we could eat good-quality food. Once, we gatecrashed the wedding reception of a minister's son where the menu consisted of

100 non-veg delicacies. Balya ate so much that the next day, his face was swollen. I would have fun with him for a few hours and then return to my schedule.

I filled out the form for the MA examination which was to be held in the month of October. There were three reasons behind this decision. Firstly, if I managed to score good marks, it would get me admitted into the hostel again. Secondly, if I completed my MA, I would at least be able to work as a teacher. Thirdly, while studying MA-level history, my preparation of history, world history and contemporary history for the UPSC would be done simultaneously.

One had the choice of writing the papers in English or Marathi. I opted for both languages—wrote some papers in English and others in Marathi. I wanted to experience the powerful style of writing history in English. I linked my studies for MA with preparation for the main examination, so I found the MA papers easy.

It was difficult for me to study alone in the room at Ambivali. Besides, travelling to and from the Chhatrapati Shivaji Terminus took up a lot of time. Shivaji Nimat was living alone in a rented tiny one-BHK flat in the Shivajinagar area of Thane. He was so studious that once he sat down to study, he would not get up for eight hours. I moved to Thane, thinking that his company would encourage me. The area around the MHADA colony was serene and tranquil. I had procured audio cassettes of the UPSC prelim examination from Delhi. I would go to Vihar Lake in the evening and listen to music on my Walkman, trying to ignore the couples there. The movie *Rangeela* was the current super hit. I would also listen to Urmila's hit songs like 'Hai Rama' and imagine a lover running towards me as I walked along the lane, the way it was shown in the film *Roja*.

The 'high' of studies and the euphoria of dreams are closely related to each other. Around that time, *Mukta*, a very good Marathi film, had been released. It has excellently sung songs, penned by the poet N.D. Mahanor. The songs would ignite a fire within me. The mess was located about one and a half kilometres away from my lodgings and its owner was a peon with the municipal corporation. He would lovingly use swear words with his wife but addressed her respectfully too. While leaving for the office he would say, 'Hey, Madam Witch, I am going to the office. Do you want me to bring anything for your puppy to eat or to study?' Listening to such sentences, Shivaji Nimat and I would smile and continue eating.

A beautiful Sai Baba Temple was located next to the mess. Visiting it rejuvenated me. I would sit in the temple premises for hours. Nimat would get bored after a short while and leave. At times, we would reach at the time of aarti. The ringing of the bell would give me a sense of immense peace. Besides, several young women residing in Thane visited the temple to offer prayers. They provided a pleasant relief to the eyes too. I had read about Maslow's hierarchy of needs, which states that man looks for the fulfilment of psychological needs after his physical needs are addressed, and, after his psychological needs are addressed, man turns to spirituality and attaining self-actualization. None of my needs were getting fulfilled. Our emotional world during the days of youth is always overwhelmed with darkness and confusion.

Cleanliness was never next to godliness for me. I used the same towel for a month and the same bedsheet and mattress for a year without washing them. The toilet was never cleaned with disinfectants. The landlord would cover his nose to before entering our room. He had threatened to evict us if we didn't clean the toilet.

I was tempted to steal a glance at the girl next door when she dried clothes in the balcony but would turn to my books when her father stared at me angrily. Such were the allurements in Mumbai and Thane. I tried to be careful and away from temptations. On Sundays, the aroma of mutton curry or fried Bombay fish would overpower my senses. A year had passed since I had savoured the taste of non-vegetarian dishes, but I was firm in my resolve. I had entered into an agreement with God. I had to keep my word. My firm resolution gave me enormous strength. The humiliations of the past would flash before my eyes. I was ready to do the impossible to become successful. I was determined to emerge victorious even if it meant flaring up like a torch flame, picking up a bow to shoot or roaring like a lion. I told myself, 'I will not get tired, I will not bow down to circumstances. I will keep on walking, running and overcoming adversities to emerge victorious.'

Since I had failed in the first attempt of the UPSC prelim examination, I was not willing to take any more chances. The prelim exam required speed with accuracy. One needed to understand the multiple options with speed. More than understanding which of the four options was right, it was important to understand which three were wrong. I started taking mock tests, thrice a week, in the last three months of my preparation. I collected as many question paper sets as possible. Keeping an eye on the clock, I solved 120 questions of the optional subjects and 150 questions of general studies. We did not have a negative marking system. I could select options which sounded logical even if I wasn't sure about them.

Thanks to persistent study and practice, my mock score started increasing, day by day. This gradual improvement did wonders for my self-confidence. That year, the MPSC had announced that it would conduct its examination to fill up 350 vacant posts of Class I and Class II officers. I filled out the form. I had also appeared for the examinations for the Class III post of PSI and STI, and had passed both with flying colours.

I got a call for the physical test for the post of PSI a week before the prelim exam of the UPSC. I was not used to exercising; besides, I had lost weight due to the unhealthy food that I ate in Mumbai and Thane. I could hardly do a couple of push-ups. I could not sprint for the required 800 metres. On the day of the physical test, I went to the police ground at Naygaon. I met with PSI Kamble, who hailed from the neighbouring village. Many a time, he would visit the area near Petit Library in style, riding a Bullet motorcycle and wearing Ray-Ban sunglasses, to meet his friends. We mingled with his friends, in the hopes that he would offer us tea. He came close to me, patted my back and wished me heartily, saying, 'You are lucky, Vishwas. You must emerge victorious today. Such an opportunity comes only once in a lifetime. You too must prove that you are a tiger, like me, from the banks of the Warna River. You are sure to become a police sub-inspector.'

I mustered up my courage and strength. Teams of six candidates each had to complete two laps on the 400-metre-long track at full speed. I picked up speed immediately after the whistle was sounded but suffered cramps in my stomach after 200 metres. My speed reduced and I did the second lap walking. PSI Kamble was cheering me on, but I had no strength left to run. When I stepped out of the track, a frustrated PSI

Kambale shook me and rebuked me, saying, 'Only a loser would give up this God-sent opportunity.' I said, 'Sir, if Lady Luck smiles at me, you will be saluting me around this time next year.' He said, 'You are free to have unrealistic big dreams. Now go and study instead of wasting your time making empty promises. If you become a big boss, I would not be ashamed to salute a tiger coming from the banks of the Warna.'

Tired, I returned to my room. My entire body was aching. Nimat gave me a tablet of Combiflam. I had to revise for the prelim examination. To successfully accomplish this, I had maintained a 500-page register for general studies preparation, with 100 pages allotted to each section. Whatever I found important, I jotted down in the relevant section of the register. This ensured that I was not just dragging through the track, but carefully picking and plucking the flowers. I had stored these pearls of knowledge in the register, and it was time to realize their worth. I had also highlighted important sections in the general studies study kit and Tata McGraw Hill.

While studying, I started by reading the entire chapter first, though I understood little. During that preliminary reading, I underlined the difficult words, found their meanings in the dictionary, assigned them a number and jotted down the meaning on the margin of the same page. In the second reading, I lay emphasis on comprehension, underlining the important lines. In the third reading, I wrote down the précis of every paragraph in a line or two in my micro notes. I marked these notes with blue, red or black pencils, depending on the importance of the content. As a result, I found it easy to revise the important parts.

These three readings made my preparation wholesome and complete. Children do not get bored of reading while studying but they find writing to be tiresome. I was different as I liked to write. Therefore, I was able to jot down essays ranging from fifty to 250 words and answers to questions ranging from 60 to 200 marks without referring to other essays. This strategy helped me prepare for the main examination too. Since I had jotted down the notes meticulously, I found it easy to re-read the material. For answers to questions asked in university exams, one writes long introductions. Here, I approached the topic directly, understanding the question and writing the answer in accordance with the nature and scope of the question, doing comparisons while explaining topics. As a result, the subject was reflected in a holistic manner in my answers. Finally, I concluded my answers logically. Thus, my comprehension of the subject and capability to take decisions improved and my point of view on complex and controversial incidents became mature. My emotional and intellectual levels were enhanced to the level of an officer's. My thoroughness in my studies was reflected in the fact that I was able to correctly guess the psyche of the examiner and write my answers accordingly.

Chapter 10

Combined Campaign

When I procured admission to the arts stream, I was under the wrong impression that once I obtained a degree in arts, it would be easy to become an IAS officer. However, as I learnt more about the examination pattern, I woke up to the harsh reality the students of the science stream, particularly young engineers and doctors, dominated the final list of candidates. Those who studied in English-medium schools, especially those that followed the Central Board of Secondary Education (CBSE) syllabus, had an upper hand in the preparation of the general studies subject. Of the successful candidates, 70 per cent were either technocrats or holders of professional degrees like medical science, agriculture or law.

When it came to the Maharashtra Public Service Commission (MPSC), candidates from an agricultural background dominated because of the weight given to subjects like agriculture and horticulture. Even in the UPSC, the elite class coming from the IITs had established a monopoly by opting for high-scoring technical subjects. Once candidates with a background in medical science and engineering got acclimatized with the syllabus, they would procure question papers, reference books and notes of coaching classes. Lo and behold, they would make it to the UPSC merit list in large numbers as compared to those from other backgrounds. IIT candidates would choose mathematics and physics as optional subjects and achieve high scores and select the easy but high-scoring subjects of humanities, like geography, psychology or anthropology, master them and carve a place for themselves in the toppers' list.

To rein in these technocrats, the UPSC devised an effective strategy of introducing a new paper of essay writing of 200 marks. Candidates appearing for the examination had to write an analytical essay on a given topic over three hours. The expected word limit for these essays was 3000 to 3500 words. Engineers were unable to pretend to have expertise in this field and gain marks. For scoring in this paper, one required logical construction, mastery over language, in-depth knowledge of the subject and good handwriting. However, the UPSC tactic proved futile, as professional coaching classes geared up to this challenge.

Gradually, candidates from technical backgrounds began to crack the essay-writing paper as they procured the required knowledge. Students of engineering and medical science scored well by opting for subjects like arts and literature and writing them in Marathi or any other vernacular language. However, I could not take such a drastic and reverse decision. Having studied the science stream in my junior college, I understood topics related to statistics and science in the general studies syllabus of the UPSC. Strategies of students from the technical background and their easy adaptation to changes in the examination pattern of the UPSC—overcoming the essay paper hurdle, for example—would stress me out as it made me doubt my decision of switching to the arts stream. However, one must remember, while preparing for this competitive examination, that one is bound to face confusion, uncertainty and stress.

The pattern of the UPSC and MPSC examinations shift with changing times, with the objective of attracting quality, committed candidates. However, sometimes such policies prove harmful to the interests of the rural students. The papers of the prelim exams are set only in English or Hindi. Speed and accuracy are of prime importance in this preliminary stage. Candidates must choose the right answer from the four options provided to them, using the elimination method. From the year 2000 onwards, the UPSC implemented the system of negative marking. This means that you lose one-third of a mark if you choose the wrong option. This has upped the difficulty level of the exam as candidates cannot take a shot in the dark. The problems faced by students educated in the Marathi medium are even more complex.

Even multiple-choice questions are a big paragraph. Students from the Marathi medium take more time to read and comprehend the elaborate questions. The options provided for the answers too are lengthy and tricky. Sometimes, two or three options form a combined answer. This puts the candidate in a confused, Sudoku-like situation. Hence, there is no set formula for success in the prelim exam except relentless practice. When we appeared for the examination, we had an optional subject. Now, it has been replaced by the Civil Services Aptitude Test (CSAT). The CSAT puts rural students at a disadvantage. Candidates with a technical background emerge victorious in this paper while humanities students lose out.

Similar changes have been made in the main examination too. When we appeared for the examination, there used to be two optional subjects. One's rank would depend on the final score of these two subjects of 600 marks. Engineers from IITs would opt for physics and mathematics and score so high that we, the students of history and literature, could not come anywhere near their score, no matter how hard we studied or how well-written our answers were. Sometimes, candidates preferred odd subjects like Pali literature, psychology and anthropology because they were high-scoring subjects. We had to overcome several such contradictions and challenges. Today, things have improved as there is only one optional subject and the number of general studies papers has increased as well.

I had inadvertently blown my own trumpet, having decided to appear for the MPSC as well as the UPSC examinations. The previous year, I had successfully passed all three steps of the MPSC examination process. But in case of the UPSC examination, I was yet to succeed. If I viewed the challenge with an open and objective mind, it appeared impossible. In Greek mythology, King Sisyphus attempts to roll a huge boulder up the side of a mountain but it would roll down, over and over again, without ever reaching the top. I found myself in a similar position. However, when I closed my eyes, I could see my dreams clearly and they recharged me with the spirit and hunger to emerge victorious. I believed that I would indeed be able to face this challenge. I did not want to go wherever fate would take me. I preferred to carve my own path, consciously and judiciously. I wanted to acquire such capabilities and credentials that would allow me to script my future. It is not the situation that makes or breaks a man; it only tests his capacities.

Shivaji Maharaj was just fifteen years old when he dreamed of forming his own empire—Swarajya. He was faced with an enormous challenge—defeating the Muslim rulers. His own people put many obstacles in his path. How did he win forts and territories? How did he create an oasis of Swarajya in the deserted Sahyadri? It could only be done because he had confidence in himself, which was his biggest strength. He came, he saw and he conquered. One should find inspiration in the conviction that was reflected in his disposition, meticulous thought process and his bright and courageous life. You cannot choose your background, but your inner strength will decide your fate.

Dr Babasaheb Ambedkar's great struggle is another example that changed the course of history by turning mankind towards freedom and equality. The challenge that I was facing was small in comparison. I made a resolve to wage a war against the competitive examinations with all my might. Incidentally, there was a gap of only eight days between the prelim exams of MPSC and UPSC. The MPSC Board had made some changes, including complex subjects like agricultural factors, scientific attitude, economics, finance and so on. By now, I had developed the skill and technique of solving multiple-choice questions. Though I lacked adequate knowledge, I could zero in on the right option for the answer. I found the MPSC prelim exam quite easy. After that, I was in two minds about whether to appear for the UPSC or concentrate fully on the MPSC examination. Of course, my success was guaranteed. I went straight to the Sai Baba Temple in the Vartaknagar area of Thane to attend the evening aarti. I closed my eyes and meditated for half an hour on one of the benches. While doing so, I had a vision that I would appear for the UPSC examination. Over the next eight days, I reviewed my work of the past two and a half years. I read and re-read my micro-notes. The examination centre for the prelim examination was Sydenham College. I reached my old hostel early and had a 'cutting chai' with the watchman. The Sai Baba Temple in the barracks was closed but I took darshan of its door and left for the exam hall.

The question paper and answer sheets had been computerized. The order of the questions was different in the question papers given to every four candidates who were seated next to each other. Initially, writing the seat number and other details on the answer sheets was tedious. However, the answer sheets were distributed half an hour early, to allow time to fill in the details. General studies was the first paper. I had a tough time writing it in my previous attempt in 1994, having prepared myself by reading *Frontline*, *Manorama Yearbook* and *The Hindu*. After two and a half years of relentless hard work, I could understand English better but could not solve questions with the desired speed. This time, to study the science subject, I had referred to the McGraw Hill kit in large font. I had also read half of D.D. Basu's volume on the Constitution of India, and browsed through the expansive volume by Datt and Sundaram for economics along with NCERT's *Evolution of Economy*.

My understanding of history was enhanced by reading books by noted authors like Bipin Chandra, Romila Thapar, A.L. Basham and S.A. Rizvi. This helped me solve questions, which I had found difficult, with relative ease. The history paper, my optional subject, was scheduled after a gap of two hours. Thanks to my increased fluency in the English language, I could understand complex questions. The Hindi translation of questions was available in the adjoining page; however, this was even more difficult to comprehend. Nevertheless, by referring to both languages I could zero in on the right answer.

Though I had a firm grip on Indian history, the same wasn't true for world history. In Indian history, 120 questions are asked from the period between the Harappa civilization and the independence struggle. Of those 120 questions, 50 per cent were based on ancient history and the rest on the middle ages and modern India. In the ancient history section, questions pertaining to the culture and literature of south India proved tricky. I was thoroughly confused by words like Thiruvalluvar, Silapathikaram and Pattiruputtu. I had visited the Nehru Centre in Worli and studied the live exhibition on *The Discovery of India* for three consecutive days.

The pictorial exhibition on Nehru's book had taken me through the relevant era of history. I had found several pictorial references in it. Complex terms became easy to understand with the cloth and clay models, and the detailed descriptions scripted on the wall next to them. Some questions were related to the spread of the culture and religions of India to South-East Asia and I found their answers in the Angkor Wat Hindu Temple in Cambodia, which was also showcased in that exhibition. Today, information is readily available at your fingertips. We had to study the atlas carefully, including the appendix and indexes.

Keeping the vast syllabus in mind, one had to search for references from different books which was taxing. These aspects of study are boring and provide little joy, compared to the pleasure one derives from entertainment, friends, movies and television programmes. Sitting in a room and immersing yourself in books is a punishment. Ramdas Swami had also written about this penance that one needs to undergo during youthful years. Indeed, there is no alternative to this penance. Once we come to terms with this, the main challenge is to make one's studies easy and entertaining. Once a parrot is comfortable in his cage, he does not wish for freedom. Similarly, once we are immersed in our studies, we don't feel like breaking free. We enjoy being its slave. Since I enjoyed studying, I found the prelim exam to be easy. I was confident that I would clear it in the first attempt but that only meant that I would join the horde of 50,000 candidates, from the crowd of up to 3,50,000 candidates. The prelim served to eliminate the not-so-serious candidates, leaving only the real competitors in the race. I now had four and half months to prepare myself to compete with the serious candidates.

The main examination was of 2000 marks. There would be two papers of general studies of 300 marks each; two papers of 300 marks each of two optional subjects; and a paper on essay writing of 200 marks. Thus, the marks scored in a total of seven papers, to be solved in three hours, would be counted for the final score. Besides, passing in the compulsory papers of English and Marathi, of 300 marks each, was also required to qualify. It would have been foolish to wait for the results of the prelim exam and then start studying for the main examination. Time was precious.

I had appeared for the first year MA exam in October of the previous year and had passed with flying colours. This helped me get admission to the university hostel in Churchgate again. I was given a single-occupancy, sea-facing room on the sixth floor. This tiny room was a godsend for me. The world here comprised a cot, a table, a chair, a table lamp, a tiny gallery outside the room, a large window and me and my relentless studies. I kept my bags in the room and stood in the gallery, facing the sea. The sea breeze filled me with enthusiasm. I could not have found a better place in the whole of Mumbai. My eyes glittered with the dreams of a golden future in store for me.

There was a knock on the door and five to six seniors, pursuing their LLM at the Law College, barged into the room with a pair of binoculars. I was confused and angry. If they wanted to watch the sunset, why couldn't they watch it from the terrace? Expressing my disapproval, I told them, 'Please leave. If you want to watch the sea, please go to the terrace.' Their answer shocked me. They said, 'Wait for fifteen minutes. The bathing scene that unfolds in the apartment building across can be seen perfectly only from this room.'

They were not ready to listen to me. I did not want to spoil my first day in the hostel or my positive mood arguing with them. In a short while, the lights in a bathroom in that flat were switched on. These perverts could only make out glimpses through the gaps in the glass panes, but they enjoyed themselves nevertheless. One could not even make out whether the person bathing was a man or a woman and yet they were getting some measure of pleasure out of it. The photograph of Swami Vivekananda that hung on the wall of my room gave me the strength to politely ask them to leave my room, with a warning that I would lodge a complaint with the warden if they ever returned. Mumbling abuses at me, the group of boys left. I then went downstairs and bought some old newspapers and nails, covering the window that faced the apartment and vowing not to uncover it till the main examination was over. I did not want any distractions to hamper my studies. My penance as a student was manifested through giving up non-veg food and staying away from all temptations, at the age of twenty-two.

I began studying for the subject of Marathi literature. I kept Bhushan Gagrani's neat and to-the-point notes in front of me. His notes were a blessing for candidates appearing for the UPSC examination in the Marathi medium. Born in a Marwadi family in Kolhapur, Gagrani knew Marathi better than any professor of Marathi residing in the Sadashiv Peth area of Pune. His notes had been photocopied a thousand times. Reading his notes used to be the primary obligation of every candidate who had chosen literature as a subject. Thanks to his notes, I could comprehend the criticism and appreciation of literature.

Earlier, I was ashamed of being a Marathi manoos in Mumbai. As I began reading literature, I started feeling proud of being a Maharashtrian. The abhangs of Tukaram would give me immense pleasure. I memorized 'Pasayadan' and reciting it every day gave me tremendous self-confidence and energy. Through literature, I felt true enrichment. Whatever I understood, I noted down. My handwriting became clean and beautiful. I would write my answers and then read them. If I was not happy with them, I would write them again.

My aim was to make my answers sound logical and to ensure that they reflected my thoughts precisely and fluently. I took care to ensure that they were not mundane or monotonous. This was important. In addition to your knowledge, writing neatly in a simple way and structuring your answer precisely determines whether you'll score well or not. Literary experts like Kamlesh Walavalkar, Hemant Nimbalkar and Praveen Chavan were studying in the SIAC hostel then. I would mingle with them to discuss the style of writing and structuring answers. They gave me helpful tips. The foundation was strong, and the structure was in place; it just needed to be adorned with the appropriate language skills to tempt the examiner into shelling out more marks.

History was my favourite subject. Since I had scored sixty out of sixty in the SSC Board examination, I had chosen it as the optional subject for the civil services examination.

I had scored 90 out 100 marks in ancient Indian history in the final year of BA. I was a part of the batch where internal tests were introduced for the arts stream. These tests carried 25 per cent marks in the evaluation of the result. Good handwriting and correct grammar were my strengths. I had done my basic studies of history for my BA, but compared to the syllabus of the UPSC examination, it was like scaling the small Kalsubai Peak as opposed to climbing Mount Everest.

Over the last two and a half years, I had relentlessly worked towards developing a historic point of view, increasing my understanding of history manifold. I made a resolution to read books by acclaimed authors for my prelim examination, completing half of that reading. Nevertheless, it is the precision with which you write answers that matters for the main examination. I procured notes of Rao from Delhi, which were based on previous years' question papers. The structure of these notes filled the gaps in my knowledge, using the background information from the original books, in a concise and logical manner. I would enhance my answers with maps, which upped their quality. As for *Modern History of the World*, I used visual aids like maps and started putting them in an appropriate chronological order.

The history paper included essay-type questions worth sixty marks and short notes worth twenty. This made understanding the questions crucial. The question itself would be elaborate and consist several sub-questions. It was important to estimate how many marks would be allotted to the main question and how many to the sub questions. The keywords in a question, such as Discuss, Compare, Elaborate, Analyse, Explain and Elucidate and so on, determined the structure of the answer. The structure of the answer was as important as turning the sail of the ship towards the direction of the wind. Once I understood the concept, the appropriate words would flow from my pen. I had to work hard to translate the concepts from the notes of Rao to Marathi, which I did through the balanced use of the dictionary, notes, notebooks and books. The concepts that resulted from this hard work are still embedded in my memory. Writing down these concepts was a laborious task due to the non-availability of material in Marathi. When a larva transforms into a butterfly, it must undergo a world of struggle and it is this hardship that gives it the strength required to survive.

Candidates giving their examination in Marathi were in a similar situation, but adversity gets the best out of you and these candidates scored well in their finals. Nowadays, Marathi translations of almost all the books are available in the market. Coaching classes too have translated their old notes to Marathi. This ready-to-use study material has considerably reduced the struggle. We had to break big boulders to make pebbles. Nowadays, pampered candidates can buy a finer version of this translated material. As a result, the chances of achieving success are more for those who use their own language and style of writing. This is my experience and it is the key to success.

I was immersed in my studies, often connecting and comparing contemporary incidents in my history answers. Whenever I came across a number that I had to memorize, I would select a year out of that and memorize the events that had taken place in that year. Because of this habit, transformations taking place in Europe would feature in my answers to questions on Indian history, giving them an intellectual twist. The impact reflected in the marks.

In order to be in the toppers list, one had to score at least 60 per cent marks. I decided that my strategy would be to show leniency towards the time given to write answers where I took a calculated risk. One had to solve four out of six questions of sixty marks, giving one thirty-five minutes per question. Instead of going at this, I first solved the questions that I was the most confident about, allocating up to forty-five minutes to write a comprehensive and perfect answer. Then I would address the question for which I was less prepared, allocating thirty-five minutes to it. Then I would address the remaining two questions and take thirty minutes each to answer them.

This was how I maintained the balance between time and focus. If the examiner was impressed with the first answer and gave 40 out of 60 marks for it, he would examine the remaining answers with the same impression to evaluate my intellectual capacity. Common sense told me that in such circumstances he would give me 30–35 marks each. The risk here was that if the examiner decided to examine the paper backwards, my strategy would backfire. However, examiners seldom check papers in this manner. Nevertheless, I had to work out my strategy after considering various possibilities. I would write the remaining four short notes and the 60-mark question using visual aids like maps. Lastly, I reserved the last seven minutes to cross check my grammar.

However well you may prepare for the examination, only those who plan their answers beforehand and concentrate during the three-hour examination are successful. It takes a lot of hard work to create a three-hour-long movie. The music, acting, plot and direction are all vital. Film-making is a combination of fourteen schools of knowledge and sixty-four schools of arts. If the editing goes haywire, the film too meets the same fate. This means that there must've been a miscalculation as to how successful the film would be during the planning process. One must properly plan how to amalgamate various facets of one's strategy and fix it well before the examination. I have observed that intelligent candidates are beaten only because they did not plan ahead. As the old saying goes, 'If we fail to plan, we plan to fail.'

Time management and smart study are the deciding factors for success. It is vital to work out a minute-to-minute plan for the three hours of solving a paper, just as one plans one's studies for a year, a month, a week and a day. Relentless practice is the mantra of success, establishing one's expertise and giving one the upper hand. However boring it may be or even if you are not in a proper frame of mind and feel like throwing away your books, you must not give up on practice and revision. Once we make such a resolution, studying becomes easy.

Several candidates appearing for competitive examinations approach me to ask me the secret of my so-called success. I tell them that there is no such secret—the only secret lies in your willpower, planning, preparation, revision and hard work. This reminds me of an inspiring tale about the philosopher Socrates. A youngster met Socrates to ask him the secret of success. Socrates took him to a lake and pushed him into the water. When the water was neck deep, Socrates pushed his head under the surface of the water with his hand. When he turned black and blue and began suffocating, Socrates loosened his grip and dragged him out. Once out of the water, the youngster started breathing deeply. Socrates told him, 'You can easily achieve your target if you strive as hard for success as you struggled to inhale your breath.' There is no shortcut in the struggle to succeed in the competitive examinations.

There was no need for me to laboriously prepare for the compulsory papers of English and Marathi. The marks scored in similar languages in the MPSC examination would be counted in the final score. However, the essay paper concerned me. What and how much should be written on a topic? The marks obtained in this 200-mark question are counted in the final score. One had to write an answer on any one of the four given topics. My first task was to decide which subject of which field I should choose.

I knew that I would not be able to write a quality essay of 3000 words on subjects related to economics, science or technology. I decided to attempt an essay related to the subjects of politics, sociology or humanities. I read up on various subjects, making a 300-page notebook for writing essays. I noted down a list of thirty subjects in it and, whenever I found any new information on them, I would write a rough draft of the essays and take account of the time taken for writing them. I memorized quotes, poetry and thoughts. This helped me not only in my examination then but also now while working in the field and interacting with youngsters. Simultaneously, I was preparing the material and structure of my answers. Of the three hours available to me, I allotted the first half hour to preparing the skeletal frame of the essay. I jotted down points to plan the flow and logical structure of the essay and wrote the essay without changing the structure. I would take precautions to ensure that the qualities as well as the positive attitude required to become an officer were reflected in my essay.

And suddenly, one day, the result of the MPSC prelim examination was declared. I had passed. The result of the UPSC prelim examination was still a fortnight away. My preparation for the UPSC slowed down. For me, the bus to Delhi, which was going at top speed, suddenly halted due to a punctured tyre as the MPSC had again announced recruitment for 350 posts. Insecurity, doubt and fear of the future started haunting me again. There was no point of leaving the one bird in hand for two in the bush. I gave up on my Delhi aspirations and started studying for the main examination of the MPSC, in right earnest.

Some randomly bought books came in handy. I prepared for Paper II of general studies, concentrating on Maharashtra. In the previous attempt, I had scored well by choosing sociology though I had studied it only for a week. This time, instead of relying solely on a 150-page book, I bought books written by Iravati Karve on sociological concepts. I was already well prepared for the papers of history and general studies Paper I due to the UPSC examination. However, the nature of the examination and the standard of questions asked in the two examinations were different. I needed to steer the train of my preparation in another direction. There was too much confusion and too little time.

A fortnight later, the results of the UPSC prelim examination were announced and I had passed it too. I was in two minds now. Which examination should I prepare for? Where should I focus my energies? If I started preparing for both simultaneously, I would end up nowhere. Thankfully, the MPSC had recently changed its syllabus along the lines of the UPSC. Earlier, preparing for both the examinations simultaneously was akin to walking a tight rope. An optional paper that would give you success in one exam would mean failure in the other—so diverse was the approach. Even the schedules of the two examinations would often clash. Experts in those days would advise candidates to choose one examination.

Thankfully, recently the MPSC decided to adopt the examination pattern and syllabus complementary to the UPSC examination, to support UPSC candidates from Maharashtra. If one does some preparation centred around Maharashtra while preparing for the UPSC examination, one can secure a Class II job through MPSC. That was not so in our days. Both examinations would clash with each other, adversely impacting the candidates from Maharashtra. They would not succeed in either of the examinations. I too faced a similar situation, but there was no alternative to play a twenty-twenty match. I resolved to make a boundary for every oncoming ball and worked out a schedule and a strategy to appear for both examinations. Since I had the experience of going through the main examination of MPSC, I had an inside view of the examination process. Therefore, I aimed to conquer Mount Everest by reassuring myself that I would be able to conquer Kalsubai Peak too. I got serious and devoted myself to the preparations.

One needs to do selective and intensive study for the main examination, analysing the question papers and the syllabus of the previous years and predicting the questions likely to be asked. I picked up clues from whatever I could lay my hands on and fit it in my study frame. I read everything from the government-run magazines *Yojana* and *Lokrajya* to reference books for the civil services. It was difficult to write on subjects like political science, science and technology, and statistics in Marathi. I had to face several complex questions and difficult situations simultaneously. Maybe it was a preview of the situations one faces while battling natural calamities, law and order skirmishes or terrorism, working as a government servant. It tested my capacities and my personality to the fullest.

With every passing day, I could feel my brain becoming sharper and more versatile. When I was the district superintendent of police in Thane, eighteen dacoits had struck a jewellery shop in Vikramgarh, seriously injuring the jeweller and fleeing to the forests with jewels worth lakhs of rupees.

They were the dangerous fraternity dacoits belonging to the Jhabua district of Madhya Pradesh. Their speciality was to hurl stones at the people chasing them while they were running. I happened to be present at the Wada Police Station, twenty kilometres from the crime scene.

I summoned reinforcements, sought help from the local villagers and laid out a plan. We nabbed seventeen dacoits and the eighteenth one was killed after he opened fire. The police arrested the dacoits as well as their weapons and recovered the stolen goods. The government awarded our team with a prize of Rs 1 lakh, a considerable sum back then. We had studied the strategy and psychology of the dacoits well and taken into confidence the locals who knew the forests inside out. We had obtained their physical descriptions from the CCTV footage and put everyone on alert. Around 300 policemen and 1000 locals cordoned off the entire forest and the plan proved successful.

The examination was no different. One who identifies the enemy's strategy, chooses the right weapon and uses it effectively in conjunction with the right tactics is bound to win. Keeping your weapons sharp and practising with them is also equally important. As the great philosopher Confucius said, 'I hear and I forget, I see and I remember, I do and I understand.' Thus, what one only hears, one is bound to forget. What one only sees, one is bound to remember only for a few days but what one does by practising, one will retain forever. The one who practises by writing will both comprehend and remember.

Both the main examinations were scheduled within two months of each other—sometime during the months of October–November in 1996. Luckily, none of the papers clashed. I had to solve six papers of a total of 800 marks including two language papers, two papers each of general studies and my optional subjects for the MPSC exam.

For the UPSC exam, I had to solve nine papers for a total of 2000 marks consisting of two papers of general studies, four papers of optional subjects, two papers of language and one essay paper. In short, I had to solve a total of fifteen papers, of three hours each. These did not comprise the multiple-choice objective questions like in the prelim exams. They contained detailed answers which meant that every answer sheet would contain 4500–5000 words and would be as long as thirty-five pages.

I had to familiarize myself with every subject, the context, the types of study and acquire the material required to have firm knowledge base. I had to build it brick by brick. Only then could I succeed in these exams. My Luxor pens became my sword. Vikas was in Mumbai. He would see to it that I was provided with my daily tiffin and stationery. He would travel to Dadar to get 0.6 point Zebra or Luxor pens for me. I had subscribed to the monthly tiffin as I had vowed to be a vegetarian. I ate only to survive and not to savour the taste of food, curbing the risk of suffering from gas or acidity. Remembering all that Dr Uncle had taught me, I began practicing pranayama every day.

My brain sharpens through the recital of Omkar, and breathing exercises like Bhasrika, Kapalbhati, Anulom-Vilom and Bhramari recharged my battery. I was gearing up for the fight, round the clock. I had to learn about global and national issues, conquering fifteen battlefields of examinations, the way Napoleon had proved his might across Europe or the way Chhatrapati Shivaji Maharaj had conquered Karnataka. I had to display similar willpower and war strategies. Finally, the day of the combat arrived.

In November 1996, the nation was celebrating the Hero Cup. I could hear the shouts and cries raised during the cricket match at the Wankhede Stadium in my hostel room. The entire hostel would gather in front of the television set in the canteen to watch these matches. My concentration wavered and distraction settled in when I would find out that Sachin was batting. Since they were day and night cricket matches, the noise continued until late in the night. I had to ensure that I slept soundly on the night before an examination. I would drink half a litre of milk straight from the plastic pouches to ensure a good night's sleep.

For breakfast, I would have two bananas. I would always keep two packets of Glucon-D and Parle-G biscuits and two bananas in my haversack. The top pocket of my haversack contained the sacred ash of Ninai Devi, which my mother had sent from the village. The middle pocket contained a writing pad and micro notes for the subject of my examination that day. My compass box contained four Luxor pens, two pencils, an eraser, a sharpener and a ruler. In case my wristwatch stopped working, I would also carry a small desk clock. I would also carry a water bottle, which I would finish before the paper got over. After the exam, I would go to a restaurant or the water faucet at the railway station or any other public tap to refill it. Today, I find it risky to drink even the purified water in restaurants. When I order mineral water, I tell my children about the past. They tease me saying, 'Bhide Guruji, do not lecture us.' How can I blame them when I sneeze and my throat gets sore if I accidentally gulp water kept in a steel utensil on the table when I attend programmes? Perhaps the body's immunity reduces as one grows older.

When I was young, mosquitoes, bed bugs, fleas, flies, rats and cockroaches would bite me as I slept. However, I slept so soundly that I would not even realize it. I would guess which insect had bitten me, going by the size of rashes on my body the next morning. At times, rats would nibble at my legs, but I never suffered from fever or any other disease. Maybe the daily encounters with insects built up my resistance to disease. Today, if a mosquito strays into my room, I cannot sleep until I find it and kill it. The mere sight of a rat in the house makes us feel as if we have already caught an infection from it.

While I was training at Gadchiroli, we were asked to go with the C60 team for Long Range Patrolling (LRP). The commander did not permit us to carry water. My throat was parched after walking twenty kilometres in the humid weather, carrying a haversack and AK-48. We spotted a fly-infested swamp with murky waters. The commander said we could drink that water. When one faces adversities in a war-like situation, one does not get five-star facilities. And yes, on the night of 26/11 Mumbai terror attack, we had entered the Taj around quarter to ten at night on an empty stomach. After a five-hour long battle, when we reached the ballroom on the first floor, we were forced to eat a half-eaten apple thrown by someone and pieces of wafers, crushed under people's feet, to regain our energy. This is the reason why preparation for the civil services examination tests your capacity and patience to the fullest. The examination process may seem challenging in the beginning. Ultimately, it moulds you to use your personality, chiselled out of penance, and overcome any trials and tribulations without feeling exhausted or defeated.

Finally, the exhausting, merciless and deceptive main examination commenced. The first two papers were of language, which I wrote without any difficulty. I had to return to the room at the earliest, to get the maximum time to study for the next paper, which was general studies. To hasten my return journey, I boarded a taxi at the Sales Tax Bhavan in Mazgaon. The next paper was in two days. In the syllabus of general studies, I liked the topics of modern Indian history, with the thoughts of Gandhi, Nehru and Tagore, the Indian political system, current affairs and geography. However, I could never keep up with economics, statistics and science and technology, like a wrestler who neglects to build one part of his body which becomes the weak link.

Examiners would have found it difficult to do a balanced evaluation of my knowledge of general studies. The paper was made up of a variety of questions, from 250-word short notes to definitions in under twenty words. Patiently, I read all the topics within two days and I felt as if my performance was akin to that of a batsman playing a twenty-twenty match. I put in my best efforts to solve all the questions as speedily as I could. VOIP phones and microwave ovens were newly introduced in the market. I attempted to explain them in Marathi without really knowing anything about them. On the question on the partition of Bengal, I wrote my answer like a batsman who goes all out to hit a sixer on a full-toss ball.

I wrote a lucid note on habeas corpus, explaining its contemporary importance in spreading awareness about human rights. I explained Gandhiji's concept of the 'Seven Social Sins' in elaborate detail, linking them to his quote, 'The world has enough for everyone's need, but not enough for everyone's greed.' I interpreted this thought by first identifying the dangers of the seven sins—politics without principles, knowledge without character, science without humanity, pleasure without conscience, commerce without morality, wealth without work and religion without sacrifice—then referring to our virtuous and glorious past, rectifying our mistakes in time and linking the modern approach with the traditional for the next generation to prove to be superior—physically, mentally and spiritually. I do not recall if questions related to economics were asked.

Since I was a student of the science stream in high school and had a flair for mathematics, I found both statistics papers relatively easy. At last, I had rid myself of the burden of 600 marks and felt relieved.

The next paper was essay writing. Sitting in the same spot for three hours and writing an essay of 200 marks was a major challenge. I would get a mental block even while writing sixty marks worth 650–700-word answer for optional subjects. Writing a 3000-word essay would be my final test of English comprehension. I held one page in my hand. For the essay, I had to choose from one of the three topics provided in the question paper. The first topic was 'Safety and Empowerment of Women'—this was not only related to humanities but it was one of the five topics that I had prepared for in advance. Since I was well versed in it, I did not have to plan the structure of the essay. Straightaway, I began writing, penning down my thoughts on this sensitive yet important topic. Of course, I started my essay by linking it to ancient Indian culture and quoting the Sanskrit couplet:

यत्रनार्यस्तुपूज्यन्ते, रमन्तेतत्रदेवता:|
यत्रेतास्तुनपूज्यन्ते, सर्वास्तत्राफला: क्रिया||

(The gods reside where women are respected and where they are humiliated and subjected to atrocities, nothing proves successful.)

After this positive note I elaborated on how, barring a few exceptions, the fundamental rights of women were denied in the ancient and middle ages and how they were forced to live under degrading circumstances. Referring to customs and traditions like the humiliating life of widows, sati, denial of education, female foeticide, child marriage, custom of purdah (veil), jauhar (mass self-immolation of women to avoid capture by invaders during war), *devdasi* (a girl dedicated to a deity in a temple), *janana* and dowry, I elaborated on how such negative customs and traditions resulted in the unabated exploitation of women and their treatment as subhuman members of society. I also put forth the groundbreaking and pioneering roles assumed by women diplomats and politicians like Razia Sultan, Chand Bibi, Rani Durgavati of Gond, Noor Jehan, Jijau as well as women saints like Akka Mahadevi and Janabai.

I proceeded to discuss the contributions of the British rulers and Indian social reformers towards the empowerment of women. I also wrote in detail about the range of measures taken post-Independence through provisions laid down in the Constitution of India and various laws to uplift Indian women. I also delved into the importance of education in women empowerment as well as the representation of women in politics and positions of power. I referred to the atrocities faced by women, starting right from the household, including pre-natal sex discernment and female foeticide, domestic violence, eve teasing and molestation, sexual harassment in the workplace, rape, dowry deaths, acid attacks and so on. I expressed my views on the present situation relating to the enforcement of laws, the loopholes in them and the lackadaisical attitude of the judicial system along with the changes required to transform the current pathetic status.

I had touched upon all the possible angles of the topic including if the mere promulgation of laws could change the situation. But I wondered if my thoughts were enough to drive home my point of view. Comparing the situation of women when I wrote that essay to the present time, I can easily recall several terrifying cases that have led to stronger laws for women's protection. One can cite several legal remedies such as women's safety committees, fast-track courts, Criminal Law (Amendment) Act of 2013 and POCSA law, the Protection of Women from Domestic Violence Act, IT Act, Vishakha Guidelines, Damini Squads, PCPNDT Act and PITA law, but do our sisters feel safe in this society? Why hasn't the situation prevailing in rural areas changed? High-profile cases like the Nirbhaya case continue to shock the entire nation and raise a question mark on the safety of Indian women at international forums.

Once I had gone for a surprise visit to the police station in Shikrapur near Pune. A village woman was sitting in a corner of the police station with her three daughters. I approached her and tried to understand her problem. She had balled up the end of the saree to cover her mouth. When she saw me approaching, she removed the blood-stained ball and I saw blood oozing from her lips. She opened the fist of her left hand to show me the six or seven teeth she had lost. She was unable to speak clearly. Her eldest daughter, who was about eight or nine, yelled, 'Our father bashed her face with a grinding stone because we have no brother.'

The girl's words made me boil with anger. I yelled at the police inspector there for making her sit in the police station in that condition and directed him to take her to the hospital immediately. I also ordered him to file a case of Indian Penal Code section 307, which deals with attempted murder, based on her first information report (FIR), and arrest her husband. When the motherly soul realized the orders I had given, she fell at my feet even in that condition, pleading, 'Sir, please do not jail my husband. My three daughters will be forced to beg on the street if that happens. He drinks and beats me up. He does not give me money for household expenses. Just make life tolerable for me.'

I failed to understand her psyche. When I studied women's empowerment, I did not know that such incidents took place. How long would she suffer brutality at her husband's hands? One day, when she could no longer take it, she would take the drastic decision of ending her life along with her daughters'. Such incidents happen every day. We choose to remain silent, apathetic spectators. Does a woman find true liberation wearing jeans and T-shirts or using four-wheelers and mobile phones? The urban woman, free from the chulha and children, is now trapped by ovens and television serials. She is busy attending kitty parties. How many educated women have come forward to help their hapless rural sisters? I have no answer to these questions. I just don't know. I am flummoxed.

Twenty years ago, the poet Kusumagraj wrote a poem titled 'Swatantryadevatechi Vinavani' (Prayer to the Goddess of Freedom). Its two lines are directed at men. They are:

समान मानव माना स्त्रीला, तिचीअस्मिता खुडू नका
देवी म्हणुनी भजू नका की दासी म्हणुनी पिटू नका

(Consider a woman as a fellow human being. Do not hurt her self-esteem. Do not worship her as a goddess or do not treat her like a slave nor thrash her.)

What does a woman expect from us men? Respect, affection, a glance of love and a secure environment. Whom should she believe when she leaves her parents, her house, erases her entire past and enters a new world? Even in this age when LPG stoves have become common, stove explosions occur after marriage, a newlywed slips into the well while washing clothes and the life of a battered woman is lost.

The grieving parents cry themselves hoarse and relatives intervene but, in most cases, money silences the noise. In rare incidents, cases are filed.

Jewellery, utensils and the dowry given in the wedding are returned and an amount of Rs 50,000–60,000 exchanges hands to silence the girl's family. The parents accept this compromise, keeping the future of their other daughter in mind. Everybody asks, 'Will approaching the police revive the dead girl?' It only takes a few days for everybody to forget about the incident and the husband soon remarries. The girl's parents wed the other daughter with much pomp. But the spirit of the dead woman remains restless. Her small dreams had come to an untimely end. Every day two or three such cases of accidental death take place in the district. Deputy superintendents of police visit the scene of crime but due to their indifference, 90 per cent of such cases are disposed of. In the remaining incidents, cases are filed but to what end? The blood relatives turn into hostile witnesses when the case comes to trial and sell themselves for a few rupees, unmindful of the young woman whose life has been snuffed out. Those related to her and those who are a part of the justice process are silenced, by hook or crook.

After all this, we claim to follow our age-old customs and traditions. Women are worth worshipping and protecting because they tend to the home and bear children. But what does she ultimately get? All her life, she has been a giver. What is her own identity? What is the purpose of her existence? In most cases, labouring for everyone around her, she fades from her life one day, leaving behind the fragrance of her good deeds and blessings for every member of the family.

Therefore, the only way to women empowerment and safety is the relentless pursuit of studies and untiring hard

work. These issues will be addressed only if girls resolve to
stand on their own feet. In our batch of seventy Indian Police
Service probationers, five were women. One of them was
Bharati Jajoria. When there were swimming competitions
during the aquatic meet, male probationers would swim in
different tracks, but Bharati alone won medals in all the events
including freestyle, breaststroke, backstroke and butterfly. She
also won horse-riding competitions. This proves that we need
to think outside of common stereotypes. All terminologies
attributed to women, such as 'delicate', 'housewife', 'helpless'
and 'beautiful' need to be done away with and women need
to become strong, independent, self-reliant, competent and
powerful. They can do that by studying, being ambitious and
putting in maximum effort.

When my daughter was seven years old, I took her
to meet A.P.J. Abdul Kalam. She couldn't get enough of
listening to him on television. She could not comprehend
all his words, but she could fathom his love for children, the
positivity he effused and his desire to help the needy. Only
those who dream reach their destinations. Kalam Sir taught
us how to dream. He gave us a new-found confidence, a new
hope and the optimism to fight for our dreams. When Sir
asked Janhavi, 'Yes, my child, what do you want to become
in your life? Do you want to become an IPS officer like your
father?' Janhavi promptly answered, 'No Sir, I want to become
Dr A.P.J. Abdul Kalam.'

One must aim high. At the top, competition is scarce,
though the road is tough. There are several idols like Mother
Teresa, Kalpana Chawla, Sunita Williams, Helen Keller, Rani
Laxmibai, Mata Jijau and Savitribai Phule who overcame all
odds with hard work and carved a space for themselves during
their lifetime. Girls must believe that they too can fly high

and become victorious like them. Swami Vivekanand says, 'No bird can fly with one wing.' Indeed, the need of the hour is to strengthen both wings of society to make the whole of India powerful and capable. One must resolve to strengthen their wings to bring their dreams to reality. Women must become so capable and independent that nobody would ever dare to say that women and animals must be flogged.

Major amendments were made in the Indian Penal Code (IPC) after the Nirbhaya case. The definition of rape has been made more comprehensive. Provision of capital punishment for those committing rape on two or more occasions has been made. The scope of the offence of molestation has also been increased. Medical tests, which were humiliating for victims, have been done away with. Measures have been taken for the rehabilitation of such victims under the Manodhairya Yojana. The POCSA Act has provided for stringent punishment for offences against children. Despite these measures, such offences are taking place every day. What can be done to prevent such crimes? Statistics of the last five years show that in 7380 of the total 7850 rape cases, the victim was acquainted with the accused. Further analysis revealed that 37 per cent of them were neighbours, 17 per cent were friends, 8 per cent were lovers, 6 per cent were relatives, 3 per cent were parents and 1 per cent were teachers. Of the total number of victims, 35 per cent were in the age group of fourteen to eighteen years. Most importantly, a majority of rapes take place in the home. How can we make our homes and society safe and reliable?

I would like to share with my young sisters some knowledge that I have gained. The first step towards self-protection is to have proper knowledge of the surroundings and the intention of the attacker. It is most important to shock the attacker before physical contact is made, and escape from his clutches. When I was working as additional commissioner of police in the western Mumbai region, an unfortunate incident took place. An offender who had been arrested for several crimes previously had raped a German girl brutally. We arrested him within twenty-four hours.

A lesson should be learnt from that incident. Both watchmen deployed in the apartment where the young girl lived were fast asleep on the night of the crime. Hers was the only flat which did not have a safety grill on the windows. The burglar, therefore, targeted her flat. He climbed up a sewage pipe to the fourth floor of the building, a la Spider-Man. The girl had not closed the window from the inside, enabling him to force himself inside the flat. Even her bedroom door was ajar. Therefore, the burglar, who had broken into her home with the intention of committing a theft, was able to attack the helpless girl with a kitchen knife.

She somehow managed to escape and started banging on the door of the neighbouring flat, unaware that it was locked from the outside. The burglar pounced on her again. She could have escaped had she run down the staircase. The incident would have been averted had she shut the doors and windows properly before going to sleep, if safety grills had been installed on the windows of her flat, if she had known about the absence of her neighbours, if the security guards had been awake and alert, if the building had a wall compound or if the sewage pipes been covered with barbed wires. Therefore, making use of your sixth sense is of utmost importance. One should practise escaping from such a situation over the option of attacking the attacker, through simulated practice.

However, if launching a counterattack is your only option, you should do so, without holding back. One needs to be fully trained in self-defence. The woman puts herself in more danger by getting confused or opting to cooperate with the perverted attacker, fearing that a counterattack may anger him further. It is also of vital importance that you should launch the attack; moreover, ensure that the attack is rapid. You may get the opportunity to attack only once and you should never waste it. Target the delicate parts of the attacker's body like the throat, stomach, temple, chin, eyes or kneecaps. If he is standing in front of you, kick him in the groin with your knee. If he is trying to overpower you from behind, hit him in the stomach with your elbow. Make use of items like a pen, a pencil, lemon juice, a keychain, an umbrella or pepper spray that are readily available to you. Use your brain and body, as the situation warrants.

In today's era of information technology, you may come across con artists and frauds on social media who may try to exploit you emotionally. Therefore, one must be extremely cautious while sharing one's real identity, name, address and photos with others on Facebook or WhatsApp. Parents must keep a watchful eye on the online activities of their wards. Instead of policing their wards, they should ensure that there is mutual confidence between them. Teenagers hardly ever understand the difference between good and bad things. Parents must monitor the whereabouts of their children. Your daughter may be inadvertently going to a dangerous place with a potential rapist, camouflaged as a boyfriend.

One should never be in the company of those who speak about aggression, violence, drugs, liquor or weapons. One should be cautious about those who intentionally bring up sexual topics while chatting. Always remember that in case of a sexual assault, escaping is possible only in the few initial moments. One must use all means available to them, without inhibition. Lastly, if unfortunately a girl falls prey to such atrocities, she should never blame herself. She must find the courage to come forward to ensure that the offender who has committed the crime against her is punished. Never let yourself slip into the mire of frustration or guilt. In such circumstances, it is essential for parents to be compassionate and sensitive to help their child overcome the shock and trauma.

I was immensely relieved after sitting for the essay-writing paper. Next, I had to prepare for history, a subject I had ably mastered. The scope of history is enormous so I had prepared on various periods of history such as ancient and the middle ages, modern history of India and modern history of the world. Questions were generally asked on kings and emperors, wars and treaties and contemporary civilizations. The format of the question paper was such that questions were asked on a wide range of topics, from art, literature and culture to the social and general conditions of the lowest strata of society.

The paper was for 300 marks, containing three questions of 60 marks each and six short comments of 20 marks each. One of the questions was invariably on maps. We were asked to pinpoint the given places on a map and describe their importance in fifty words. My proficiency in history was undeniable. I shouldn't say it myself, but I did write with creditable speed. I checked it too, front to back and then back to front, and still managed to complete five minutes before time. I handed it over to the supervisor with a triumphant mien.

There is a vast difference between the examinee's body language before he gets the question paper and after the last bell tolls. Still, the war was far from over. The paper on Marathi literature was a fortnight away. But I had to write six papers in three days for the MPSC final. This was a truly warlike condition. My fingers ached; my brain power got thoroughly drained; my limbs began to hobble. But I firmly stood my ground and never got diverted from the thoughts of the race. I was fighting the war of life.

During life-threatening situations, your abilities are whisked out of the bedrock. It happened to me too, not only this once but several times later as well. I remember I was an SP, posted in Latur, about to celebrate the first birthday of our daughter Janhavi. Since the day before our house had been crammed with guests. So I had decided to 'rest' at the rest house of the main police station. My plan was to go home in the morning and enjoy the day. I had spent the after-duty hours doing my share in the function. So I was bone-tired and slept like a log the moment I touched the bed.

At 3 a.m. I got whisked to wakefulness by the ring of the phone. A robbery had been perpetrated at Karepur, close to Renapur. An eighty-year-old woman had been murdered during it. The police managed to locate three of the robbers near a farm at Renapur. A chase ensued. With the help of the locals, we formed three concentric circles round the area, continuing to chase the perpetrators all the time. After a chase of sixty-two hours, we succeeded in apprehending them.

One of them hit back at us with stones; but he then jumped into a well and died instantly, for the well barely had 6 inches of water. The other two we nabbed. The young criminal who had committed suicide had fingernail marks on his face. Remnants of his skin were found under the old woman's nails.

The duo that we had taken captive had a hair-raising account to share. The robbers had tried to take off a necklace that the old woman was wearing. Her resistance had been unforgettable—truly of a very high order. She had clawed at them with her sharp nails. Aggravated, they had slashed her abdomen with a sharp weapon, and even after taking away her necklace they had strangulated her. But till her final breath she had continued to claw. Her fight had been unbelievably nonpareil!

The robbery, one of the most monstrous and horrifying, had been perpetrated by members of a particular tribe. The crime brought to our notice one striking detail: the devils had run a distance of sixty-two kilometres within five hours. Their speed and stamina were of a very high order. That suddenly stemmed an oblique thought: 'Young men! If at all you had participated in the Olympic games or in a marathon and given an example of your outstanding speed, you would surely have won at least one medal for our country.' Such talented youngsters are found all over the country. There is a dire need to provide them with constructive outlets that would get their energy on to a proper track.

Investigation of that crime had squeezed the last drop of my strength and truly tested my worth—I was distress about the old woman's incomparable struggle in her hour of death as well as struck by the robbers' amazing determination to run for their life. As I have said before, such ability is whisked out of one's bedrock only when one's very existence is threatened. The UPSC is one such life-threatening situation. Anyone who jumps into the fray with all his might, willpower and preparedness, fearing and therefore confronting the life-ending situation, emerges a winner.

Recently, I have been obsessed with running marathons of twenty-one kilometres. In the beginning, covering such long a distance at a steady speed of 10 or 11 kmph seemed unachievable. But when I saw octogenarian women completing the run, my interest in it, and confidence in myself, got triggered.

In 2013, I fixed a goal to complete a half marathon in two hours. I began to practise with a group of young policemen. I made a small beginning with a distance of five kilometres. Then, I began to increase the run by 2 km every week. Small though it was, it did a lot to bolster my confidence. By December I was confident that I would complete a 21-km run in two hours, give or take a few minutes.

But by a strange coincidence, Umang, a function organized by the police force, coincided with the eve of the marathon. I happened to be given charge of its management. I had been standing for eight hours the day before the marathon. Earlier, at another function, a stampede in Mumbai had claimed twenty-eight lives. The incident had spread shadows of deep anxiety. Everybody in the force, including the commissioner, laboured under enormous stress.

The function ended at 1 a.m. By the time I had dinner and made it to the office, it was 2.30 a.m. What with the late meal and the stressful day, I had a splitting headache. I tried to catch a few winks at the Bandra office but failed. I couldn't fall asleep. I still might have caught half an hour's slumber, but it was not to be! The ring of the 5 a.m. alarm that I had set got me out of bed. I had severe body ache. Acidity, too, was giving me pain. Not a single organ in my body flashed the green signal. However, my mind kept dragging me to the starting line of the marathon at the Bandra Sea Link.

The poet Bahinabai has said:

Mind is but a bird. How can I describe its wont?
Now it was here; now it went up in sky.

Once the mind hits irrepressibly on something, the body has no choice but to comply. I got into my sports kit and reached the starting line barely 2–3 minutes before the starting whistle. Krishnaprakash and Anil Ambani were already there, going through the preliminaries. Atul Karwal, our ADOD at the academy, had come with his daughters to participate in the run. Karwal Sir rushed to me as soon as he saw me; he held my hand in a strong grip and gave me good wishes. That touch galvanized my entire body. The aches and pains vaporized magically. This IPS officer, fifty years old, and a maverick, has climbed Mount Everest. He has travelled all over India on a bicycle and has the highest belts in martial arts. He is still lean, smart and stern, and has a penetrating glare.

I had been Karwal Sir's favourite probationer at the academy. I now wanted to prove to him that I had followed in his footsteps and improved my fitness level. At the sight of him I felt such uncanny energy that I took off like a horse. But when I reached the Peddar Road climb, I kept losing my breath; I panted and had cramps in my calves. Both sides of the road were thronged with people who were cheering and whistling to motivate the runners. But here I was slowing down! By now I had a twitch in my foot too. Four jawans of Force 1 caught up with me. 'Collect yourself, sir. Pump a tad strength into your body. Only a slight distance remains,' they said in an assuring voice.

I did. The exhaustion was swept off by their concern. My legs caught up speed. The climb, too, was over. I got back into my earlier rhythm and began to run with the jawans. Rupa, my wife, and Janhavi and Ranveer, my children, had been standing at Marine Drive for a long time.

'Run, Daddy! You have to be the first!' Ranveer said as he handed to me a bottle of Gatorade. Hundreds of runners were ahead of me already. But then the boy always regarded me as Superman. He was no different from all the other sons who put their fathers on a high pedestal.

I did overtake a few jawans. That elevated the boy's fervour. 'That is the spirit, Daddy! Pick up speed!' he yelled. I crossed Churchgate and reached Hutatma Chowk, from where I could see the last stretch of 500 metres. My wristwatch showed four minutes short of two hours. My target had been to cover the distance in two hours. Keeping that in mind, I commanded my aching legs to go for the final sprint. They did. I crossed the finishing line with ease. The watch showed 7:57:15.

I had completed the marathon. But as soon as I stepped beyond the finish line, my strength got drained. I nearly collapsed. My aides propped me up, seated me and took off my shoes. When they peeled off my socks, they saw that the nails of both my big toes had fallen out. Unsightly blood drops were dripping out of them. I was rushed to the Bombay Hospital. Yet I remained impervious to the pain, for I had had the satisfaction of having reached my target. The point is, any competitive exam is precisely like the above experience. It tests every fibre in your body and mind.

In the timetable for the main exam of the UPSC papers on literature followed the mainstream papers, approximately after a gap of a month. However, during this month I had to face the MPSC the challenge of the main exam too, which had had a timetable that was intertwined with the UPSC's. But I had the previous year's experience to fall back on and was more proficient in sociology. My mellowness had doubled during the past year a and a half. I had begun to randomly catch up with my reading about Maharashtra. *Yojana* and *Lokrajya*, periodicals published by the Government of Maharashtra, had solidified my base of general knowledge. The magazine *Guide to Competitive Examinations* had automatically got me ready for paper II. *Circle*, too, was of immense help.

Generally, in the timetable of the UPSC main examination, the literature paper would be scheduled a month after the main subjects. During that period, I had to simultaneously face the challenge of appearing for the main MPSC examination. I had the experience of the previous year in my repertoire. I now knew the subject of sociology. In the previous one and a half years, I had matured twofold. I had read about the various schemes implemented by the Maharashtra State Government and read every issue of the *Lokrajya* magazine in detail. This strategy strengthened my foundation for the preparation of the general studies paper. Study Circle's *Spardha Pariksha Margdarshak* magazine also proved to be helpful. I prepared for the general studies Paper II, laying emphasis on Maharashtra while preparing for the last interview. I solved all eight papers of the MPSC examination in four consecutive days and appeared for two papers a day. I would reserve the last ten minutes of the examination time to crosscheck my answer sheets. I could foresee my future success in those thirty to thirty-two pages and felt a sense of satisfaction. When you run a marathon, your toes are bound to get injured. The condition of fingers after continuously writing answers without a break is similar. Moreover, I had the bad habit of holding the pen tightly and pressing it hard on the paper. As a result, my fingers would stiffen up like those of a corpse, due to rigor mortis. After the exam, I would massage them with oil, preparing for the papers scheduled for the next day. At times, sitting for two papers without a break and spending another six hours studying at my desk would make my back ache. But the exercises of Suryanamaskara and push-ups provided a measure of relief. Once, I did two sets of Suryanamaskaras while chanting the name of the sun god and found that every disc in my spine and every cell in my body was recharged with new energy and vigour.

Ten days after the main MPSC examination, my last two papers of Marathi literature for the UPSC examination were due. I had thoroughly revised Marathi literature. As India reached the finals of the Hero Cup tournament, winning all the matches one by one, I revised every chapter till the night before the examination. India was to face South Africa in the finals of the Hero Cup on that night. The cheers that arose with every ball could be heard in my room. I was trying to give the finishing touches to my preparation, but I could not concentrate. I increased the speed of the fan and tried to fall asleep, but the cheers and whistles resonated in my ears. India had won the Hero Cup; I too wanted to win the battle of UPSC. I woke up early and freshened up. I could not find any taxi to reach Chhatrapati Shivaji Terminus (CST) due to the hangover of the Hero Cup finals.

So decided to walk to the station via a short cut. This entailed crossing the CST railway track through a tunnel, and I was scared of getting caught by the ticket checker. At times, druggies too assaulted a lone walker. I was drenched in sweat by the time I reached this spot. The upshot is that I made it to the CST, boarded a train, got down at Mazgaon and again had a walk of ten minutes to make it to the Sales Tax Bhavan. The first paper was criticism, grammar and history of literature. I had a sound grip over criticism and history of literature.

In the second paper I discovered a question on Saint Tukaram, a known non-conformist. I bubbled with joy like a small boy who had been given a lollipop. I had read the entire collection of Tukaram's verses. So my answers turned out to be perfect. I handled the questions on Hari Narayan Apte's

Pan Lakshat Kon Gheto? and Ram Gadkari's *Ekach Pyala*, too, with the flair of a batsman hitting a six. And, hey presto!—the exams were over! Still, I had no idea if I would cross this final hurdle or would get back to the zero position as in a game of snakes and ladders.

Anyway, this time I had appeared for both the exams of the Public Service Commission. So my flicker of a hope was blooming into a blaze that hinted that I would hit the target board at some place, if not the bull's-eye, and find some government job. That led to my having fulsome fun in Mumbai. My definition of fun was to wander through the milling crowds, see a couple of Bollywood movies, visit relatives and, if possible, have a few meals at restaurants. At all times, my friends from Kokrud and a posse of relatives from the village remained my source of comfort. I never got sight of the side of the city that I see these days.

When I was barely twenty-three years old, I was deeply curious about and attracted by the lifestyle of Mumbai's upper echelons. My eyes widened when I witnessed the crowd in pubs. I felt envious when I saw beautiful girls hugging their drunk boyfriends. I would see the crowd at discotheques after watching the night show of a movie and watch the spoilt brats of rich and influential fathers. However, when I became additional commissioner of police in Mumbai, I clashed with this maddening night life. When I conducted raids on rave parties at pubs and discotheques, I came under fire from the so-called elite class for encroaching upon their 'privacy' and several doubts were raised. I could watch this culture closely. Today, I feel pity for the same youngsters. I feel it is my duty to address youngsters with a few horrifying experiences I had during raids conducted at raves.

It is of the utmost importance to understand how frivolous and bogus the world that attracts us in our twenties is. Post the raids, the blood and urine samples of the young boys and girls who had participated in these parties were sent for analysis. The medical examinations had proved that, of the 500 boys and girls who had participated in the three rave parties handled by me in Pune and Juhu, more than 90 per cent had consumed drugs. This figure should awaken society, which is high on the modern lifestyle. Rave parties are all-night dance events with intoxicating music and drugs aplenty. Under the effect of drugs, every sensation is amplified. The perversions of Western culture have had a huge impact on Indian youngsters, which I found painful to witness at first hand. The smoke billowing from the *chillum* while smoking hashish, the maddening instrumental beats played by the DJ and the children dancing lewdly were unbearable to watch. Eighty per cent of them were weak, skinny and looked as if they were ailing. Upper-class youngsters have all the comforts in their twenties. They have money, mobile phones and other electronics, cars and, at times, even separate flats in the name of privacy. Many of them tread the wrong path. Addiction to cigarettes and alcoholism is common. Moreover, some of them get addicted to drugs and ruin their bodies and lives forever.

The first drag, puffed, just to get a kick, makes one addicted. One runs after the euphoria of drugs which drives away all worries. The amphetamines consumed to stay awake during the examinations drive you to drugs like cocaine and speed. The consumption of tablets of the barbiturate group gets one hooked to opium, morphine and heroin. The hallucination one experiences with a drag of hashish drives one to LSD.

This kick gradually takes over the function of the central nervous system. The substances seep into every blood cell and enslave the brain. That is just the beginning of the monstrous perversions. These youths are tempted to commit crimes and attempt suicide when they fail to get drugs. Several tread the murky paths of the underworld. Several become mental patients, landing up in correctional institutions for a lifetime, finding themselves mired in the imaginary whirlpools of hallucinations.

What is the solution to all these issues? How do we stop the young generation from losing their conscience and consciousness in this 'masti ki pathshala'? Nobody addresses these issues in schools or colleges. When a raid is conducted, debates are held in the electronic and print media for TRPs and columns in newspapers are filled, and gradually things go back to square one. Thanks to the changed economic policy, our social and family lives are undergoing a sea change. Trends from western countries are knocking at our doors, sneaking into our daily lives through the internet, print and audio-visual media. The arrival of positive, constructive and healthy changes is always welcome. Should we accept something that is going to ruin the next generation, mentally and psychologically, destroy our family system and raze our values and ethics to the ground? Confused by information overload, today's generation is getting lost in the maze of social media and trance parties. We need to find solutions to such problems. In the yesteryears, one would buy a house and a vehicle when one reached one's fifties. Today, youngsters in their twenties, who work in the IT sector, are buying luxurious houses and four-wheelers as they are handsomely paid. We have a culture of closed doors. In the concrete jungles, one does not even know their neighbour's name.

Earlier, when a child was born, the grandfather would cut its umbilical cord with a sickle and bury it in black soil. As a result, generations with deep attachment to the soil would be born. Today, who knows which gutter the umbilical cord lands up in as medical waste? The terrible possibility is that we have a generation with an attachment to muck. Grandparents are viewed as unwanted people in the house. Unfortunately, the new generation is often heard saying, 'Old people are such a bother. Their thoughts are so backward. They say such mean things without even giving a thought.' When the elderly are ill-treated, who will inculcate good values? Villages are facing a similar situation. In rural areas, you find a school, a college, liquor store and permit room at the centre of the village. Children watch their parents and teachers visiting these liquor shops and tread the same path.

Youngsters get a false sense of enjoyment from consuming drugs, dancing to wild music and indulging in perversions. The health minister of Russia has officially announced that 50 lakh youngsters have become addicted to drugs over the last decade. A thinker says, 'Tell me what songs the young generation in your country sings and I can predict the future of your country.' What will be the future of a society in which youngsters sing the songs of the devil and dance to Satan worshipping trance music?

To give you another example, a daughter of a businessman tried to commit suicide. The reason: her mother did not allow her to go to a nightclub for a day. Since her father was one of my acquaintances, he brought her to me for counselling. She said she could not live without the party culture. I was stunned. When one comes across such incidents, one wonders whether life is all about dancing and being wild. It's easy for such people to be deeply affected by emotional trauma because they have never experienced reality. I had keenly observed the investigation of the death of a Bollywood heroine. Her lover started achieving new heights of success. The moment he got his big break, he started planning to break up with her. During one of their fights, they used abusive language with each other. Finally, he sent her a bouquet with a break-up message. Angered, she threw it in the garbage bin and committed suicide by hanging herself from the ceiling fan. 'The End!' Life is God's gift. Dead bodies, even of those born with a silver spoon in their mouth, stink while decomposing. A Marathi family from Satara had migrated to Mauritius two generations back. A young girl from the family became Miss Mauritius and came to Mumbai to try her luck in Bollywood. She did not get her big break. Instead, she got an opportunity to work in a condom advertisement. She fell out of favour in highbrow society. A businessman's son used and discarded her. She ended her life, leaving a message of 'You killed me', mentioning his name. The businessman got away scot-free for want of evidence but unfortunately, the life of a beautiful girl was wasted. This proves the age-old saying, 'All that glitters is not gold.' Thus, the path of addiction leads to ruin.

There's a right time for everything. We must wait for that time patiently. We can never conquer if we fall for such vices. If one maintains restraint, defies temptation and becomes successful, one fulfils all of one's worldly desires. Vice is like opium and selfish, antisocial elements try to push it down the throat of our youth. This was how Kasab and his accomplices were misled and provoked to kill innocent citizens. They were led astray under the pretence that their path would lead them to Jannat. What was the result? Their corpses were left to decompose in the mortuary of JJ Hospital for months.

I have watched the movie *Dilwale Dulhaniya Le Jayenge* many times. Many people teach their children to enjoy life when they're young, the way Anupam Kher, in the role of Shahrukh Khan's father, did in the film. People are encouraged to look for his or her Shahrukh or Kajol. But what stuck in my head was a dialogue from the film. When Kajol's mother insists to Shahrukh that he and Kajol should elope, he holds her hand and says, 'At every crossroad in life, one has to choose one of the two options. One is a shortcut—a simple, straight beautiful road that is a bed of roses and the other is a long, difficult route. If we choose the shortcut, it creates the illusion of reaching the destination, but it is just the beginning of failure. Soon disillusion follows and the grave reality makes us handicapped forever. If we choose the long route, we must face hardships initially. We face risks and pains but finally our victory is assured. The hardships and risks make us so powerful that we can face any challenge and become successful.'

This dialogue from the movie is deeply etched in my mind. Whenever I was tempted to take a shortcut, I would remember these words and overcome the temptation. Several candidates ruined their lives taking such shortcuts by trying to get hold of leaked papers. Scam artists prey on such candidates. Many even mortgage their land to finance such shortcuts and are subsequently cheated. Therefore, in this game of snakes and ladders, we should not get discouraged if we suffer a fall. If we are required to face the storm, we should not get exhausted; we must get up and continue our journey on the tedious route, keeping our eyes fixed on the lighthouse.

We should be relentless in this endeavour and there should be no room for any doubt until we reach our destination. Indeed, Bollywood has given me a helping hand when I faced tough challenges. I had jotted down, in my diary, several inspiring dialogues from Bollywood such as: 'Make yourself capable and success will follow you'; 'The right time to score is when everybody else in the world thinks that a particular task is impossible'; 'I want to stand up and run. It does not matter if I fall down while running but I don't have either the will or the time to halt'; 'One should think of loss in the distant future rather than gain in the near future'; 'One is a winner till he loses out'; and 'This world has both winners and losers and every loser gets at least one opportunity to become the winner'. Whenever my battery runs low, I look at myself in the mirror and utter these dialogues, imitating the heroes. Besides motivation, this also provides some entertainment to me.

I returned to my village. I was happy because my exams had gone well. I spread my arms like wings to fly high in the sky, took a deep breath and closed my eyes to call out to God. Behold, I found myself flying higher than the sky. Energy flowed through my veins like the water flowing in the Warna river. The hillock in my village would always recharge my energies; my challenges seemed like a piece of cake. I had identified my 'happy spot'. One finds many such 'happy spots' in one's life. They come to our rescue when we feel depressed. They embrace us, caress us and rid us of our sorrows and stress. My mother's lap, my father's lap, my grandmother's godhadi, the school bell, Bapu's theatre, strings of kites, swinging on the hanging roots of banyan trees, a dive in the river . . . I had several such happy spots and still continue to find more, so that my emotional life is beautiful, full of laughter and pleasure. The ruckus of my children, motorcycle rides with my wife, early morning runs on Nariman Point, exercise in the gym, a dip in the swimming pool, playing the guitar, watching a good movie, looking for old memories in the fields of my village, are some of my other happy spots. When I get depressed,

I go to such a spot and disconnect from the world. These spots inspire me to continue living my life. They give me strength to fight back. They transform my struggles into goals. They make my ambitions a reality.

This time around, I didn't say a word about my examinations. I wanted to give a tight slap to those who had looked at me with contempt and laughed at my failure. I had resolved that, this time, I would keep everything a secret. My friends and I went for a long drive in a jeep. We stayed in Konkan for a week. The lush greenery freshened me up. We paid our obeisance to Lord Ganesha at Ganapati Pule and swam in the sea. I considered the challenges that I would be taking up in the future while riding the waves. Like the sea, our life faces moments of high and low tide. At times, we experience a tsunami too. If we sail and steer in an appropriate direction, facing such waves becomes easy. Ordinary people cannot sail in the rough sea. Small or weak boats capsize. To survive, one needs a strong boat. Ordinary people survive the tides but fail when a tsunami hits. Life is the same. If one wants to live like an ordinary man, one will stick to the shallow waters along the beach but if one wants to swim in the deep sea, one will need the personality and physique of a strong, sturdy ship.

The UPSC examination is like the deep ocean. In its three stages, it swells and roars, springs up tricky challenges and tests our abilities. If we do not prepare ourselves adequately at any stage, we are slated to drown. I could see the peak of Mount Everest and needed to make the final ascent to conquer it. I needed to be cautious and alert about my situation. I was having fun with my friends but deep within me, a storm was brewing. The ship of my life was not designed to stay rooted at the docks. God did not grant me life for that. Yes, it would be safe on the shore but what is its use if not to enter the waters? I had decided to sail into the rough sea and now I would sail across it. I had chosen to mount an uncontrolled horse and now I had to rein him in. Weathered in the village, my body was built for it. If I must build a hut at the place where fate wants to strike a bolt of lightning, I would do it. The world around me might turn upside down but I would not let it break me. I would ride that uncontrolled horse and gallop from one peak to another. If God was testing me, he must have big plans for my future.

Travelling with friends also meant staying in temples or dharmashalas. Everybody contributed to pay for the fuel. We ate whatever roadside food we could afford, cracked jokes and laughed. We teased each other, talked about delicate matters and sighed with relaxation. It was a happy life; we took dips in the shallow waters along the shore. Sometimes I wondered, if everything was fine and I was happy, why should I compete with the rough seas? In the same vein, I would think, what would have happened had Columbus or Vasco da Gama had thought the same? They were mighty explorers who changed the world for the better. My task was not as Herculean. The sea in Konkan signalled me to take off. I bid adieu to my friends and returned to Mumbai to start preparing for the interview.

I moved out of the university hostel. I lived in the SIAC with my friends as a parasite but needed a place of my own to sleep. I met with Deshmukh Saheb. He gave me the keys to his air-conditioned room in the MLA hostel. My journey began from room no. 105 in the Majestic MLA Hostel. In fact, it was the only AC room in the entire MLA hostel. A window AC was installed in it because it was directly above the canteen's kitchen. There was a settee outside the AC room where anybody from the tehsil could camp. Around six people could be seen camping there, seemingly forever. They would get up early in the morning, bathe, eat vada pav and visit Deshmukh Saheb. Each one of them wanted a job but none of them took any initiative. They would roam around Colaba Causeway, whiling away time in the evening. I kept my trunk under the cot and took out a few select books. My routine was to get up early in the morning and go to Petit Library or the SIAC and return to the MLA hostel late at night only to sleep. Since I had appeared for the main examination, the new entrants in the SIAC treated me respectfully. They would come and talk to me to clear their doubts. I also started entertaining a couple of candidates for tea and discussions. Sometimes Deshmukh Saheb's relatives from the village would come to live in the MLA hostel. They also had the key to the AC room. When I returned to the room after studying throughout the day, I would find them lying on the bed, wearing striped boxer shorts and baniyans and snoring away.

Hoping that I would become a saheb, Tatya bought a second-hand motorcycle for me. I would get confused riding it on the crowded streets of Mumbai. Besides, there was the problem of finding a parking space during the night. I parked the vehicle at the chawl behind the MLA hostel for a few days, but some nasty character put a kilogram of sugar in its petrol tank. I had to get the entire bike repaired because of this incident, spending three days at the garage. One fine day, I took Shivjya with me and rode 400 kilometres on the serpentine roads of Konkan to reach my village and left my motorcycle there. On the way, we swam in lakes and the sea. We whistled and sung songs like 'Yeh Dosti, Hum Nahin Chhodenge' as we rode to the village. We gave an outlet to our feelings through these songs. We observed the picturesque bloom on the slopes of the hills. We watched birds flying high in the sky and felt our minds and bodies relax.

Chapter 11

The Victorious Last Lap

Acing the interview is no mean feat and requires some basic skills. You need to be well-spoken and should be able to put your point forth effectively. Your language should be polite and you should be able to speak extempore. Your pronunciation and accent should be correct, clear and flawless. Your thought process should be rational. These are some of the established norms.

I thought of an innovative way to master these skills. I walked into a private coaching class in Dadar and met with its director. I expressed my desire to teach the Constitution of India to the new batches. He readily accepted my request and offered to pay me Rs 100 per hour. I started earning Rs 600 for putting in two hours a day and three days a week. I also took up teaching in two other coaching classes—the Dadasaheb Gaikwad Centre and Sthaniya Lokadhikar Samiti. In addition to earning money to meet my expenses, this helped me gain mastery over the art of speaking. Besides, it boosted my confidence. To further sharpen my oratory skills,

I needed to teach in English in a class being conducted at Chabildas School, where students mostly hailed from convent schools. Here, one can find many dedicated people preparing for exams for the Indian Institutes of Management, chartered accountancy or corporate law courses. However, it is rare to find people like me, dedicating their full time in preparing for the MPSC or the UPSC. In Mumbai, a corporate job is given preference over a government one. A handful of youngsters prepare for the civil services examinations part-time, while also pursuing a job. As a result, local coaching centres in Mumbai are rarely attended by brilliant or serious students.

In Chabildas School, I could hardly pass for a teacher, being only a couple of years older than the students. My English was not very good, and when I started teaching, the students would ask me tricky questions in their convent-educated accent and try to catch me on the wrong foot. This propelled me to prepare thoroughly for my class, silencing them.

Simultaneously, I started working on preparing my biodata for the interview. I began to read *Lokrajya* and *Frontline* magazines to stay up to date on Maharashtrian news and happenings. I also made it a habit to read *The Hindu*, allowing me to comprehend various issues in depth and expanding my knowledge base. I started attending as many public lectures as I could fit into my busy schedule. These lectures provided insights into the thoughts of several prominent figures and experts on the globalization and liberalization of the economy in the modest hall of the Indian Merchants' Chamber. I made it a point to listen to public speeches given by former civil services officers like J.F. Rebeiro, Nana Patil, Chandra Iyyangar and Avinash Dharmadhikari. I also started tuning in to the *Spotlight* programme that was broadcast on All India Radio. Besides, television debates and panel discussions also helped in broadening my point of view.

I dug deep into my personal background, family, village, education, hobbies and so on and compiled all that information. I formed questions on this information from several perspectives and wrote down the answers. I prepared answers for questions that might come up during cross-questioning. I conducted mock interviews with my friends. I went with Santosh Patil to meet big names in the civil services. I would study their personalities carefully. Santosh would study with us but he spent more time loitering in the Mantralaya than studying. He had given the interview for the State Public Service Commission twice, but was more inclined towards industry, business and politics. He changed his track in time and said goodbye to competitive examinations. Today, he is a successful entrepreneur. He had connections in high places. Even as a student, he would easily get a pass to enter the Mantralaya. He was well acquainted with several gazetted officers and thanks to him, I met several senior officers. I gained interview tips from all of them.

He was acquainted with Bapat Sir, who was a member of the MPSC. He took me to him too. During the Mumbai riots of 1992, he had worked as police commissioner, Mumbai. I amassed a lot of information from him about maintaining *bon entente*, learnt how a stressful situation is handled and how policing is done in mofussil sectors.

He had a fine sense of humour. He used to jest: 'Ganpati Bappa grants whatever one asks for—knowledge to a student; prosperity to those who want to be rich; a child to the childless; Moksha to those who pray for it. But for the police he has nothing but tension. Any why is he so indiscriminate? He is because our viewpoint regarding him is flawed.'

Even today, after twenty years of experience in police service, I think his point remains relevant. Anyone working in the police department is confronted daily with new issues that inevitably engender new questions. These problems can't be cured by a common antidote. We have to invent a new formula every time and base a new remedy on it. The slightest negligence, even a marginal error, can cause the cure to fail.

It is imperative to promptly identify the germs and viruses that are seen to be infecting society, and to destroy them in time without yielding to the least pressure and, if it comes to that, even resort to venomous means. However, on occasions when we go to the extremes, the protectors of human rights begin to beat their drums. Whenever a doctor's motive is suspected, the illness grows worse and rudimentary measures fail to work. The same applies to police work, too.

Bapat Sir's analysis was very accurate. Constructive conversations with officers made my concepts lucid. I came to have a better understanding of the challenges that could raise their ugly heads on the field. Now I was eagerly looking forward to the result of the main exam and a call for the interview.

Additionally, I was also preparing for the prelim examination again. Just like an Abhimanyu, the fighter who never accepts defeat, I had made up my mind to appear for the civil services examination again, if I did not get the call for the next round. I decided that I would continue to reappear for the examination, until my age made me ineligible. Pandu Patil had arrived in Mumbai to prepare for the examination. When I got bored in the evening, we went outside to relax. Just like actor Rajesh Khanna would accost any stranger in the Bollywood movie *Anand*, we too would accost any Mumbaikar who was walking past us in a hurry, saying, 'Hey Mr Kangude, what are you doing here?' The already harassed Mumbaikars abhorred this. They usually gave us look of scorn and walked away. Their priority was to board the next train and get home; they didn't have time for our antics.

The Bagdadi restaurant, which was located behind the Taj, served chicken tangdi for Rs 20. I had pledged to be a vegetarian but still never failed to meet with friends at Bagdadi on Sundays. PR and Shivaji never tired of slurping the crimson delicacy, served at an affordable rate. Till today, I have not been able to figure out how the shop procured such large chunks of chicken at such a throwaway price. I watched a movie recently. It had a scene related to eating the tasty and affordable 'crow biryani' which was made with sketchy 'chicken'. While eating the tasteless vegetarian dish at Bagdadi, I would voice various possibilities relating to the origin of the 'chicken', but it all fell on deaf ears. After supper, we would stroll to the Gateway of India and return to the room, taking precautions to avoid stepping on couples romancing on the Colaba Causeway or trampling the people sleeping on the footpaths. All in all, my routine was set, as I waited for the results with growing anxiety.

Finally, the results of the UPSC main examination were announced. To my delight, I was selected for the interview round. I had to prepare a strategy to ace the interview which would take place in Delhi. I was fortunate to have carved out a place among lakhs of candidates, as only a few thousand were selected for the interview round. I needed to make sure that I would join the ranks of the few hundreds who would be selected after the interview. My days became busy as I needed to run errands to prepare for the interview. I needed to buy everything, right from a necktie to a new pair of shoes. I also needed to book a train reservation to Delhi and look for a place to stay in the national capital for a month.

Mock interviews began in the SIAC. Several experts and senior officers started visiting the campus to prepare the candidates. Group discussions began in full swing.

The atmosphere of the SIAC was charged with enthusiasm. The candidates started preparing for the internal as well as the external aspects of the interview. Each person expressed his opinion on every aspect of one's appearance and attire. Embarrassing stories from previous years' interviews started doing rounds among the candidates.

The matter of hobbies was a deep one and every aspirant chose a hobby that suited his personality. On a previous occasion, Kharge Sir had stated 'visiting forts' as his hobby and had scored well in the interview. Therefore, some opted for the same hobby and started reading *Bakhars* (historic accounts). One's hobbies and preferences are associated with one's natural tendencies. A hobby helps one relax; it is a passion pursued for the sake of enjoyment. Instead of opting for genuine hobbies, most succumb to 'herd mentality' and try to adopt a hobby. This is where the trouble starts. How can you expect to justify your hobby if it isn't genuine? Faking a hobby to impress interviewers is how most candidates dig their own grave. A friend had written that his hobby was daydreaming. He would imagine incidents wherein he fought injustice like Singham. Nobody could guess how the interviewers would take to this hobby. Another wrote 'paintings and sculptures' as his hobby and, before the interview, he sidelined his studies to visit all the museums and painting exhibitions in Delhi.

I appeared for a mock interview but did not fare too well. The interviewing panel asked me to be more confident. My current affairs were not up to the mark, so they advised me to read *Frontline* and *The Hindu* more attentively. Doubtful as to whether my English would improve any further, they advised me to try and give my interview in Marathi as far as possible.

I met Kasar Saheb and reserved a second-class sleeper coach ticket to Delhi on the Nizamuddin Express. My twenty-eight-hour-long train ride to Delhi began. It was my first long journey in a train. Carrying my books, important documents and a trunk containing my clothes, I located my berth. My seat number was the upper berth in the triple-tiered compartment. Two north Indian women sat on the lower berth, occupying all the space. I did not know one could sit on the lower berth even if they were allotted the upper berth.

Too shy to ask if I could sit with them on the lower berth and also afraid they would be rude to me, I awkwardly sat in the middle berth throughout the day and tried to prepare myself for the interview. I managed to catch up on some sleep at night but couldn't sleep a lot as I was worried about my certificates, which were in my trunk, getting stolen. Finally, I reached Delhi. I immediately noticed how hot it was; the scorching Delhi sun was unrelenting. Candidates who had come from the SIAC had checked into the Maharashtra Sadan. I boarded a taxi to reach there. As the taxi meter kept going up, my heart started palpitating. I had indulged in an argument with the barbershop owner just before going for the MPSC interview and that had ruined my dialogue. I cautiously avoided arguing with the taxi driver and quietly paid him Rs 250 when we reached the Maharashtra Sadan.

Eight candidates had already checked in and were camping in a non-AC room. I was the ninth one to join them. I could feel my body literally burning on the inside. I got some relief after taking a cold shower. Refreshed, I reached the temporary interview room at the Maharashtra Sadan. Each one of us had to explain his strategy for conquering Delhi. Everybody had taken admission to the Vajiram classes. I too followed suit and paid the fee of Rs 2800. Several candidates like me, who had passed the main examination, were preparing with the help of experts to answer the questions that had the most probability of being asked during the interview. Some of the candidates hailed from upper-class families, some from middle-class families and a few like me had come from rural areas. I felt suffocated in this environment. The urge to leave everything behind and return to my village suddenly took over me. I told myself to buckle up for the interview; I had resolved to pass the civil services examination with flying colours and the interview was a part of it. The day of the interview was approaching steadily and, with practice, I was able to rehearse the answers to more and more questions.

Delhi witnesses extremely high temperatures during the summer. Particularly in May, the sun is scorching hot. The fan didn't do much to reduce the heat and one sweated profusely throughout the day. The nights were spent restlessly. Gradually, I got used to the heat during my month-long stay in Delhi. The interviewers who came to conduct our interviews would form panels. Every panel conducted discussions to analyse and assess how the questions would be asked during the interview. Every interview panel would hold detailed discussions on a candidate's good and bad habits, beliefs and thought process.

During the planning process, discussions were on leftist leanings, how to counter them and how to sidestep questions that were tough or beyond one's expertise. Current affairs were discussed in elaborate detail and plans devised as to how to talk about relevant news topics. Some candidates started frequenting the nearby Laxminarayan Temple to pray for the interviewing panels of their preference. Lying on the lawns of India Gate, I could see the South Block and the North Block ahead; I dreamt of the day when I would serve in those buildings. Secretarial service is normally listed as the last preference. Even if I did not do too well in the final merit list but got selected for the civil services, I would be able to become a desk officer or babu in the Secretariat in Delhi. Vehicles whose tops blazed with red, blue and amber beacons plied on the roads, manifesting the VIP culture of Delhi, spurred my expectations.

Tatya occasionally sent me a letter. In those times, even if one wished to make a phone call, there was no guarantee that one would get through, despite waiting for a couple of hours. Sending a letter by post was a better option as it was delivered in a week's time. In his latest letter, my eighth-grade-educated father had penned down his expectations of me. He apprised me of the financial condition of our family: the loans we were forced to take for Seematai's wedding, the total loss of yield we had suffered in the fields due to pest infestation and how he awaited news of my success patiently. He penned down all this, in his broken Marathi, in that letter. I am known as Bhavdya in my village. To sum up his letter, Tatya had written a line that set me on fire. He wrote, 'Bhavdya, I want to see you coming to our village in a car with red beacon before I die.' I had studied day and night to fulfil my illiterate father's dreams. This letter prompted me to resolve, yet again, that I would not return from Delhi empty-handed. I would ace the interview and emerge victorious. Finally, the D-Day of the interview arrived.

On the day of the interview, my clothes were crisply ironed and my face clean-shaven. My moustache was uneven, so I trimmed it. I wore a light blue shirt, navy blue trousers, a black belt and Oxford shoes. I was still unsure about whether to wear a necktie or not. I tried to tie a Windsor knot three or four times but could not adjust the length of the tie. It was either too long or too short. With successive failed attempts, the tie was wrinkled, and I had to drop the idea of wearing it. I grabbed my certificates and other documents and reached Dholpur House on a cycle rickshaw.

I entered the UPSC building for the first time. I checked my name on the notice board and next to it (where the names of the interviewers are written) was the name of Lieutenant General Surendra Nath. I broke into cold sweat. He was the then chairman of UPSC. I had heard rumours that he held a bias against those who were not from English-medium schools. Supressing my fear, I walked in. Bapu too reached there. He was also one of Surendra Nath's preys. His problem was that he was a die-hard addict of *gutka*. I sat with the clerk and got my certificates and documents verified. After submitting the required documents, I walked into the tiny waiting hall outside the conference room where the interview panel was seated. Bapu, meanwhile, lost his patience and opened a gutka pouch. After chewing it for about ten minutes, he felt rejuvenated. He had carried his toothpaste and toothbrush along and brushed his teeth to remove the odour.

The conference room was adjacent to the waiting hall. The candidates were seated as per their number on a bench as they waited for their turn. Every candidate was interviewed for twenty to twenty-five minutes. My turn was after a candidate from Nagpur. Even in the sweltering Delhi heat, he had chosen to wear a three-piece suit for his interview. I got acquainted with the smart candidate who spoke fluent English. He was extraordinarily talented. His academic record was astonishing. He had done his BTech from IIT Mumbai before finishing a master's in management studies (MMS) from IIM Ahmedabad. He had rejected a fat-salaried job offer from a US-based multinational company to join the civil services. I browsed through my own biodata. I possessed only one degree and that too a BA (History) degree from Shivaji University, Kolhapur. He and I were worlds apart. My inferiority complex would often rear its ugly head during such incidents. On such occasions, Tatya's letter acted like a salve. I took out his letter from my pocket and read the last line again. A wave of energy flowed through my veins. I had regained my confidence by the time my turn came to appear for the interview.

Cautiously, I pushed the door open and asked, 'May I come in, sir?' The chairman, without lifting his head, replied, 'Yes, please.' With my file in hand, I walked up to the chair and wished all the members of the interviewing panel good morning. The method of interviewing here was novel. The candidate's chair was placed at a short distance from the table across which the interviewing panel was sitting. As a result, the panel could observe the candidate's movements and body language. The panellists gestured for me to sit down. A woman came and sat on a chair next to me. She was introduced to me as Mrs Kulkarni. She was the interpreter. Since I had chosen Marathi medium, she was there to translate the conversation for the benefit of both parties.

The chairman skimmed through my biodata. Anyway, its contents weren't of any interest to him. There was a 'C' certificate of NCC, silver medal won at a university level shooting competition, a BA degree and a village boy sitting across the table. That's it. He bowled his first googly, 'Mr Narayan, you have opted for Marathi medium for the personality test. Why don't you speak in English?'

I was confused. I managed to say, 'Sir, I am from a rural background. My English is not that good. May I express myself in my mother tongue, please?' I felt as if I was pleading like a beggar pleads for alms.

He insisted, 'You try in broken English, Mr Narayan.' He had addressed me with my father's name for the second time. In Maharashtra, the custom is to write the surname first, then your first name and your father's name, last. My name ended with Narayan. I guessed that had probably confused the panel. I could not resist myself from pointing it out.

I mustered up courage and said, 'Sir, Narayan is my father's name. My name is Vishwas!' Daring to say this was of crucial importance. Avinash Hathgal had goofed up when he had faced a similar situation in the previous year. For the entire duration of his interview, they addressed him by his father's name, Ramrao. He ignored it thinking, 'What's in a name?' And finally, as he rose to go out after the interview, the chairman had bid him adieu, saying, 'Thank you, Avinash.' He scored less. All this had been discussed while we were preparing for the interview. Therefore, I showed presence of mind and set the record straight. I told myself, 'We too have been told the tale of "The Monkeys and the Cap Seller" by our predecessors,' which stood for the tales of those candidates who had appeared for interviews earlier.

The interviewing panel insisted on conducting the interview in English. Overcoming my inferiority complex was of utmost importance to me. I agreed, saying, 'I will try, sir.' I did not miss the mischievous smile on Surendra Nath's face. He had another look at my biodata and asked me in English, 'Mr Narayan, sorry, Mr Vishwas, you graduated in 1993. No further degree? What were you doing during these four long years? Were you exclusively preparing for the civil services?' I promptly replied, 'Yes, sir, I am simultaneously doing some constructive social work to bring about positive change in my village. The villages are affected by many negative, disruptive and backward tendencies.

The droughts and poor yields have brought pessimism and lethargy, resulting in delinquency, mainly in the youth. Sir, we have established one NGO in my village which works for the upliftment of the rural youth as well as for disseminating rational, scientific and viable ideas among the rural folks. We have already begun our work and established a well-equipped library and study centre for the students preparing for SSC, the HSC and various other competitive examinations.'

I answered this in fluent, flawless English without stumbling. Pleased, other members of the interviewing panel looked at me appreciatively over the edges of their spectacles. Surendra Nath smiled and said, 'Mr Vishwas, you speak fluent English! Very good!' How was I to tell them that I had worked hard on memorizing this answer? I had been expecting this question. Normally, all candidates are asked this question and it was obvious that I would score a sixer on this full-toss ball.

Soon after, my real English surfaced and left me exposed. Abraham, an IAS officer of Maharashtra cadre, was also a panellist. He asked me for my optional subjects and when I told him that 'Marathi literature' was one of them, he bowled another bouncer to me, saying, 'Mr Vishwas, can you explain why the drama *Ghashiram Kotwal* became controversial?'

I knew the answer but didn't know how to word it out. Fumbling, I started, 'Sir, *Ghashiram Kotwal* is a Marathi play written by Vijay Tendulkar in 1972 as a response to the rise of the Shiv Sena. The play caused controversy because some people believed that it hurt the feelings of the Chitpavan Brahmin community and that it showed Nana Phadnavis, the well-respected statesman, as "behind women" person.'

My hodgepodge pronunciation and the fact that the interviewing panel could not understand what I meant by 'behind women', threw me off. I looked at Kulkarni Madam and said, 'Madam, please tell them "behind women" means "स्त्रीलंपट" (womanizer).' When Madam explained the meaning, the interviewing panel broke into laughter.

I relaxed a little. I felt like a batsman who had settled down with his bat on the pitch. Anna Hazare's agitation was in the limelight at the national level at that time. They asked me about Anna's Ralegan Siddhi Model. I had been to Ralegan Siddhi with friends and stayed there for two days. I explained to the interviewing panel in detail, in Marathi, the changed mindset of the village through sterilization, prohibition of all addictive substances, ban on cutting trees, ban on grazing, contribution of labour, economic self-reliance attained by the villagers and the water harvesting scheme. Kulkarni Madam, on her part, translated it excellently into English for the benefit of the interviewing panel.

The next question—How would privatization and globalization make their impact on the rural economy and how would they change the lives of the lowest strata of society?—deserved an honest answer. I detailed the positive and negative aspects of privatization and globalization, in the light of constitutional provisions, fundamental rights and the scope and expanse of the concept of state. I handled everything, ranging from the amenities and assistance provided to the backward classes to the onslaught of urbanization. Answering this question consumed five minutes of the total duration of my interview. However, the next question on an international issue—How can the UNO be restructured?—bowled me out completely. I did not know the then structure of the UNO well. What would I have to say about its restructuring?

The next question was on history and it too was tricky. Which personalities in Indian history fascinate you? History has a huge scope. Moreover, great personalities belonging to the various eras of history were incomparable in terms of their importance, achievements and brilliance. I pondered for a moment and replied, 'Personally, my life and thoughts bear the influence of three great personalities—Chhatrapati Shivaji, Mahatma Gandhi and Dr Ambedkar!'

The next question was related to the previous one—What was the difference between the policies of Gandhiji and Babasaheb relating to the eradication of untouchability? Whose views do you admire more? It was tough to give an exact answer to this question.

I started, 'Both advocated for a social structure based on the principles of social justice and equality. But the means they adopted to achieve the ends were different. Gandhiji wanted to reform the caste system while Ambedkar wanted to destroy it totally. Ambedkar felt that untouchability would prevail as long as the caste system existed. Gandhiji did satyagraha and fasts to change the mindset of the upper caste, but Ambedkar argued that satyagraha was a useless tool for this purpose. The differences between the two reached their peak at the time of communal discord. Gandhiji wanted to end untouchability while remaining a Hindu while Ambedkar tried to address the issue by renouncing Hinduism and converting to Buddhism.' The answer was okay.

The next question was about the king whose very name swells every Marathi's chest with pride: Chhatrapati Shivaji. The interviewing panel bowled its next googly, 'What was the concept of "Swarajya" and why is Shivaji considered to be a great noble king?' I had to think about how I would answer this question and talk about the pride that I felt for this deity-like figure, worshipped by the entire state of Maharashtra.

I started narrating in my mother tongue: 'Swarajya is the sovereign welfare state formed for the common citizens. Chhatrapati Shivaji's approach emphasized that the citizenry is the owner of Swarajya and as a ruler, he was its trustee. Swarajya is the reformatory and effective system created by Shivraya using disciplined military and constructive administration. In that era, customs like considering women as property, to be looted in the wars, destruction of places of worship, slavery and forced conversion were prevalent. Shivaji Maharaj curbed them. The life and work of Chhatrapati Shivaji is no less than a miracle. It is astonishing to observe that a singular man could achieve so much in one lifetime. He changed the rules of military tactics, created independent roles, changed the tax structure, eliminated bribery and corruption, made morality, discipline and credibility the main sources of administration and adopted the principle of equality. His policies for agriculture and environment, the adoption of new concepts and techniques by him, his way of inspiring colleagues, the chain of command formed by him, the balance in powers and duties achieved by him, his adaptation of guerrilla warfare, the intelligence network formed by him, his effective use of cavalry and the navy, his planning, leadership, dedication, far-sightedness, his trade policy, the forts constructed by him, the respect he had for women and other communities mark out his different and liberal approach. His great and magnanimous personality stands out because of his words and actions. In fact, it would be most appropriate to call him the founder of modern nationalism and the secular sovereign of India. The resistance that the Marathas put up against the Mughals for twenty-two years after the demise of Shivaji Maharaj stands as the living proof of nationalism and patriotism inculcated by

Shivaji.' The panel stopped me midway. They did not want me
to linger for too long in my area of expertise.

As expected, the interviewers proceeded to ask me about
shooting. I had prepared myself well on this topic. The
question was, 'What do you have inside you to hit the bull's
eye?' I replied, 'One needs to practise keeping his body still
while shooting. The movement should only be in the finger
pulling the trigger. Your weapon, your bullet and your target
are different. One needs to focus on one's own shooting
technique rather than thinking about the capabilities of his
competitors. Only then will one be able to hit the bull's eye.
Sir, I have demonstrated the highest level of patience and
I have complete control over my mind. I can pull the trigger
very well. I have mastered the practice of precise and accurate
aiming. I focus on what I am doing in the present rather than
thinking about the past or the future. I have no doubts about
my own capabilities. I have immense willpower. A disciplined
mind is the base of my skill.' As I spoke in Marathi, I paused
after every sentence or so for Kulkarni Madam as she was
translating it to English with the same vigour for the benefit
of the interviewing panel.

It had been half an hour. Lieutenant General Surendra
Nath then said, 'Mr Vishwas, I shall ask you the last question
in Hindi.' He asked me in Hindi, 'Why have you come to
this world? Please explain.' This question was difficult to
comprehend. I was confused. This was the last ball of the
innings and I needed five runs to score a century. Hitting
a sixer was my only option. But how does one answer
such a question? Firstly, God and secondly, my parents are
responsible for bringing me into this world. Did I choose to
be born? Such an answer would be a naïve one. I understood
the answer expected for that question. The interviewing panel

wanted to find out what my life's aim was. They wanted to know the direction in which I would be steering my life in the future. Had I replied saying that I was there to become a district collector or commissioner, it would have shown my intellect at a mundane level. Had I replied that I wanted to serve people and work for the masses, it would have sounded like a run-of-the-mill answer. For a moment, my past flashed before my eyes. A boy wearing shorts with patches stitched to conceal its holes, I had made my way to Dholpur House to be interviewed by highbrow and accomplished seniors; passing this interview would make me a part of the country's most prestigious service: the Indian Civil Services. In that moment, I recalled the poem 'La Mancha', taught by my English professor, which was etched into my memory.

I told the panel, 'Sir, I feel my aim in life is reflected in a poem a teacher taught me. If you would permit, I would like to recite it for you.' The interviewing panel granted me the permission and I recited the inspiring, effective last lines of the poem, with great vigour:

To dream the impossible dream
To fight the unbeatable foe
To bear with unbearable sorrow
To run where the brave dare not go
To right the unforgivable wrong
To love the pure and chaste from afar
To reach the unreachable star
This is my quest.
To follow that star
No matter how hopeless, no matter how far
To fight for the right, without question or pause
To be willing to march into hell for that heavenly cause.

'Sir, I have come to this world for this struggle. I have reached so far, struggling against adversities. If I enter the system with all this struggle, I will continue to overpower the negative, the bad and the antisocial tendencies in society for the rest of my life.'

This was my answer. The interviewing panel was amazed by my emotional and sensitive approach. Lieutenant General Surendra Nath wished me well, saying, 'Thank you, Vishwas. Best of luck!' My interview was over. I stepped out. Seeing the victorious expression on my face, Bapu said, 'Bhavdya, it seems you have won a jackpot.' I was not sure whether the panel had looked at me as an emotional fool or a committed candidate. There was no point pondering over it. I bought good-quality sweaters for my mother and Tatya as well as some books for myself. I packed my bag and left for Mumbai aboard the Nizamuddin Express. On the train, the last few lines of the poem 'La Mancha', which I had not recited in my interview, came to my mind:

> And I know if I'll only be true
> To this glorious quest
> That my heart will lie peaceful and calm
> When I'm laid to my rest.
> And the word will be better for this
> That one man scorned, and covered with scars,
> Still strove with his last ounce of courage
> To reach the unreachable star.

Often, I compare these lines with my mindset today. What lies behind this unexplainable attraction to death? Why do I feel that I need to make the supreme sacrifice for my country? Why does the idea of a dignified death call to me? I lived

these lines while I was battling against the terrorists on the
night of 26/11. The dead bodies, carelessly scattered in pools
of fresh blood, marked the aura of death on that night when
my bodyguard Amit Khetale and I entered the Taj. The firing
of AK-47 and booms of grenades were the sounding bugle,
as if connoting that my final goal was near. At the thirteenth
minute, we had a skirmish with terrorists on the second floor
and the three rounds fired from my pistol met with a response
of thirty fired from AK-47s. I was convinced that the Taj
would become my burial ground. I had the guerrilla warfare
tactics taught by Chhatrapati Shivaji to bank on.

I charged with presence of mind and attentiveness. Your
position is always more important than any weapon. I reached
the sixth floor. Thanks to the unexpected firing from our side
at the twentieth minute, the terrorists did not fire a single
round for the next one hour. They wanted to stretch the
ordeal for as long as possible because they wanted the eyes
of the world to be on them. They focused on consolidating
their own position. We reached the ground floor, conducting
searches on the fifth, fourth and third floors.

Deathly silence prevailed. We thought that they had fled
but at that very moment there were two grenade blasts. While
we were checking the south wing, the terrorists had reached
the sixth floor of the north wing. I went to the main entrance
of the Taj to summon reinforcements. Two State Reserve
Police Force (SRPF) jawans, Rahul Shinde and Samadhan
More, were standing there, holding their position behind a
Gypsy van. Seeing me at the main entrance, they came out
and saluted me. I asked them about their platoon. They told
me that they had been detailed to take position near the
main entrance. It was as if a drowning man was trying to save
himself by grasping at a straw. Inside, the dance of death and

destruction had resumed. I told my team that they would
never again get an opportunity like the one we were facing to
prove their patriotism and love for the country.

I hopped into the lift and reached the sixth floor of the
north wing. We chased the terrorists till half past twelve.
Though we were making some headway, we knew death
was chasing our tails. Finally, we reached the CCTV room.
We could ascertain the accurate position of the terrorists.
They had taken five innocent citizens as hostages. The brutes
had tied their hands, hitting them and pushing them to reach
downstairs. Using a wireless set, I apprised commissioner of
police Gafoor Saheb and joint commissioner of police Maria
Saheb about the situation. Gafoor Saheb ordered us to engage
the terrorists there till the navy commandos arrived. Without
mincing words, I reassured him, 'We will not allow them to
come down, even if we die.' This grim conversation is logged
and recorded at the control room. Our small team fought the
terrorists till quarter to three, keeping them confined to the
sixth floor.

We were able to keep an eye on their movements from
the CCTV room. Whenever they tried to move downstairs,
we were able to take them by surprise and open fire. However,
at around quarter to three, they worked out our position
and attacked the floor we were on with grenades. The entire
floor, decorated with woodwork, caught on fire. The flames
and smoke started filling the CCTV room. We decided that
fighting till our last breath by stepping out of the control room
was better than being roasted alive or dying from suffocation.
In a line formation we exited the CCTV room, but they had
already trained their AK-47s on us.

The sudden onslaught of bullets forced us to scatter and
take cover. Our weapons weren't death machines, like the

terrorists'. Rajvardhan and I managed to reach the ballroom. Amit was wounded as three bullets had hit him. A bullet which brushed against his stomach ultimately hit Rahul in the chest. Police Inspector Dhole and Police Sub-Inspector Kakade suffered burns. Employees of the Taj, Puru and Nausher, were injured too. They could leave the hotel using the back door. Rahul, however, lost his life.

The next day, when I went to claim Rahul's mortal remains, his body had stiffened up, his uniform was gutted but the butt of his rifle was still on his shoulder and his finger was still on the trigger guard of the rifle. The bayonet of his gun was pointed upwards, and his eyes were still open as if reassuring me that he had lived up to his words. The fifty-five-year-old police officer, Tukaram Ombale, pounced on the AK-47 wielding Kasab, holding only a lathi in his hand, overpowering him and maintaining his grip despite taking hits from five bullets. Thus, a terrorist was caught alive. When death comes calling as you fight for the nation, a heavenly power embraces you. Why does this virtue of hara-kiri fascinate me? Why does dying a hero, even one hundred times, seem more appealing to me than living a humiliating, cowardly life? I face this dilemma constantly. This is the coincidence of tendency. Tendencies are formed by the values one is born with and those inculcated intentionally. This forms the character of a human being.

Somewhere, I had read an ancient tale of China. The Chinese resolved to live a peaceful life, so they decided to build the Great Wall of China. They built the wall so high that they felt no enemy would ever be able to scale it. However, within 100 years, they suffered three successful aggressions and the enemy armies managed to cross the Great Wall and infiltrate their country. The enemy had bribed the corrupt security men and entered, without facing any counterattack. The Chinese built the Great Wall but forgot to build the character of the soldiers guarding it. Thus, traitors were born. Building your character is more important than achieving worldly success. We must consciously include this in the basic curriculum of students.

An oriental thinker says: there are three ways of destroying any civilized culture. First, destroy the family system, then corrupt their education system and lastly, dishonour and malign their idols to such an extent that society will start looking down on them. To destroy the family system, destabilize the mother of that family. If she feels ashamed of being a homemaker, she will fail to inculcate values in the next generation. To destroy the education system, reduce the importance of teachers in the society. Insult them to the extent that their image in the eyes of the students will be maligned. To do away with the idols in the society, humiliate the intellectuals, carry out their character assassination, spread doubts about their thoughts to such an extent that nobody will tread on the path shown by them.

Once the rational mother disappears, the goal-oriented guru (mentor) is demoralized and the committed intellectuals are ruined, who will educate the new generation about the importance of values? If the new generation falters or strays, who will show them the path of righteousness and honesty? This reminds me of the following lines written by the legendary Kusumagraj:

सूर्यकुळाचा दिव्य वारसा प्रिय पुत्रानो तुम्हा मिळे
काळोखाचे करून पूजन घुबडाचे व्रत धरू नका,
तरुणाईचे बळ देशाचे, जपा वाढवा तरुपरी
करमणुकीच्या गटारगंगा, त्यात स्वत:ला श्राळू नका.

(My dear sons, you inherit the great legacy of the family of the Sun. Do not worship the darkness, thereby adopting the resolve of the owl fraternity. Youth is the strength of the country and hence must be protected and nurtured like trees. Do not allow yourselves to rot in the filthy gutter of crass entertainment.)

Nowadays, children have busied themselves with television and mobile phones to such an extent that one day they will have to be shown the courtyard, the backyard, clean floors plastered with cow dung, milking of buffaloes and corn ears blooming in the fields, through the eyes of the Internet. They are under the impression that milk comes from the milkman and a machine produces popcorn. The present generation is smart, intelligent and fast. My views may seem backward but I feel that today's youth are mindless, chasing worldly pleasures. Their emotional world is online. They are getting trapped in the web of social-media sites like Facebook and Twitter.

This point of view can be elaborated through Bapuji's philosophy. These days, Bapuji's philosophy needs to be taught through films like *Lage Raho Munnabhai*. Munnabhai needs to answer ten questions on the life of Bapu to impress a beautiful radio jockey. He asks his friend Circuit, 'Hey, who is this Bapu?' Circuit replies, 'Hey, Bapu is the one whose image is printed on Rs 500 notes.' A curious Munnabhai further asks, 'Was he in the police force or the army?' Circuit replies, 'No, his body isn't built like a soldier's. He did not even wear much of clothing, but he ruined the British.' Today's generation needs Bapu but finds him only on bundles of currency notes. They find Bapu's teachings to be out of date. What are the reasons behind the increasing moral degradation and decay of schools of thought? When we attained freedom, utmost importance was attached to the sacrifice of the high-brow class for the betterment of society. As a result, concepts like Swaraj and Surajya evolved. Vinoba Bhave's movements like Bhudan (donation of land), Gramdan (contribution for the village), Sampattidan (contribution in terms of wealth) were based on the philosophy of Bapuji. Today, the greed of a few is valued above the needs of lakhs.

Charity begins at home. I will begin from myself, be the messenger and implement the reforms expected by Bapu. The strong, powerful India envisaged by Bapu was not a nation laced with sophisticated weapons and missiles, ready to go to war. It was a prosperous, democratic state that is rich in inclusive philosophy and culture and committed to serving humanity.

I was lost in this whirlwind of thoughts until I reached Mumbai. I left my bag at the MLA hostel and went for a stroll to the Gateway of India. The prelim examination was to be conducted again after one and a half months. If, unfortunately, the result turned out to be negative, I would have to start afresh. I reached Petit Library. Since I had appeared for the UPSC interview, my status had risen. Everybody treated me with respect. I was able to enjoy this special treatment for at least some days. I visited the SIAC too. Sipping a cuppa, I narrated the tale of my interview to the freshers.

While I was in Delhi, the results of the main MPSC examination had been declared. I was selected for the interview. I had cleared the main examination for the post of sales tax inspector. With these opportunities knocking at my door, I felt the comforting presence of success. Normally, in any competitive examination, the number of candidates called for an interview is about thrice the number of posts.

I was selected for interviews for three separate posts. Going by the general rule of probability, I was slated to be selected for at least one of the three posts. The real question remained: Would I win the UPSC jackpot or land a small-time MPSC job? The interviews for the posts of sales tax inspector and deputy collector were lined up one after the other. I had already been hunting for the tiger and now these interviews were like hunting for rabbits.

I appeared for the interview for the post of sales tax inspector. Coincidentally, the interviewing panel was led by then chairman Shinde. He had failed me in the MPSC interview conducted in 1994. Most probably, it had proved to be a blessing in disguise for me as I had reached the final stage of selection for the UPSC because of that. I was confident when I appeared for the interview. I was asked difficult questions on sales tax and VAT. I answered all the questions saying, 'I do not know' or 'I am sorry, sir'. I had not studied the topic and didn't have the time to prepare in advance. Therefore, I kept answering in the negative.

Frustrated, he asked me a question on the subject I had graduated in—history. 'Do you feel the new generation should study history?' I firmly answered in the affirmative and cited my reasons. I started with the couplet, 'तारीख ने कुछ ऐसे मंझर भी दिखाए है, लम्हों ने खता की थी सदियो ने सजा पाई है' and proceeded to stress that the study of history helps us understand the transition of society and gives us the vision and direction needed to steer ourselves into the future. History introduces us to our culture and traditions, inspiring us. Our morals and value systems become strong. Knowledge of history is essential to become an upstanding citizen. It is not just related to erstwhile kings and emperors. It involves the study of the economic, political, cultural and social structure of the society. The study of revolutions and movements organized by workers, farmers, labourers, poets, and artists forms the very fabric of history. I also explained how the study of history is important for the upliftment and welfare of the subaltern or depressed classes.

The panel was astonished by my answer. A candidate who could not answer a single question on sales tax had analysed history so exceedingly well. Unable to resist, the chairman asked me, 'You would benefit society more by becoming a professor of history instead of becoming a sales tax officer. Why have you appeared for this interview for a Class III post?'

Politely, I told him the truth, 'I have done my graduation in history and presently I'm doing my post-graduation in the same. I have chosen history as an optional subject for the UPSC examination too. Thus I could do history justice. In fact, the syllabus of the examinations, be it for a post in revenue, police, sales tax or the excise department, has nothing to do with the work in those posts. Selected candidates are trained in specific subjects and the department they are going to work for. If you feel that I am an expert in history and select me for the job in the sales tax department, I will acquire professional skills and expertise in that too. I have appeared for the final interview of the UPSC. I have not yet been selected in it. If I fail, I will have to return to my village and till my farm. If I become a sales tax inspector, I would at least have a source of income.' They did not ask me anything after that. I left. However, I scored 55 out of 60 marks in the interview, standing second in the merit list for the post of sales tax inspector.

My experience with the MPSC interview for the post of deputy collector was similar. The last time I had appeared for this interview, I was tense. I had zero experience. I was not mature enough. I did not even have a full beard. This time, however, the situation was different. I had the experience of three interviews. Experience with Lieutenant General Surendra Nath had helped me overcome my fear of an interviewing panel. Since it was my third MPSC interview, I was acquainted with such a panel. I recognized the panel members too. I was yet to experience rewinding and replaying the cassette. In this interview, I answered the questions confidently.

I batted well on fundamental rights and the directive principles of state policy; I explained the difference between the two and delved into their importance. I recited the Preamble of the Constitution of India, which I had memorized. I also made analytical comments on the basic structure of the Constitution of India with reference to the judgment in the Keshavanand and Bharati case. I discussed the Indian political system. In response to the question on whether the 30 per cent reservation provided for women by constitutional amendment was appropriate, I put forth the concept of 'Sarpanchpati' and explained, with reasons, that it was an ambitious step towards the empowerment of women.

A question was asked on judicial review and judicial activism. I commented on the right to judicial review, separation of the judiciary from the executive and the legislative branches as well as the autonomy of the judiciary. I explained how this right is instrumental in protecting the basic structure of the Constitution. I had memorized the five rights provided from Articles 32 and 226. I critically analysed them with references. I opined that though judicial activism had encroached upon the jurisdiction of the executive, the judiciary was working for public interest and public welfare. I was well-versed with the questions asked on subjects related to humanities. I gave sound answers in the interview and scored well. I was also selected for the post of deputy collector. This was the second sixer that I scored.

However, these interviews were minor battles. The war would be won when I cleared the final stage of the UPSC. That was a point of honour, the ultimate reward for my years of hard work. My name is Vishwasrao and I was trying to win over the crown of Delhi. I was constantly worried whether my efforts would be in vain, like the Battle of Panipat that was disastrous for the Marathas. In those days, the results were not published on a website. They would be put up on the notice board of the UPSC and a copy would be faxed to the State Information and Broadcasting Department of the government. I was living as a parasite at the hostel on B Road at Churchgate. My anxiety about the result had reached its peak. Vikas, in the meanwhile, had secured admission to the SIAC.

The doorbell of my room rang on 15 June 1997. Sweaty and out of breath, Vikas stood at the door. For a moment, his haggard appearance made me panic. I wondered whether any bad news had come from our village. The moment he saw me, he hugged me tightly and said, 'Bhau, you have scored your rank. You have become an IPS officer.' I could not believe it. As I processed the news, I felt elated. Four years of hard work had paid off. I had conquered. I had lived up to the dreams envisioned by my father for me.

I was anxious to touch Tatya's feet and deliver him the news. In his old age, this news would give him new strength to live, his ageing eyes would see a new hope. I closed my eyes and thanked God. Then I called Tatya and informed him that I had been selected for the Indian Police Service. Vikas had already told him. He burst out sobbing. He kept on repeating, 'Bhavdya, my cub.' In the background, I could hear my mother's voice, choked with emotion, saying, 'The purpose of our life has been served.' I visited all the temples to thank God. My relatives thronged to my aunt's house and showered me with praise. Viju Akka's husband, who had once scorned at my ambition, took me close and proudly said, 'Bhavdya, you have done it.'

In my village, Anand Pawar had come to know of the news. He had not understood what IPS meant. He went to the police station in the village and asked the head constable there, 'Our Bhavdya has become IPS. What does it mean?' He too knew only that the district superintendent of police is an IPS officer. Hiding his ignorance, he said that IPS stood for Indian police superintendent! I had become IPS but the 'S' in IPS stands for 'service' and not 'superintendent'. At that early age, I had to shoulder the responsibility of serving the nation. In fact, it was only a semicolon. I was now on the threshold of a mission that begins in one's twenties and continues till one is sixty. I had secured a position on the frontlines of the war. I have been at war for the last eighteen years, struggling, continuing my battle.

Today, when I look back, sometimes I feel a sense of satisfaction and at times I am overpowered by dejection. I recall my successes and failures, the whirlpools of hope and despair and my glorious success in the face of adversities. Sometimes, this chronology is disturbed due to the pendulum swinging between morality and principles. I have had many differences and disputes with the system. However, every day in my life has brought in new experiences. My emotions change with every incident and experience. I have lost seniors who guided and supported me, colleagues who put their lives at stake for me on that fateful night of 26/11. Their memories wring my heart, but their supreme sacrifice continues to inspire me.

26/11 changed my views on life. The person that I was before 26/11 is unrecognizable to the person I have become. Indeed, change is the rule of nature. All my strength was put to the test during that night. Like Sita proving her piousness, I had to prove myself inside the aflame Taj. I suffered. In the end, truth prevailed. Sometimes, truth takes time and one becomes restless. Until then, the confusion between hope and despair troubles us.

The Ram Pradhan committee systematically inquired into every response of the police. The procedure was long drawn. Statements were recorded. All documentary evidence was checked. Everything, including the CCTV footage and telephone recordings, was studied. Mr Balchandran, an experienced former IPS officer who had worked with the Research and Analysis Wing (RAW), was a member of the inquiry committee. Former Union Secretary for Home Ram Pradhan and Balchandran Sir visited the cites of each incident. They interviewed senior officers and submitted a detailed objective report, comprising elaborate professional recommendations to the state government.

Their report begins with evaluation of performances of me and my young colleagues in the following words:

The committee was greatly impressed with speed and urgency with which the Mumbai Police machinery, as a whole, reacted to unfolding of events at five different venues in a short span of time. Also, we note with appreciation, the initiative exhibited by younger police officers who showed exemplary courage and enterprise. Among them, we would like to mention two in particular—Shri Vishwas Nangre Patil, deputy commissioner of police of Zone I and Shri Rajvardhan Sinha, DCP, SB-2, who tried to ferret out terrorists from within the Heritage Taj. Also, Shri Sadanand Date, Additional CP, who determinedly faced terrorists in the Cama Hospital and was seriously injured.

The committee's inspiring and praiseworthy words gave me enormous strength.

They wrote a detailed note on the preparations made to foil any incident prior to the brutal attack and praised the preventive measures I had taken. I had passed the test on both counts—prevention and response. These two are the most important aspects of life. If we prevent untoward incidents and hazards, we automatically respond cautiously and successfully. Whenever we receive any information from the offices of our seniors, analysing it seriously and taking appropriate steps in time is of vital importance.

One and a half months before the attack, I had myself walked through every nook and corner of the Taj. I had reviewed the security there and held discussions with the administration. I had written down everything on paper and submitted twenty-eight detailed suggestions for implementation. All this study helped me while fighting the terrorists. Since I knew the deceptive layout of the Taj, I did not falter or stray. The guerrilla warfare tactic employed by Chhatrapati Shivaji lives on in the blood of the present generation of the people of Maharashtra. Displaying presence of mind, I launched attacks at the right

places and at the right time and succeeded in saving the lives
of many innocent people.

The office of the President of India, in the notification
published in the Central government's gazette while
honouring me and my team with the President's Police
Medal for Gallantry, described our action in the following
appropriate words:

PRESIDENT'S SECRETARIAT
Notification

New Delhi,   the 29th November, 2013

No. 139-Pres/2013-The President is pleased to award the
President's Police Medal for Gallantry/ Police Medal for Gallantry
to the under mentioned officers of Maharashtra Police –

S/Shri

01. Vishwas Narayan Nangre Patil,   (PPMG)
    Dy. Commissioner of Police
02. Deepak Narsu Dhole,   (PMG)
    Inspector
03. Nitin Digambar Kakade,   (PMG)
    Sub Inspector
04. Amit Raghunath Khetle,   (PMG)
    Constable
05. Arun Sarjerao Mane,   (PMG)
    Naik
06. Ashok Laxman Pawar,   (PMG)
    Naik
07. Saudagar Nivrutti Shinde,   (PMG)
    Constable

Statement of service for which the decoration has been awarded –

The well trained ten most dreaded terrorists attacked the metropolis of Mumbai at six different places on the night of Nov. 26, 2008. Mumbai city police, ill equipped compared to the weapons of the terrorists, still gave a tough fight and nine of them were killed in the fierce encounter, which lasted for more than 59 hours with the police and National Security Guards, and one was captured alive. These terrorists were stocked with lethal automatic weapons like AK-47, pistols, hand grenades and RDX with ultimate motive of waging war against country. They killed 183 civilians and 20 security personnel including police and grievously injured about 300 civilians/police, creating chaos and anarchy in the city. At hotel Leopold, 9 persons died and 19 persons, including two policemen, were injured, while at Hotel Taj, 34 persons died, including Major Sandip Unnikrishnan and one SRPF Constable and 24 persons were injured, including 7 policemen.

On 26th Nov 2008, at about 21.40 hrs, two out of the ten well trained dreaded terrorists opened indiscriminate and berserk fire of AK-47 inside the C.S.T. railway station. Another pair of terrorists stormed into Hotel Oberoi. At the same time, six terrorists headed towards Colaba and a pair of those trained terrorists struck the Nariman House, Colaba. Two of them opened similar indiscriminate and berserk fire at hotel Leopold and subsequently went to hotel Taj, Colaba to join their remaining two associates there. Before going to Hotel Taj, they planted two powerful RDX bombs around the hotel in the vicinity of Gateway of India.

At Hotel Taj, the four terrorists then continued with their indiscriminate fire and lobbed grenades on the innocents. The quick response and entry in the hotel by the team of DCP, Zone-1, Vishwas Nangre Patil and surprise counterattack and firing on the terrorists injuring one of them, put the terrorists on defensive *mode. The teams chased the terrorists almost on all the floors of hotel Taj for next 1 hour and 30 minutes, obstructed their free movements, protecting hundreds of lives. Later monitoring from CCTV control room and cross firing from second floor could hinder the movements of the attackers for the next three hours on 6th floor of old Taj. The tenacious resistance by police team confined and incapacitated the terrorists and enabled the rescue of more than 500 innocent people from the various halls, rooms, chambers and restaurants and could prevent the entry of terrorists in new Taj. Throughout the whole operation, the team voluntarily risked their lives with utmost motivation and commitment.*

Individual Role

1. Role played by Shri Vishwas Nangre Patil, DCP Zone-1, Mumbai

On 26/11/2008, four terrorists attacked Hotel Taj with AK-47 guns, grenades and IEDs of RDX at 21.40 hrs. Vishwas Nangre Patil, then DCP, Zone-1, rushed to the spot at 21.47 with his Radio Operator (RTPC) Khetle and reached Taj within 7 minutes. At Taj, he took along the security chief of Taj, Sunil Kudiyadi and reached second floor and noticed that three terrorists were moving towards upper floors. He fired 3 rounds from his glock pistol (at 22.02 as per the CCTV record), of which one round hit the leg of one of the terrorists.

Seeing the grave danger from the armed terrorists, he took cover behind a ledge when the terrorists retaliated with AK-47 burst. Along with Mr Kudiyadi, he searched the whole of 6th, 5th, 4th and 3rd floors of South wing. By coincidence, the terrorists were on the 3rd floor of North wing, when he was searching (as seen in CCTV recording later). He came on the ground floor and reached the Royal Staircase when the terrorists threw one grenade on his party. In retaliation, Vishwas Nangre Patil Fixed two rounds in upward direction to contain the terrorists.

He then called two constables of SRPF, Rahul Shinde and Samadhan More, and rushed to 6th floor of North wing of Old Taj. The team searched the whole floor, but could not locate them. Hence, he blocked all the gates with available manpower that he had since reached the spot and gave a call to control room seeking Assault teams.

Vishwas Nangre Patil and his team could jam the routes of the terrorists on the basis of this visual apprehension of the movements of terrorists. The terrorists had taken 5 men as hostages. Whenever they tried to come down with hostages, he and Rajvardhan opened crossfire from 2nd floor. They did not allow them to come down by effective retaliation up to 03.00 am. During this interregnum, the Taj management guided the guests on intercom and mobiles resulting in evacuation of 650 persons.

At 03.00 am, the terrorists located the room from where they were getting cross fire operations as well as the floor had got massive fire. Nangre Patil and his team got out in the corridor.

Seeing them in the target area, the terrorists threw grenade and fired from AK-47 where in Police Constable Rahul Shinde lost his life and two constables got seriously injured due to bullets and splinters. Two officers and two constables were injured by fire.

In the encounter S/Shri Vishwas Narayan Nangre Patil, Dy. Commissioner of Police; Deepk Narsu Dhole, Inspector; Nitin Digambar Kakade, Sub Inspector; Amit Raghunath Khetle, Constable; Arun Sarjerao Mane, Naik; Ashok Laxman Pawar, Naik and Saudagar Nivrutti Shinde, Constable, displayed conspicuous gallantry, courage and devotion to duty of a high order.

These awards are made for gallantry under Rule 4(i) of the Rules governing the award of President's Police Medal and *consequently carries with it the special allowance admissible under Rule 5, with from 26/11/2008.*

Before the attack, I had written a semi-official letter to my colleague officers. Concluding that letter, I had said: We frequently receive alerts, anonymous letters or phone calls regarding a terrorist attack. Often, we turn a blind eye towards them, thinking it is an oft repeated, routine, nonsensical and boring alert. Sometimes an emergency arises and we find ourselves in a pickle. There has not been a single major terror strike in the USA after the 9/11 attack because of their 'broken window response' system. Under that system, even shattering a windowpane is presumed to be a terror attack and the situation is handled in a professional and skilful manner. It takes only a few minutes for a country like Israel to be war-ready. Every citizen is imparted military training at a young age. As a result, they know what they should or shouldn't do in case of an emergency and can easily face any situation. Along with the discipline of individuals, discipline in society is equally important.

We face several major and minor emergencies at various stages of life. When one is astride a horse, the animal immediately realizes how strong the rider is, by how strong his grip is and how sternly he pulls the reins—it then gallops in the direction and speed deserving of the rider, without causing any trouble. It is the same with emergency situations. If we display dismay or confusion, we are slated to get defeated. If we face emergency situations systematically with courage, they are gradually phased out. They test your patience and courage. Once they realize that you are not the one to collapse or give up, they cannot sustain themselves for long. Instead, you can overcome them and convert the emergencies into opportunities and glorious victories. Only unwavering self-confidence, relentless willpower and willingness to work hard is needed. That's it! Of course, it also needs honesty and complete dedication.

I recall a story I once read. A famous painter wants to draw a painting of God. He talks to his friend who suggests, 'Choose a six-year-old child and make a painting of that child. It would look just like Lord Krishna.' Heeding his friend's advice, the painter selects a cute boy and makes a painting of God, using him as a model. The picture indeed resembles Lord Shri Krishna. The painter makes a fortune. After twenty years, the same painter gets into the mood to paint a monster and asks the same friend for advice. The friend says, 'Go to a jail, select a prisoner who has committed several serious crimes and make a painting using that prisoner as a model.' Again, he heeds his friend's advice. He visits a jail, consults the jailor and selects a savage-looking criminal and starts painting the image of a monster using him as a model. His eyes blood-red and hair long grown, the prisoner, out of curiosity, asks the painter, 'What are you using me as a model for?' The painter replies, 'I am sorry, but I am painting the image of a fearsome devil, a merciless monster, using you as a model.'

On hearing this, the criminal is stunned for a moment and tears roll down his eyes. The painter is shocked and tries to console the criminal, 'You are just a representation of that evil. Why are you shedding tears over it?' The criminal's unexpected answer makes the painter rethink. He says, 'Mr Painter, you have not recognized me. I am the same boy whom you had used as a model twenty years ago to draw the painting of Lord Shri Krishna. Over the last two decades, the God in me has become weak and the monster, stronger.'

In the same manner, two contrasting tendencies are constantly at war within each one of us. One of them represents vices like fear, anger, jealousy, hate, sorrow, selfishness, guilt, inferiority complex, falsehood, vanity, pride, and arrogance while the other represents virtues like peace, love, mercy, hope, generosity, helpfulness, friendship, truth and piousness. This is the battle between the deities and demons, sin and virtuosity, good and evil. Which side wins? The side which is nurtured by us.

I had to face many a conflict and dilemma while sticking to my conscience and to truth. Yet, doubts crop up in my mind, now and then. The wolfish, evil tendencies try to capture my mind at times. On the night of 26/11, I was racing towards death and still I emerged, alive and unscathed. Indeed, God must have granted me a lease on life. He must have some constructive plans for me. Therefore, I have made some resolutions, nurtured some dreams.

Firstly, I want to overcome the remaining fear in my mind. I want to live with my head held high, keeping myself focused on my purpose, to the very end. I want to acquire more knowledge, read, know more about the world. I want to learn new things. I want to free myself from my shortcomings, the restraints which make me shallow and narrow-minded. I want to apply the test of truth to every word I utter. I want to chase perfection. I want to destroy those negative habits which kill my sensitivities. I want to adopt a scientific approach and rationality to the end. I want to extend the boundaries of my actions and thoughts. I want to awaken myself. I want to maintain a positive and constructive attitude forever. I may become successful or unsuccessful, but I want neither to be dejected by failure nor overjoyed by success. I want to remain balanced. I want to not succumb to the lure of gain attained without hard work.

Wake up

The sun, the moon, the stars are all in your blood.

Get up and fight back.

Take blows and give blows but do not resort to deceit to become successful.

Be it on the warpath, victorious march or walk on the fire,

Face every test by fire with courage.

Fight back every attack on your warpath

And enrich your victorious march with small victories,

Which are meaningful on the test of rules, values and context.

Weapons to be used on this warpath

Are not lathis, sticks, swords and guns.

The weapon to be used on this warpath

Is only the peaceful service of humanity.

Continue a meaningful journey of life

By providing affectionate relief

To the wounds and pains of poor, helpless victims.

Whenever possible and if possible,

Lend a helping hand and cooperation to those in trouble.

For eighteen years while serving the police force and till the last breath;

I want to proceed on this path without a break, without getting fatigued, incessantly, fearlessly, without any confusion.

I have only one aim in my life—

When I embrace death

The wrinkles on my face will speak of my love, my service, my observance and my honest efforts and;

My self-pride will never take a beating,

I shall never fall in my own eyes.

I will continue my progress

Without getting tired, incessantly, fearlessly, without any confusion;

For the service and protection of my motherland, the nation that is India . . .

Jai Hind!